G000242056

AUTHE
Italian Riviera

Touring Club Italiano
President and Chairman: *Roberto Ruozi*

Touring Editore
Editorial Director: *Michele D'Innella*
Editorial coordination: *Cristiana Baietta*

International Division
m.rondinelli@giunti.it
http://internationaldivision.giunti.it

Senior Editor: *Paola Pandiani*
Editor: *Monica Maraschi*
Researchers: *Monica Maraschi, Agostina Pizzocri*
with Banca Dati Turistica for Pratical info
Translation and page layout: *Studio Queens, Milan*
Maps: *Touring Club Italiano*
Design: *Studio Queens, Milan*
Cover photo: *The colorful houses by the seafront in Portovènere*
(P. Barbanera/Panda Photo)

Advertising Manager: *Claudio Bettinelli*
Local Advertising: *Progetto*
www.progettosrl.it - info@progettosrl.it

Printing and Binding in China

Distribution
USA/CAN – *Publishers Group West*
UK/Ireland – *Portfolio Books*

Touring Club Italiano, Corso Italia 10, 20122 Milano
www.touringclub.it
© 2008 Touring Editore, Milan

Code K8AAF
ISBN-13: 978 – 88365 – 4220 – 8

Printed in February 2008

AUTHENTIC
Italian Riviera

TOURING CLUB
OF ITALY

16   HERITAGE

Liguria might be small and narrow, but many of the towns and cities, with Genoa leading the way, contain wonderful and surprising elements of art, culture and history that are well worth exploring.

Genova/Genoa
Day trips: Borzonasca, Camogli, Chiàvari, Portofino, Rapallo, Santa Margherita Lìgure, Santo Stéfano d'Àveto, Sestri Levante.
La Spèzia
Day trips: Brugnato, Castelnuovo Magra, Cinque Terre (Riomaggiore, Manarola, Corniglia, Vernazza, Monterosso al Mare), Lérici, Lèvanto, Luni, Portovènere, Sarzana, Varese Ligure.
Savona
Day trips: Alàssio, Albenga, Andora Castello, Castelvecchio di Rocca Barbena, Finale Lìgure, Noli, Sassello, Toirano, Zuccarello.
Imperia
Day trips: Apricale, Bordighera, Cervo, Dolceàcqua, Pigna, Sanremo, Taggia, Triora, Ventimìglia.

84   ITINERARIES

In Liguria, the mountains, sea and beaches are quite literally crammed together, making this region ideal for all types of outings, from a day at the beach to a challenging trek.

Beaches
Parks
Marine Protected Areas
Children
Cinema

Sport
Walking
Historical Itineraries
Biking Routes

114   FOOD

The dense physical nature of the region is clearly reflected in the cuisine. The centuries of trading brought many exotic items to this land, but the knowledgeable locals then combined them carefully to make numerous wonderful delicacies.

Traditional dishes
Pasta
Hams and Salami
Cheese
Oil

Wine
Liqueurs and drinks
Cakes
Food and Wine festivals

The close links both to far-off lands and nearer regions have made Liguria into a center where one can find a delightful array of items. Local crafts also abound, ranging from glass to rival Murano to furniture that was once found in the best European courts and delightful ceramics.

Arts & crafts
Markets
Fashion

Liguria is awash with festivals, feasts, trade fairs and musical events. Genoa leads the way with the more commercial trade fairs and for music, but many of the small towns and villages across the region host a lot of lovely festival, normally in conjunction with the local confraternity.

Music
Folklore

In this region, nature and beautiful landscapes create an ideal atmosphere for relaxation and rejuvenation. Yet, these wellness centers are as much about physical health as mental wellbeing and emotional balance, bringing to life a new adage that "beauty is created, not born".

Alàssio   Portofino
Bordighera   Rapallo
Pigna   Uscio

The Practical Information is divided into sections on the hotels, restaurants, farm holidays and places of entertainment we recommend. The category of the hotels is indicated by the number of stars. In the case of restaurants we have awarded forks, taking into account the price of the meal, the level of comfort and service, and the ambience.

WHAT IS THE TOURING CLUB OF ITALY?

Long Tradition, Great Prestige

For over 110 years, the Touring Club of Italy (TCI) has offered travelers the most detailed and comprehensive source of travel information available on Italy. The Touring Club of Italy was founded in 1894 with the aim of developing the social and cultural values of tourism and promoting the conservation and enjoyment of the country's national heritage, landscape and environment.

Advantages of Membership

Today, TCI offers a wide rage of travel services to assist and support members with the highest level of convenience and quality. Now you can discover the unique charms of Italy with a distinct insider's advantage.

Enjoy exclusive money saving offers with a TCI membership. Use your membership card for discounts in thousands of restaurants, hotels, spas, campgrounds, museums, shops and markets.

These Hotel Chains offer preferred rates and discounts to TCI members!

JOIN THE TOURING CLUB OF ITALY

How to Join

It's quick and easy to join.
Apply for your membership online at
www.touringclub.it
Your membership card will arrive within
three weeks and is valid for discounts
across Italy for the entire year.
Get your card before you go and start
saving as soon as you arrive.
Euro 25 annual membership fee
includes priority mail postage for
membership card and materials.
Just one use of the card will more than
cover the cost of membership.

Benefits

- Exclusive car rental rates with Hertz
- Discounts at select Esso gas stations
- 20% discount on TCI guidebooks
and maps purchased in TCI bookstores
or directly online at
www.touringclub.com
- Preferred rates and discounts available
at thousands of locations in Italy: Hotels -
B&B's - Villa Rentals - Campgrounds -TCI
Resorts - Spas - Restaurants - Wineries -
Museums - Cinemas - Theaters - Music
Festivals - Shops - Craft Markets - Ferries -
Cruises - Theme Parks - Botanical Gardens

ITALY: INSTRUCTIONS FOR USE

Italy is known throughout the world for the quantity and quality of its art treasures and for its natural beauty, but it is also famous for its inimitable lifestyle and fabulous cuisine and wines. Although it is a relatively small country, Italy boasts an extremely varied culture and multifarious traditions and customs. The information and suggestions in this brief section will help foreign tourists not only to understand certain aspects of Italian life, but also to solve the everyday difficulties and the problems of a practical nature that inevitably crop up during any trip.

This practical information is included in brief descriptions of various topics: public transport and how to purchase tickets; suggestions on how to drive in this country; the different types of rooms and accommodation in hotels; hints on how to use mobile phones and communication in general. This is followed by useful advice on how to meet your everyday needs and on shopping, as well as information concerning the cultural differences in the various regions. Lastly, there is a section describing the vast range of restaurants, bars, wine bars and pizza parlors.

TRANSPORTATION

From the airport to the city
Public transportation in major cities is easily accessible and simple to use. Both Milan and Rome airports have trains and buses linking them to the city centers. At Milano-Malpensa, you can take a bus to the main train station or a train to Cadorna train station and subway stop.

Subways, buses, and trams
Access to the subways, buses, and trams requires a ticket (tickets are not sold on board but can be purchased at most newsstands and tobacco shops). The ticket is good for one ride and sometimes has a time limit (in the case of buses and trams). When you board a bus or tram, you are required to stamp your previously-acquired ticket in the time-stamping machine. Occasionally, a conductor will board the bus or tram and check everyone's ticket. If you haven't got one, or if it has not been time-stamped, you will have to pay a steep fine.

Trains
The Ferrovie dello Stato (Italian Railways) is among the best and most modern railway systems in Europe. Timetables and routes can be consulted and reservations can be made online at **www.trenitalia.com**. Many travel agents can also dispense tickets and help you plan your journey. Hard-copy schedules can be purchased at all newsstands and most bookstores.

Boats in Manarola, the Cinque Terre.

Automated ticket machines, which include easy-to-use instructions in English, are available in nearly all stations. They can be used to check schedules, makes reservations, and purchase tickets. There are different types of train, according to the requirements:
Eurostar Italia Trains **ES★** : Fast connections between Italy's most important cities. The ticket includes seat booking charge;
Intercity *IC* and **Espresso** *E* Trains: Local connections among Italy's towns and cities. Sometimes *IC* and *E* trains require seat booking. You can book your seat up to 3 hours before the train departure. The seat booking charge is of 3 Euro.
Interregionale Trains *iR* move beyond regional boundaries. Among the combined local-transport services, the *iR* Trains are the fastest ones with the fewest number of stops. No seat booking available.
Diretto *D* and **Regionale** *R* Trains can circulate both within the regions and their bordering regions. No seat booking available.

DO NOT FORGET: In Italy, you can only board a train if you have a valid ticket. Tickets without seat booking must be time-stamped prior to boarding (each station has numerous time-stamping machines).

If you don't have a ticket – or did not stamp before boarding – you will be liable to pay the full ticket price plus a 25 euro fine. If you produce a ticket that is not valid for the train or service you're using (i.e. one issued for a different train category at a different price, etc.) you will be asked to pay the difference with respect to the full ticket price, plus an 8 euro surcharge.

Taxis

Taxis are a convenient but expensive way to travel in Italian cities. There are taxi stands scattered throughout major cities. You cannot hail taxis on the street in Italy, but you can reserve taxis, in advance or immediately, by phone: consult the yellow pages for the number or ask your hotel reception desk or maitre d'hotel to call for you.

Taxi drivers have the right to charge you a supplementary fee for every piece of luggage they transport, as well as night and festivity surcharge.

Driving

Especially when staying in the countryside, driving is a safe and convenient way to travel through Italy and its major cities. It is important to be aware of street signs and speed limits, and many cities have zones where only limited traffic is allowed in order to accommodate pedestrians.

Street parking is organized using road signs and different colored street markings. No line or a white line is for free parking, blue is for paid parking and yellow is for reserved parking (disabled, residents etc). There may be time limits for both free and paid parking. In this case, use your parking disc to indicate your time of arrival. Although an international driver's license is not required in Italy, it is advisable. ACI and similar associations provide this service to members. The fuel distribution network is reasonably distributed all over the territory. All service stations have unleaded gasoline ("benzina verde") and diesel fuel ("gasolio"). Opening time is 7 to 12:30 and 15 to 19:30; on motorways the service is 24 hours a day.

Type of roads in Italy: The *Autostrada* (for example A14) is the main highway system in Italy and is similar to the Interstate highway system in the US and the motorway system in the UK. Shown on our Touring Club Italiano 1:200,000 road maps as black. The Autostrada are toll highways; you pay to use them. The *Strada Statale* (for example SS54) is a fast moving road that may have one or more lanes in each direction. Shown on our Touring Club Italiano 1:200,000 road maps as red. *Strada Provinciale* (for example SP358) can be narrow, slow and winding roads. They are usually one lane in each direction. Shown on our Touring Club Italiano 1:200,000 road maps as yellow. *Strada Comunale* (for example SC652) is a local road connecting the main town with its sorrounding. Note: In our guide you will sometime find an address of a place in the countryside listed, for example, as

"SS54 Km 25". This means that you have to drive along the Strada Statale 54 until you reach the 25-km road sign.

Speed limits: 130 kmph on the Autostrada, 110 kmph on main highways, 90 kmph outside of towns, 50 kmph in towns.

The town streets are patrolled by the Polizia Locale while the roads outside cities and the Autostrada are patrolled by the Carabinieri or the Polizia Stradale.

Do not forget:

- Wear your seat belt at all times;
- Do not use the cellular phone while driving;
- Have your headlights on at all times when driving outside of cities;
- The drunk driving laws are strict – do not drink and drive;
- In case of an accident you are not allowed to get out of your car unless you are wearing a special, high-visibility, reflective jacket.

ACCOMMODATION

Hotels

In Italy it is common practice for the reception desk to register your passport, and only registered guests are allowed to use the rooms. This is mere routine, done for security reasons, and there is no need for concern.

All hotels use the official star classification system, from 5-star luxury hotel to 1 star accommodation.

Room rates are based on whether they are for single ("camera singola") or double ("camera doppia") occupancy. In every room you will find a list of the hotel rates (generally on the back of the door). While 4- and 5-star hotels have double beds, most hotels have only single beds. Should you want a double bed, you have to ask for a "letto matrimoniale". All hotels have rooms with bathrooms; only 1-star establishments usually have only shared bathrooms.

Most hotel rates include breakfast ("prima colazione"), but you can request to do without it, thus reducing the rate. Breakfast is generally served in a communal room and comprises a buffet with pastries, bread with butter and jam, cold cereals, fruit, yoghurt, coffee, and fruit juice. Some hotels regularly frequented by foreign tourists will also serve other items such as eggs for their American and British guests.

The hotels for families and in tourist localities also offer "mezza pensione", or half board, in which breakfast and dinner are included in the price.

It's always a good idea to check when a hotel's annual closing period is, especially if you are planning a holiday by the sea.

Farm stays

Located only in the countryside, and generally on a farm, "agriturismo" – a network of farm holiday establishments – is part of a growing trend in Italy to honor local gastronomic and wine traditions, as well as countryside traditions. These farms offer meals prepared with ingredients cultivated exclusively on site: garden-grown vegetables, homemade cheese and local recipes. Many of these places also provide lodging, one of the best ways to experience the "genuine" Italian lifestyle.

Bed & Breakfast

This form of accommodation provides bed and breakfast in a private house, and in the last few years has become much more widespread in Italy. There are over 6,500 b&bs, classified in 3 categories, and situated both in historic town centers, as well as in the outskirts and the countryside. Rooms for guests are always well-furnished, but not all of them have en suite bathrooms.

It is well-recommended to check the closing of the open-all-year accommodation services and restaurants, because they could have a short break during the year (usually no longer than a fortnight).

COMMUNICATIONS

Nearly everyone in Italy owns a cellular phone. Although public phones are still available, they seem to be ever fewer and farther between. If you wish to use public phones, you will find them in subway stops, bars, along the street, and phone centers generally located in the city center. Phone cards and pre-paid phone cards can be purchased at most newsstands and tobacco shops, and can also be acquired at automated tellers.

For European travelers, activating personal cellular coverage is relatively simple, as it is in most cases for American and Australian travelers as well. Contact your mobile service provider for details.

Cellular phones can also be rented in Italy from TIM, the Italian national phone company. For information, visit its website at www.tim.it. When traveling by car through the countryside, a cellular phone can really come in handy.

Note that when dialing in Italy, you must always dial the prefix (e.g., 02 for Milan, 06 for Rome) even when making a local call. For cellular phones, however, the initial zero is always dropped.

Freephone numbers always start with "800". For calls abroad from Italy, it's a good idea to buy a special pre-paid international phone card, which is used with a PIN code.

Internet access

Cyber cafés have sprung up all over Italy and you can find one on nearly every city block.

EATING AND DRINKING

The bar

The Italian "bar" is a multi-faceted, all-purpose establishment for drinking, eating and socializing, where you can order an espresso, have breakfast, and enjoy a quick sandwich for lunch or even a hot meal. You can often buy various items here (sometimes even stamps, cigarettes, phone cards, etc.). Bear in mind that table service ("servizio a tavola") includes a surcharge. At most bars, if you choose to sit, a waiter will take your order. Every bar should have a list of prices posted behind or near the counter; if the bar offers table service, the price list should also include the extra fee for this.

Lunch at bars will include, but is not limited to, "panini," sandwiches with crusty bread, usually with cured meats such as "prosciutto" (salt-cured ham), "prosciutto cotto" (cooked ham), and cheeses such as mozzarella topped with tomato and basil. Then there are "tramezzini" (finger sandwiches) with tuna, cheese, or vegetables, etc. Often the "panini" and other savory sandwiches (like stuffed flatbread or "focaccia") are heated before being served. Naturally, the menu at bars varies according to the region: in Bologna you will find "piadine" (flatbread similar to pita) with Swiss chard; in Palermo there are "arancini" (fried rice balls stuffed with

ground meat); in Genoa you will find that even the most unassuming bar serves some of the best "focaccia" in all Italy. Some bars also include a "tavola calda". If you see this sign in a bar window, it means that hot dishes like pasta and even entrées are served.

A brief comment on coffee and cappuccino: Italians never serve coffee with savory dishes or sandwiches, and they seldom drink cappuccino outside of breakfast (although they are happy to serve it at any time).

While English- and Irish-type pubs are frequented by beer lovers and young people in Italy, there are also American bars where long drinks and American cocktails are served.

Breakfast at the bar

Breakfast in Italy generally consists of some type of pastry, most commonly a "brioche" – a croissant either filled with cream or jam, or plain – and a cappuccino or espresso. Although most bars do not offer American coffee, you can ask for a "caffè lungo" or "caffè americano", both of which resemble the American coffee preferred by the British and Americans. Most bars have a juicer to make a "spremuta", freshly squeezed orange or grapefruit juice.

Lunch and Dinner

As with all daily rituals in Italy, food is prepared and meals are served according to local customs (e.g., in the North they prefer rice and butter, in South and Central Italy they favor pasta and olive oil).

Wine is generally served at mealtime, and while finer restaurants have excellent wine lists (some including vintage wines), ordering the house table wine generally brings good results (a house Chianti to accompany your Florentine steak in Tuscany, a sparkling Prosecco paired with your creamed stockfish and polenta in Venice, a dry white wine with pasta dressed with sardines and wild fennel fronds in Sicily).

Mineral water is also commonly served at meals and can be "gassata" (sparkling) or "naturale" (still).

The most sublime culinary experience in Italy is achieved by matching the local foods with the appropriate local wines: wisdom dictates that a friendly waiter will be flattered by your request for his recommendation on what to eat and drink. Whether at an "osteria" (a tavern), a "trattoria" (a home-style restaurant), or a "ristorante" (a proper restaurant), the service of lunch and dinner generally consists of – but is not limited to – the following: "antipasti" or appetizers; "primo piatto" or first course, i.e., pasta, rice, or soup; "secondo piatto" or main course, i.e., meat or seafood; "contorno" or side-dish, served with the main course, i.e., vegetables or salad; "formaggi", "frutta", and "dolci", i.e., cheeses, fruit, and dessert; caffè or espresso coffee, perhaps spiked with a shot of grappa.

The pizzeria

The pizzeria is in general one of the most economical, democratic, and satisfying culinary experiences in Italy. Everyone eats at the pizzeria: young people, families, couples, locals and tourists alike. Generally, each person orders her/his own pizza, and while the styles of crust and toppings will vary from region to region (some of the best pizzas are served in Naples and Rome), the acid test of any pizzeria is the Margherita, topped simply with cheese and tomato sauce.

Beer, sparkling or still water, and Coca Cola are the beverages commonly served with pizza. Some restaurants include a pizza menu, but most establishments do not serve pizza at lunchtime.

The wine bar (enoteca)

More than one English-speaking tourist in Italy has wondered why the wine bar is called an enoteca in other countries and the English term is used in Italy: the answer lies somewhere in the mutual fondness that Italians and English speakers have for one another. Wine bars have become popular in recent years in the major cities (especially in Rome, where you can find some of the best). The wine bar is a great place to sample different local wines and eat a light, tapas-style dinner.

CULTURAL DIVERSITY

Whenever you travel, not only are you a guest of your host country, but you are also a representative of your home country. As a general rule, courtesy, consideration, and respect are always appreciated by guests and their hosts alike. Italians are famous for their hospitality and experience will verify this felicitous stereotype: perhaps nowhere else in Europe are tourists and visitors received more warmly. Italy is a relatively "new" country. Its borders, as we know them today, were established only in 1861 when it became a monarchy under the House of Savoy. After WWII, Italy became a Republic and now it is one of the member states of the European Union. One of the most fascinating aspects of Italian culture is that, even as a unified country, local tradition still prevails over a universally Italian national identity. Some jokingly say that the only time that Venetians, Milanese, Florentines, Neapolitans, and Sicilians feel like Italians is when the national football team plays in international competitions. From their highly localized dialects to the foods they eat, from their religious celebration to their politics, Italians proudly maintain their local heritage. This is one of the reasons why the Piedmontese continue to prefer their beloved Barolo wine and their white truffles, the Umbrians their rich Sagrantino wine and black truffles, the Milanese their risotto and panettone, the Venetians their stockfish and polenta, the Bolognese their lasagne and pumpkin ravioli, the Florentines their bread soups and steaks cooked rare, the Abruzzese their excellent fish broth and seafood, the Neapolitans their mozzarella, basil, pizza, and pasta. As a result of its rich cultural diversity, the country's population also varies greatly in its customs from region to region, city to city, town to town. As you visit different cities and regions throughout Italy, you will see how the local personality and character of the Italians change as rapidly as the landscape does. Having lived for millennia with their great diversity and rich, highly heterogeneous culture, the Italians have taught us many things, foremost among them the age-old expression, "When in Rome, do as the Romans do."

NATIONAL HOLIDAYS

New Year's Day (1st January), Epiphany (6th January), Easter Monday (day after Easter Sunday), Liberation Day (25th April), Labour Day (1st May), Italian Republic Day (2nd June), Assumption (15th August), All Saints' Day (1st November), Immaculate Conception (8th December), Christmas Day and Boxing Day (25th-26th December).
In addition to these holidays, each city also has a holiday to celebrate its patron saint's feast day, usually with lively, local celebrations. Shops and services in large cities close on national holidays and for the week of the 15th of August.

EVERYDAY NEEDS

State tobacco shops and pharmacies
Tobacco is available in Italy only at state licensed tobacco shops. These vendors ("tabaccheria"), often incorporated in a bar, also sell stamps.
Smoking is forbidden in all so-called public places – unless a separately ventilated space is constructed – meaning over 90% of the country's restaurants and bars.
Medicines can be purchased only in pharmacies ("farmacia") in Italy. Pharmacists are very knowledgeable about common ailments and can generally prescribe a treatment for you on the spot. Opening time is 8:30-12:30 and 15:30-19:30 but in any case there is always a pharmacy open 24 hours and during holidays.
Shopping
Every locality in Italy offers tourists characteristic shops, markets with good bargains, and even boutiques featuring leading Italian fashion designers. Opening hours vary from region to region and from season to season. In general, shops are open from 9 to 13 and from 15/16 to 19/20, but in large cities they usually have no lunchtime break.
Tax Free
Non-EU citizens can obtain a reimbursement for IVA (goods and services tax) paid on purchases over €155, for goods which are exported within 90 days, in shops which display the relevant sign. IVA is always automatically included in the price of any purchase, and ranges from 20% to 4% depending on the item. The shop issues a reimbursement voucher to present when you leave the country (at a frontier or airport). For purchases in shops affiliated to 'Tax Free Shopping', IVA may be reimbursed directly at international airports.
Banks and post offices
Italian banks are open Monday to Friday, from 8:30 to 13:30 and then from 15 to 16. However, the afternoon business hours may vary.
Post offices are open from Monday to Saturday, from 8:30 to 13:30 (12:30 on Saturday). In the larger towns there are also some offices open in the afternoon.
Currency
As in many other European Union countries, the Euros is the Italian currency. Coins are in denominations of 1, 2, 5, 10, 20 and 50 cents and 1 and 2 euros; banknotes are in denominations of 5, 10, 20, 50, 100, 200 and 500 euros, each with a different color.
Credit cards
All the main credit cards are generally accepted, but some smaller enterprises (arts and crafts shops, small hotels, bed & breakfasts, or farm stays) do not provide this service. Foreign tourists can obtain cash using credit cards at automatic teller machines.
Time
All Italy is in the same time zone, which is six hours ahead of Eastern Standard Time in the USA. Daylight saving time is used from March to October, when watches and clocks are set an hour ahead of standard time.
Passports and vaccinations
Citizens of EU countries can enter Italy without frontier checks. Citizens of Australia, Canada, New Zealand, and the United States can enter Italy with a valid passport and need not have a visa for a stay of less than 90 days.
No vaccinations are necessary.
Payment and tipping
When you sit down at a restaurant you are generally charged a "coperto" or cover charge ranging from 1.5 to 3 euros, for service and the bread. Tipping is not customary in Italy. Beware of unscrupulous restaurateurs who add a space on their clients' credit card receipt for a tip, while it has already been included in the cover charge.

USEFUL ADDRESSES

Foreign Embassies in Italy

Australia
Via A. Bosio, 5 - 00161 Rome
Tel. +39 06 852721
Fax +39 06 85272300
www.italy.embassy.gov.au.
info-rome@dfat.gov.au

Canada
Via Salaria, 243 - 00199 Rome
Tel. +39 06 854441
Fax +39 06 85444 3915
www.canada.it
rome@dfait-maeci.gc.ca

Great Britain
Via XX Settembre, 80 -
00187 Rome
Tel. +39 06 42200001
Fax +39 06 42202334
www.britian.it
consularenquiries@rome.
mail.fco.gov.uk

Ireland
Piazza di Campitelli, 3 -
00186 Rome
Tel. +39 06 6979121
Fax +39 06 6792354
irish.embassy@esteri.it

New Zealand
Via Zara, 28 - 00198 Rome
Tel. +39 06 4417171
Fax +39 06 4402984

South Africa
Via Tanaro, 14 - 00198 Rome
Tel. +39 06 852541
Fax +39 06 85254300
www.sudafrica.it

United States of America
Via Vittorio Veneto, 121 -
00187 Rome
Tel. +39 06 46741
Fax +39 06 4882672
www.usis.it

Foreign Consulates in Italy

Australia
Via Borgogna, 2
20122 Milan
Tel. +39 02 77704217
Fax +39 02 77704242

Canada
Via Vittor Pisani, 19
20124 Milan
Tel. +39 02 67581
Fax +39 02 67583900
milan@international.gc.ca

Great Britain
Via S. Paolo, 7
20121 Milan
Tel. +39 02 723001
Fax +39 02 86465081
ConsularMilan@fco.gov.uk

Lungarno Corsini, 2
50123 Florence
Tel. +39 055 284133
Consular.Florence@fco.gov.uk

Via dei Mille, 40
80121 Naples
Tel. +39 081 4238911
Fax +39 081 422434
Info.Naples@fco.gov.uk

Ireland
Piazza San Pietro in Gessate, 2 -
20122 Milan
Tel. +39 02 55187569/02 55187641
Fax +39 02 55187570

New Zealand
Via Guido d'Arezzo, 6
20145 Milan
Tel. +39 02 48012544
Fax +39 02 48012577

South Africa
Vicolo San Giovanni
sul Muro, 4
20121 Milan
Tel. +39 02 8858581
Fax +39 02 72011063
saconsulate@iol.it

United States of America
Via Principe Amedeo, 2/10
20121 Milan
Tel. +39 02 290351
Fax +39 02 29001165

Lungarno Vespucci, 38
50123 Florence
Tel. +39 055 266951
Fax +39 055 284088

Piazza della Repubblica
80122 Naples
Tel. +39 081 5838111
Fax +39 081 7611869

Italian Embassies and Consulates Around the World

Australia
12, Grey Street - Deakin, A.C.T.
2600 - Canberra
Tel. 02 62733333, 62733398,
62733198
Fax 02 62734223
www.ambcanberra.esteri.it
Consulates at: Brisbane, Glynde,
Melbourne, Perth , Sydney

Canada
275, Slater Street, 21st floor -
Ottawa (Ontario) K1P 5H9
Tel. (613) 232 2401/2/3
Fax (613) 233 1484 234 8424
www.ambottawa.esteri.it
ambital@italyincanada.com
Consulates at: Edmonton,
Montreal, Toronto, Vancouver,

Great Britain
14, Three Kings Yard, London
W1K 4EH
Tel. 020 73122200
Fax 020 73122230
www.amblondra.esteri.it
ambasciata.londra@esteri.it
Consulates at: London, Bedford,
Edinburgh, Manchester

Ireland
63/65, Northumberland Road -
Dublin 4
Tel. 01 6601744
Fax 01 6682759
www.ambdublino.esteri.it
info@italianembassy.ie

New Zealand
34-38 Grant Road, Thorndon,
(PO Box 463, Wellington)
Tel. 04 473 5339

Fax 04 472 7255
www.ambwellington.esteri.it

South Africa
796 George Avenue, 0083 Arcadia
Tel. 012 4305541/2/3
Fax 012 4305547
www.ambpretoria.esteri.it
Consulates at: Johannesburg,
Capetown, Durban

United States of America
3000 Whitehaven Street, NW
Washington DC 20008
Tel. (202) 612-4400
Fax (202) 518-2154
www.ambwashingtondc.esteri.it
Consulates at: Boston, MA -
Chicago, IL - Detroit, MI - Houston,
TX - Los Angeles, CA - Miami, FL -
Newark, NJ - New York, NY -
Philadelphia, PA - San Francisco, CA

ENIT (Italian State Tourism Board)

Australia
Level 4, 46 Market Street
NSW 2000 Sidney
PO Box Q802 - QVB NSW 1230
Tel. 00612 92 621666
Fax 00612 92 621677
italia@italiantourism.com.au

Canada
175 Bloor Street E. Suite 907 –
South Tower
M4W3R8 Toronto (Ontario)
Tel. (416) 925 4882
Fax (416) 925 4799
www.italiantourism.com
enit.canada@on.aibn.com

Great Britain
1, Princes Street
W1B 2AY London
Tel. 020 7408 1254
Tel. 800 00482542 FREE from
United Kingdom and Ireland
italy@italiantouristboard.co.uk

United States of America
500, North Michigan Avenue
Suite 2240
60611 Chicago 1, Illinois
Tel. (312) 644 0996 /644 0990
Fax (312) 644 3019
www.italiantourism.com
enitch@italiantourism.com

12400, Wilshire Blvd. – Suite 550
CA 90025 Los Angeles
Tel. (310) 820 1898 - 820 9807
Fax (310) 820 6357
www.italiantourism.com
enitla@italiantourism.com

630, Fifth Avenue – Suite 1565
NY – 10111 New York
Tel. (212) 245 4822 – 245 5618
Fax (212) 586 9249
www.italiantourism.com
enitny@italiantourism.com

Although, in terms of size, Liguria is one of Italy's smallest regions, it is quite difficult to summarize its dense political and cultural history, describe its considerable artistic heritage and the extraordinary variety of its landscape.

The very shape of this region—a narrow strip of land stretched in an arch around the immense "liquid plain" which so fascinated Fernand Braudel – embodies something that recalls the identity and essential characteristics of the ancient Ligurian people. A people of farmers, sailors and builders with great entrepreneurial flair, who succeeded in taming its valleys, hills, and mountains with strenuous forms of farming cleverly adapted to the landscape, dotting the land with small towns, many of which are truly charming.

They set off to conquer the Mediterranean at a time when the Mediterranean was still the center of the world, turning Genoa into a magnificent city teeming with art and history, "a regal city", as Petrarch described it, "the mere sight of it is enough to merit the title *signora del mar* (lady of the sea)...". If you come to explore this extraordinary region, and visit its towns and monuments or its many excellent museums, you will discover Liguria's secrets and be enthralled by its landscape and its history, from the earliest times to the present day.

Highlights

- The Cinque Terre: the 5 picturesque hamlets of Manarola, Corniglia, Monterosso, Vernazza and Riomaggiore.
- The mansion-lined Via Garibaldi, a UNESCO World Heritage Site in 2007.
- Dolceàcqua: Monet painted the magnificent hump-backed bridge, calling it as a "jewel of lightness".

Bold, stars and italics are used in the text to emphasize the importance of places and art-works:
bold type ** → **not to be missed**
bold type * → **very important**
bold type → **important**
italic type → *interesting*

Inside

In 1358 the Italian writer, poet and Humanist Francesco Petrarca (whom we know in English as Petrarch), described Genoa as follows: "You will see a regal city built on the mountainside, superb for its men and its walls: the mere sight of the city is enough to merit the title signora del mar (lady of the sea)...". Genoa was founded on the sea in about 500 BC. Right from the beginning (and still today) it was a crossing-point between two important transport networks: maritime routes, which led from here across the waters of the Mediterranean, and land routes, which wound up over the Apennines into the north of Italy and thence to the rest of Europe and beyond. These two networks were mainly used for trade, but, over the centuries, they also enabled people of different cultures to travel widely and for foreigners to reach Genoa. Today, the city stands in a charming setting with all the fascination and the thousand faces of a city of art and architecture with a long, complex history. Genoa is currently going through a phase of regeneration that will take the city into a new and dynamic future.

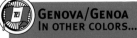

GENOVA/GENOA
IN OTHER COLORS...

ITINERARIES: pages 87, 91, 96, 98
FOOD: pages 120, 123, 125
SHOPPING: pages 147, 149, 151
EVENTS: pages 154, 158
WELLNESS: pages 166, 167
PRACTICAL INFO: pages 174, 175

Palazzo Doria Pamphilj ❶

This building, also known as Palazzo del Principe, was built for Admiral Andrea Doria. It has an elegant entrance designed by the Florentine Perin del Vaga, to whom the admiral entrusted the decoration of his entire residence (1528-33). The artist amply repaid this trust, as we can see in the frescoes of Andrea Doria's magnificent apartments: starting in the atrium (*Stories of the Roman kings and Triumphs*), we continue to the Loggia of the Heroes (ancestors of the Doria family) and the great hall of the Fall of the Giants (*Zeus hurling thunderbolts at the Giants*). In the hall is the famous portrait of Andrea Doria dressed in the uniform of the papal fleet. The Galleria contains a series of splendid **tapestries** made in Brussels in 1582-91. The south facade is just as grand: its porticoes and patios overlook the garden, laid out on a series of terraces at the end of the 16th century. In the center of the park stands the Fountain of Neptune (1599). Not far from the Porta Principe

The garden of Palazzo Doria Pamphilj, with the famous Fountain of Neptune in an old print.

train station is **Castello D'Albertis** which was given to Captain Enrico Alberto D'Albertis, a famous navigator, and now houses the collections of the Museo delle Culture del Mondo. In addition to the captain's legacy, which includes ancient weapons, nautical instruments and geographical publications, there is a collection of items exhibited by the American Catholic missions at the Great Exhibition of 1892. By walking along Via Gramsci, we see the church of *S. Giovanni di Pré*, built in 1180, and the adjoining **Commenda,** a convent dating from 1508 which now houses temporary exhibitions. Further on we turn into Via Pré, which feels like a souk with its market stalls, shops and medieval houses.

Palazzo Reale/Royal Palace ❷

The building was given its name by the Savoys, who took possession of the palazzo in 1824. Everything inside the main entrance is worthy of a royal palace, including the brightly-painted facades surrounding the main courtyard. At the far end

of it, beyond the three-arched gateway, a hanging garden overlooks the sea, with a two-color mosaic pavement made with cobbles recovered from the demolished convent of the Turchine. The staircase on the left leads to the *piano nobile*, which houses the **Museo di Palazzo Reale**. 17th-century frescoes and fine furnishings (18C-19C) enhance the setting of many important artworks. This juxtaposition is particularly striking in the *Gallery of Mirrors*, with its four fine statues (**Hyacinth**, Clitie, Amore – or Narcissus – and Venus). The Hall of Audiences contains two very valuable paintings: the *Rape of Proserpine* by Valerio Castello and the portrait of Caterina Durazzo by Anthony Van Dyck, who also painted the Crucifix in the King's Bedroom. The *silk* hangings in the Hall of Peace were painted by Giovanni Francesco Romanelli to look like tapestries. Behind Palazzo Reale is *Palazzo dell'Università*. This palazzo has a similar structure: an atrium, a raised courtyard and a double staircase in the refined 17th-century style (note the coupled columns of the

Galleria nazionale di Palazzo Reale

1 Left stair
2 Loggia
3 Room of the Battles (G.B. Pittoni, C.F. Beaumont, Francesco de Mura, F. Monti)
4 Room of Time (Domenico Piola, Grechetto, Francesco Bassano, Borgognone)
5 Room of Peace (Giovanni Francesco Romanelli)
6 The Veronese Room
7 Gallery of Mirrors (Filippo Parodi, Francesco Schiaffino)
8,9 Duke of Genoa's waiting-room and bedroom (Valerio Castello, Guercino, Gian Gioseffo Dal Sole)
10 Doge of Genoa's bedroom (Agostino Ratti)
11,12 Chapel Gallery and Chapel (G.B. Carlone, Filippo Parodi)
13 Throne Room (Luca Giordano)
14 Audience Room (Van Dyck, Valerio Castello)
15 King's bedroom (Bartolomeo Guidobono, Van Dyck)
16 King's bathroom (Maestro dell'Adorazione dei Magi di Torino)
18 Queen's Terrace
20 Blue sitting-room (Giacomo Antonio Boni)
21 Queen's bedroom (Vincent Malò, Bernardo Strozzi, il Baciccio)
23 Queen's sitting-room (Domenico Fiasella, Luca Giordano)
27 Dawn sitting-room (Giacomo Antonio Boni, Bernardo Strozzi)

An interior typical of the transition from Late Mannerism to Baroque, in the church of S. Siro.

portico). The whole palace was restored to its former glory in the 1980s and 1990s and is now open to the public. Via Balbi leads to Piazza della Nunziata, site of the **church of SS. Annunziata del Vastato,** rebuilt in 1591-1625, above a late-Gothic church. The facade is graced by two bell towers. The spectacular *interior* is built on a Latin-cross plan, splendidly decorated with inlaid red and white marble, gold-painted stuccoes and frescoes executed by the finest Genoese artists. From here we walk down Via Campo, and across Piazza Fossatello to visit the **church of S. Siro.** This was Genoa's first cathedral and dates from the 4th century. When S. Lorenzo became the city's cathedral (9C), it was rebuilt in the Romanesque style.

In 1580 the basilica was destroyed by fire, and rebuilt in the form we see today. The splendid doorway on the right facade dates from this period. The bell tower, the last vestige of the Romanesque church, was demolished in 1904 because it was thought to be unstable.

The interior, divided into a nave and two aisles by coupled columns, is richly decorated with polychrome marble and frescoes.

It has a splendid black marble and bronze **high altar.**

Palazzo S. Giorgio ❸

This building dating from 1260 was the city's seat of government for only two years. In 1407, the palazzo became the headquarters of the Bank of S. Giorgio, hence its present name. In 1570, the wing on the seaward side was added and, in 1606-08, the facade was decorated with splendid frescoes. It was altered in 1912, and carefully restored in 1990. In the majestic **Salone delle Compere** note the *Statues of the Bank's Protectors* and some fine paintings, such as the *Madonna depicted as the Queen of Genoa with St George*, by Domenico Piola (17C), Genoa's coat-of-arms and the *Symbols of Justice and Fortitude*. This is the area known as the *Porto Antico* (Old Port) which has been given a new lease of life by the famous architect Renzo Piano. The **Aquarium** is one of Genoa's greatest attractions and the third most visited monument in Italy. A few figures will explain why it is the biggest in Europe: more than 6,000 specimens of 600 marine species, 62 tanks and almost 10,000 m² of exhibition space.

One of them is the *Grande Nave Blu (Big Blue Ship),* with exhibits of fish, crustaceans and rare reptiles and plants from Madagascar.

Close by is **Porta Siberia** or **Porta del Molo,** the mighty bastion designed by

Galeazzo Alessi (1553), part of the city's 16th-century fortifications. It was important as the stronghold of the port area and was also the customs office.

Cattedrale di S. Lorenzo/Cathedral of S. Lorenzo ❹

The city's cathedral for more than 1,000 years. Founded in the 9th century, it was preferred to S. Siro because it stood within the city walls. In the early 12th century, it was rebuilt in the Romanesque style but never completed. The two **side doors**, known respectively as the doors of St John and St Gothard, date from this period. The cathedral began to take on its current appearance in the early 13th century, when the first tier of the facade was added with its motif of grey and white horizontal stripes. Other features dating from this period include the column-bearing *lions* and the so-called *arrotino* (*knife-grinder*) which actually depicts a saint with a sundial.

At the end of the same century the second tier of the facade with its two-light windows was added. The upper tier, decorated with mullioned windows and a rose window, was added in the 15th century, along with the loggia of the left tower. The bell tower and the dome were completed in the 16th century. When Via S. Lorenzo was laid out and the level of the piazza lowered, the front steps were added. The interior has a nave and two aisles. On the back of the facade is a remarkable early 14th-century fresco of the *Last Judgement* and the *Glorification of the Virgin*. In the left aisle, just beyond the entrance to the baptistery, is the

chapel of St John the Baptist*, with an elaborate front dating from 1451. At the end of the aisle, the Lercari chapel is decorated with frescoes. In the right aisle, in the Senarega chapel has an altar-piece (*Crucifixion with the Virgin, St John and St Sebastian*) painted in 1597 by Federico Barocci. Also worthy of note are the wooden *choirstalls* and the frescoes in the vault of the apse. Beyond the sacristy (door on left of presbytery) is the **Museo del Tesoro di San Lorenzo**. Steps lead down to four rooms lined with black stone from Promontorio, an interesting setting for the objects on display: the **Sacro Catino*** (holy bowl), a symbol of the cathedral, traditionally identified with the Holy Grail but

Cattedrale di S. Lorenzo

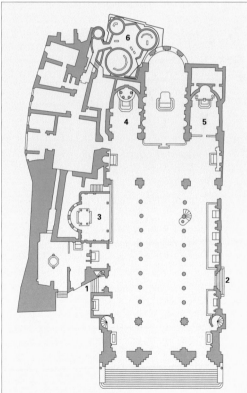

1 Door of St John the Baptist
2 Door of St Gothard
3 Chapel of St John the Baptist
4 Frescoes by G.B. Castello and Luca Cambiaso
5 Altar-piece by Federico Barocci
6 Treasury Museum

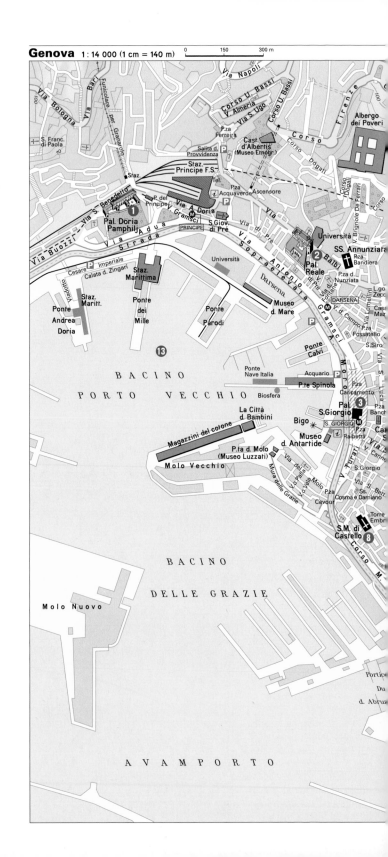

Genova 1 : 14 000 (1 cm = 140 m)

0   150   300 m

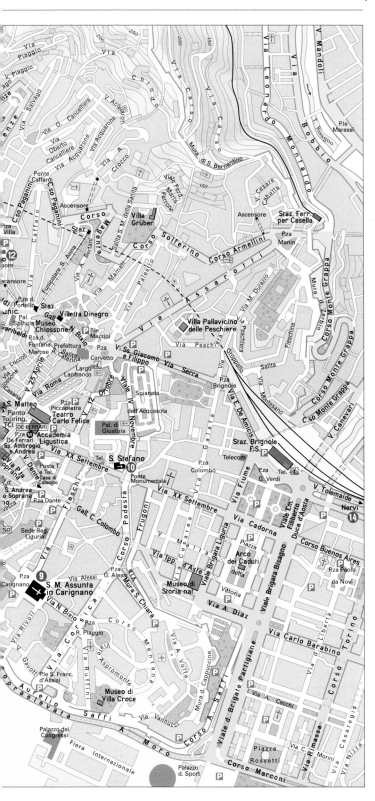

actually a work of Islamic origin; the **Reliquary of the Ashes of St John the Baptist*** by Teramo Danieli and Simone Caldera (1438-45), still used in the annual procession of June 24. The fine **Zaccaria Cross*** is a Byzantine reliquary dates from the 10th century but remodelled in the 13th century, decorated with gold leaf, pearls

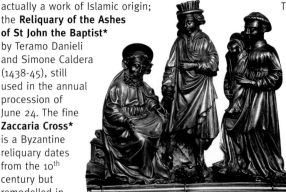

Museo del Tesoro di S. Lorenzo: detail of the reliquary containing the ashes of St John the Baptist.

and oriental gems. According to tradition, the fragments of wood inside are from the True Cross.

Piazza S. Matteo ❺

This piazza was surrounded by the mansions and the church of the Doria family. Their power is reflected in the buildings around its edge, for example *Palazzo Andrea Doria* (No. 17). On the left side of the square are *Palazzo di Domenicaccio Doria* (No. 16) and *Palazzo Branca Doria* (entrance at 1 Vico Falamonica). Their characteristic light and dark striped facades date the buildings to the second half of the 13th century.

The **church of S. Matteo*** was founded earlier (1125) but rebuilt in 1278. The Doria used it as their private chapel and the inscriptions around the base refer to the military successes of members of the family. The interior, richly decorated with frescoes, stuccoes and marble, was commissioned in the 16th century by Andrea Doria, whose remains lie in the sarcophagus below the crypt. Partly concealed, to the left of the church, is the **cloister**, with pointed arches resting on coupled columns (1308-10).

Palazzo Ducale/Ducal Palace ❻

Designed by Vannone (1591-c. 1620), the facade overlooking Piazza De Ferrari is decorated with colorful frescoes while the Neoclassical facade overlooking Piazza Matteotti has a double order of coupled columns and, on top, an attic storey topped with statues and trophies. The interior,

Genoa: the splendid, austere Ducal Palace, with its elaborate Neoclassical facade.

now used for temporary exhibitions and other cultural events, has two courtyards surrounded by columns. Two flights of stairs lead up to the loggia above, where the state rooms are arranged around the west courtyard. There is also a chapel with frescoes (*Glories of Genoa*) painted in about 1655 by Giovanni Battista Carlone, and the halls of the Great and Small Councils, which were rebuilt in 1780-83 after a fire. On the far side of Piazza De Ferraris, Via Dante leads to **Porta di S. Andrea** or **Porta Soprana****. Today this marks the dividing line between the historic center and the modern city.

The gateway stands in a position which, together with its beautiful lines has become one of the city's most famous views. The bastion, formerly part of the 9th-century fortifications, was rebuilt in 1155. Set between the two towers and built on a semi-circular plan, the bastion has a pointed arch with small blind arches, merlons and a chemin-de-ronde. Not far away is the *church of S. Agostino*, adjoining a former Augustinian monastery dating from before 1260. Its facade, divided into three parts, has the recurring motif of dark and light-colored stripes. Above the right transept, the fine 15th-century **bell tower** has a spire and four pinnacles decorated with polychrome majolica tiles. In 1995, the church was converted into an auditorium, whereas the former monastery now houses the *Museo di S. Agostino*. It contains architectural features and artworks such as the remains of the **funerary monument of Margaret of Brabant*** (1313-14) and a **Penitent St Mary Magdalene*** by A. Canova (1796).

S. Donato ❼

This church is one of the finest examples of the Genoese Romanesque style (early 12C). It has a splendid octagonal **bell tower**** with two tiers of two-light windows (the third was added in the 19C). During restoration work in the late 19th century, a rose window and the pseudo-porch with columns were added. The doorway with the deep embrasure and the arch are original. On the right side of the church is a small shrine with a dove representing the Holy Spirit, containing a statue of the Madonna and Child. The interior is divided into a nave and two aisles by columns, six of which are re-used Roman columns. Above the colonnade is a fake matroneum spanned by two-light windows. The chapel of St Joseph situated halfway down the left aisle contains a fine **triptych*** with doors dating from 1515.

S. Maria di Castello ❽

The word "Castello" refers to the fortifications built on the hill in pre-Roman times. The first church to be built on the site of the present one dates from the 10th-11th century. The Romanesque church we see today was begun in the early 12th century. It has a basilica plan with a nave

Complesso di S. Maria di Castello

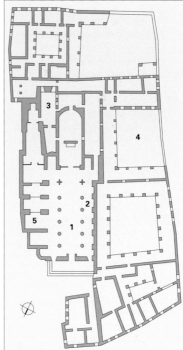

1 Church
2 Painting by Bernardo Castello
3 Works by Barnaba da Modena and Lodovico Brea
4 Cloister with fresco by Giusto di Ravensburg
5 Polyptych of the Annunciation by Giovanni Mazone

The medieval Torre degli Embriaci, on the hill of Castello.

sole tower to survive an edict issued in 1296 limiting the height of towers in the city.

S. Maria Assunta in Carignano ❾

The church stands on the top of the hill which gives it its name. Galeazzo Alessi designed it and oversaw the building work which lasted 50 years (1552-1602). It has a Greek-cross plan and consists of a cube with a central dome resting on pillars and four smaller domes at the corners.
It should also have had four bell towers, but only two were built on the main facade, which was altered in 1722. Inside, the niches in two of the pillars supporting the dome contain two magnificent statues (**Blessed Alessandro Sauli*** and **St Sebastian***), dating from 1668.
It has many fine paintings, including the **Martyrdom of St Blaise** above the second altar on the right and the **Pietà*** above the third altar on the left. Note also the painting of *St Francis receiving the Stigmata* by Guercino, and the organ (1656) with its painted

and two aisles and a fake matroneum above the arches. Many of the columns and capitals are re-used Roman material (2C and 3C AD).
In 1441, the church was given by Pope Eugenius IV to the Dominicans, who built the chapels of the great Genoese families and the convent next door. The dome, built on an octagonal plan, dates from the following century.
Inside the church (4th chapel on the right) note the *Martyrdom of St Peter of Verona*. However, the finest artworks are kept in the **Sale dei Ragusei**. These rooms can be accessed from the sacristy (door in right transept). Amongst other works, they contain a *Madonna and Child* by Barnaba da Modena and a *Coronation of the Virgin* by Lodovico Brea (1513). The convent is also very interesting and has a superb **fresco** painted in 1451 by "Iustus de Alemania".
Left of the church, 41m high, is the **Torre degli Embriaci** (12C): this is the

S. Maria Assunta in Carignano

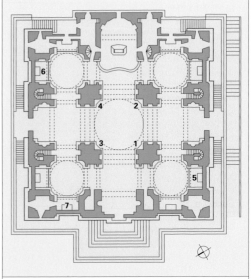

1 Statue of St Alessandro Sauli (P. Puget)
2 Statue of Sebastian (P. Puget)
3 Statue of St Bartholomew (C. David)
4 Statue of St John the Baptist (F. Parodi)
5 Martyrdom of St Blaise (C. Maratta)
6 Pietà (L. Cambiaso)
7 St Francis (Guercino)

Luca Cambiaso, *Pietà*, church of Santa Maria Assunta.

organ-doors. Not far away is the *Museo Civico di Storia Naturale Giacomo Doria*, founded in 1867 and in its present location since 1912. It has one of the finest collections in Europe, especially its splendid zoological collection.
It has many exhibits from outside Europe and is particularly proud of its entomological collection, the largest in Italy.

S. Stefano ⑩

Without wishing to do an injustice to the facade, the church is best approached from the rear, because the steps leading to it from Viale IV Novembre have lovely views of the **apse***, a masterpiece of Romanesque art, sitting on a base punctured with the small windows of the crypt.
The facade, almost suspended over Via XX Settembre, features that motif so common in Genoa's churches of black and white stripes, as well as a large rose window. It has a gable roof, another common feature in Genoa, and the bell tower stands behind.
Inside, note the superb **Martyrdom of St Stephen***, painted in 1524 by Giulio Romano. Also look out for the

cantoria on the back of the facade and the **Martyrdom of St Bartholomew** in the presbytery. By walking along Via XX Settembre you come to Piazza De Ferrari, the center of 20th-century Genoa, with its equestrian monument of Garibaldi. Facing it, the Teatro Carlo Felice (theater) has an extraordinary stage, with four mobile platforms controlled by sophisticated computer systems.

Via Garibaldi ⑪

Originally the "Strada Nuova" was laid out in 1551 by architect Bernardino as a residential street. There was no external access at the time.
Only very wealthy families could afford to build mansions there in the years between 1558 and 1583 (see the drawing on p. 28). The street was opened to traffic at the end of the 18th century. In the two centuries that followed, the houses built by the great families of Genoa were gradually taken over by the city's banks, antique shops and exclusive private clubs, which were able to maintain this considerable artistic and architectural heritage. It is now a pedestrian precinct and the street and the houses on either side of it have been declared a UNESCO World Heritage Site. The rooms of the *piano nobile* of **Palazzo Cambiaso** (No. 1), are decorated with Mannerist frescoes. Pietro Orsolino carved the reclining figures (Prudence and Vigilance) on the marble doorway of the house opposite, **Palazzo Gambaro** (No. 2), built in 1558-64.
The nearby **Palazzo Carrega Cataldi** (No. 4) was completed in 1561, and designed by Bernardino Cantone and Giovanni Battista Castello: the latter also painted the frescoes in the atrium; the *piano nobile* has a splendid Rococò gallery.
Palazzo Lercari Parodi (No. 3) has an unusual courtyard in front of the main building, making it look even more splendid, and suggests that it was built later than the houses nearby, which all follow the "enclosed block" pattern. **Palazzo Spinola** (No. 5) has particularly fine decoration on the *piano nobile*. There is a splendid hall on the *piano nobile* of **Palazzo Doria** (No. 6), with an ornate 18th-century

Palazzo Bianco

Palazzo Rosso

Palazzo Doria Tursi

Palazzo delle Torrette

Palazzo Campa[

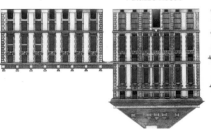

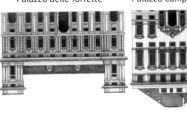

fireplace. The facade of the building dates from the late 16th century, another work by the team of Bernardino Cantone and Giovanni Battista Castello (1563-67). Between 1563 and 1566, they also built **Palazzo**

Podestà (No. 7), still privately owned, with a magnificent Mannerist facade: three tiers decorated with figures and a delightful atrium decorated with stuccoes. There is even a nymphaeum in the courtyard. Nearby **Palazzo**

Galleria di Palazzo Rosso

First floor

Second floor

First floor
1 Loggia
2 Giambono, Albrecht Dürer, Palma il Vecchio
3 Paolo Veronese, Paris Bordon, Moretto, Jacopo Bassano
4 Ludovico Carracci, Guido Reni, G.C. Procaccini
5 Guercino
6 Orazio Gentileschi, Mattia Preti
7 Luca Cambiaso, Bernardo Strozzi

9 Sinibaldo Scorza, Grechetto
10 Domenico Piola, Bartolomeo Guidobono

Second floor
11 Atrium with loggia (Bernardo Schiaffino)
12 Hall (Gregorio De Ferrari)
13 Spring Room (Van Dyck, Gregorio De Ferrari)
14 Summer Room (Van Dyck,

Gregorio De Ferrari)
15 Fall Room (Domenico Piola, Antoine-Jean Gros)
16 Winter Room (Domenico Piola)
17 Loggia
18 Giovanni Andrea Carlone
19 Giovanni Andrea Carlone, Carlo Antonio Tavella
21 Alcove
22 Domenico Parodi, Bartolomeo Guidobono

Palazzo Podestà   Palazzo Spinola   Palazzo Lercari Parodi   Palazzo Cambiaso
zo Cattaneo Adorno   Palazzo Doria   Palazzo Carrega Cataldi   Palazzo Gambaro

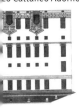
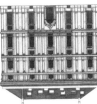
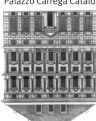
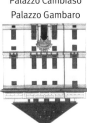

Campanella (No. 12) was altered in the late 18th century but was badly damaged by air raids in 1942.
The first things that catch the eye in **Palazzo del Municipio**** are the extraordinary dimensions of the front of the building, the length of which is three times as long as the symmetrically equal facades of the other palazzi. Its splendid staircase leads up to the colonnaded courtyard where two flights of steps climb up to a loggia. The decoration of the facades is enhanced by motifs of white and pink marble and slabs of grey slate. In 1596, the palazzo was bought by the Doria family, who, the following year, began to build the loggias at the side and to landscape the garden. More additions were made in 1820, when the clock-tower was erected. Although the palazzo is splendid architecturally, the actual decoration is comparatively restrained.
Palazzo Rosso* took six years to build (1671-77). Its name is supposed to derive from the red stones decorating the facade. One of the first works in the **art gallery** housed in the palazzo is a **Portrait of a Man*** ("Principe moscovita") formerly attributed to Pisanello, and now thought to be by Giambono; the **Portrait of a Young Man*** painted in 1506 by Albrecht Dürer bears his signature. In the next room is a

Judith with the head of Holophernes** by Veronese, also an **Annunciation*** by Ludovico Carracci and a **St Sebastian*** by Guido Reni; the **Death of Cleopatra**** is by Guercino. There are also works by Orazio Gentileschi (**Madonna and Sleeping Child***), Mattia Preti

Palazzo Rosso, *Judith with the head of Holophernes*** by Veronese.

(**Clorinda frees Olindo and Sofronia***), Bernardo Strozzi (**The Cook, Madonna and Child and the young St John***), the **Allegories of the seasons*** by De Ferrari (Spring, Summer) and Domenico Piola (Fall, Winter). Although **Palazzo Bianco*** is not so fine architecturally, it has a charming

The old port of Genoa

Genoa's Old Port area of is both the city's most modern district and the one imbued with the deepest historical significance. That explains why the plan devised by architect Renzo Piano to celebrate the 500th anniversary in 1992 of Columbus's epic voyage was so complex. It began as a project to "rehabilitate" the old port area, but in a way that would not only reinforce its historical significance but also its role as a threshold between the city and the sea. Recent changes, in particular the raised highway slicing its way through this part of the city, had transformed it into an area that was cut off from the rest of Genoa. The main aim of the regeneration of the area was, therefore, to reconnect the two parts of the city, restoring the sea to Genoa and bringing the port back to life, by building focuses of interest to the general public which

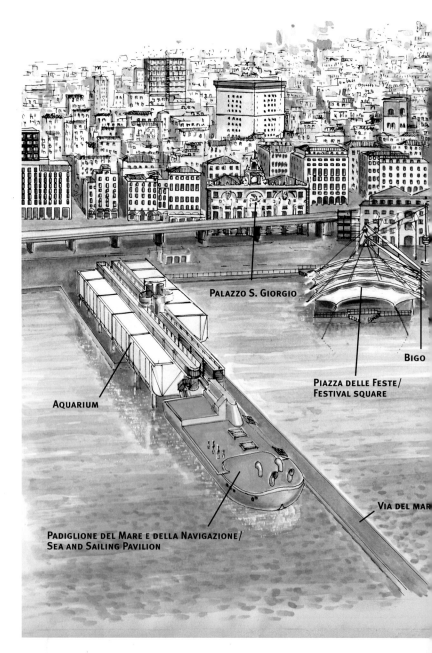

PALAZZO S. GIORGIO

BIGO

PIAZZA DELLE FESTE/
FESTIVAL SQUARE

AQUARIUM

VIA DEL MAR

PADIGLIONE DEL MARE E DELLA NAVIGAZIONE/
SEA AND SAILING PAVILION

would turn it into one of the most important cultural areas of the city. At the same time, the plan to rehabilitate the old port area was to incorporate isolated architectural features from various periods (the 17th-century free goods depot, the cotton warehouses, an industrial building from the 19th century, and the Millo building, built in the early 20th century) with new buildings which would not alter but, on the contrary, enhance the role and the historical significance of the port. In fact, the Bigio, the Sea and Sailing Pavilion, and the Aquarium conjure up the image of a ship, endowing the place with huge symbolic significance.

EDIFICIO MILLO/ MILLO-BUILDING

PANORAMIC LIFT

PORTA DEL MOLO

EX MAGAZZINI DEL COTONE/ OLD COTTON WAREHOUSES

art gallery. In the first room is an altar-piece depicting **scenes from the lives of Sts Lawrence, Sixtus and Hyppolitus***. The next two rooms contain works by 16th-century Genoese and Italian painters. Four rooms are devoted to works by Flemish painters including Hans Memling (**Christ making the sign of the Benediction****). One section of the gallery is devoted to the works of Caravaggio (**Ecce Homo***) and his followers.

Not far from here, *Piazza della Meridiana* is named after the sundial (18C) on the facade of the palazzo of the same name, built in 1541-45. Inside (entrance at No. 4 Salita S. Francesco), there are two *fresco cycles* by Luca Cambiaso.

Spianata Castelletto ⑫

A rack tramway connects Piazza Portello to the **Belvedere Montaldo*** , which has marvelous views over the old city and the old port. The Art-Deco windows of the station at the top have an old-fashioned charm.

Porto/Port ⑬

In the 10th-12th centuries work began to build the port on a site that had been used as a natural harbor in Roman times (and was, it seems, probably used even before that by the local inhabitants).

In the second half of the 14th century, a dockyard was built with an arsenal attached. At the beginning of the 17th century, the first quantum leap forward was achieved with the construction of the Molo Nuovo (new mole) and the establishment of a "free port". More building work was undertaken under the House of Savoy in the second half of the 19th century, when the whole complex was reorganized. Between the Molo Nuovo and the Molo Vecchio, 11 long jetties and 18 quays were built, protected by the 1,500m-long Duca di Galliera breakwater. Boat tours of the port leave from Ponte Spinola and Calata Zingari.

Beyond the old porto and Porto della Darsena (docks) is the area reserved for ferry traffic: cruise liners moor at Ponte dei Mille and Ponte Andrea

 TCI HIGHLIGHTS

FIERA DI GENOVA

The Fiera di Genova (Genoa Trade Fair) was created over half a century ago, in 1956, thanks to the iron will and determination of advocate Giuseppe De Andrè, father of the famous singer-songwriter Fabrizio, and the mayor of Genoa at that time, Vittorio Pertusio. The underlying goal was to stimulate the local economy. The institutional mission of the trade fair includes promoting and supporting certain productive sectors that are strategic for the surrounding area, including shipbuilding, flower growing and tourism. It has also long held major sporting fairs with substantial international participation (both in terms of exhibitors and visitors). This flexibility is helped by the fact that the buildings can easily be adapted to different purposes and are very large, allowing almost any type of fair to be hosted. A good example of this is the Palasport building, which can be used for concerts, conferences or conventions.

The fairgrounds are located in an area right near the city center, overlooking the sea. Much of the land was part of the reclamation program of the 1960s.The overall urban design of the area is the work of Luigi Carlo Daneri. The surface area of the fairgrounds is over 300,000m², but perhaps the more notable figures are the 100,000m² of water and the 8km of paths along the seaside. In short, this is a unique place, even in international terms. The sea section of the fairgrounds is divided into two main parts: the Marina, created in 1988, and the Nuova (or New) Marina, inaugurated in September 2006.

The Nuova Marina covers 60,000m² of water and includes a 12,500m² area of land. The complex has over 450 bays for boats, with a water surface area of 100,000m². Bridges, raised walkways, quays, jetties and panoramic promenades make it possible to "navigate" the exhibition area by following a path that is over 8km long.

A view of the port from San Benigno; in the foreground, the famous "Matitone" (Big Pencil).

Doria. Behind them, the modern tower-blocks of the San Benigno district, built in the last two decades of the 20th century, are more reminiscent of North America. A New York studio designed the unmistakable "Matitone" (Big Pencil), based on the bell tower of the church of S. Donato.

Nervi ⑭

So close and yet so different from the city of Genoa, Nervi is connected to it by the panoramic, winding Via Aurelia and the busy Corso Europa. In 1959, restoration work partially restored the original appearance of the church of S. Siro, erected in the first half of the 12th century and rebuilt in the 17th century. A charming 2-km walk called the **Passeggiata Anita Garibaldi**** winds along the coast past pink and yellow houses, beached boats, the mouth of a stream, crossing the occasional medieval bridge. A characteristic corner of Liguria is the *little harbor at Nervi*, protected by a dyke and the starting-point of a famous coastal walk. The English-style gardens of Villa Gropallo, Villa Serra and Villa Grimaldi are now incorporated in a large park called the **Parchi di Nervi***. Covering almost 9 hectares, the park has typical Mediterranean plant species as well as numerous exotic varieties. The setting is delightful by itself but the resident squirrel population and cultural references add to the overall feel. Another "must see", so to speak, is the garden of Villa Serra, now the *Modern Art Gallery*, with its magnificent **rose-garden***: there are an incredible 800 species, which flower from May to November.

Passeggiata Anita Garibaldi at Nervi, one of Italy's most beautiful promenades.

33

BORZONASCA [57 km]

The hills around the town are covered with dense chestnut forest. Although the town, situated on the left bank of the Sturla River, became quite important after 1805, its origins are medieval, as we can see from the church at the bottom of Via Raggio. On the slate facade of this small building with its tiny belfry at the apex of the gable, is a low relief and a plaque dated 1460. There is another slate *doorway* (1554) at the oratory of S. Rocco, situated at the junction with the provincial highway. 7km further up the

Abbazia di Borzone

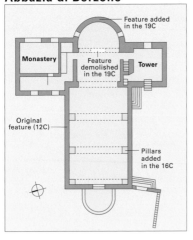

valley of the Penna Stream, the road reaches *Prato Sopralacroce*, famous for its iron-rich natural springs. Amid this unspoiled landscape, a minor road leads to Prato Sopralacroce (3km) and the **abbey of Borzone***, set in a quiet valley. A huge ancient cypress lends added charm to the abbey. According to a plaque on the eastern wall of the bell tower, it was part of the original complex of 1244. Very unusually for Liguria, the abbey has features typical of the Lombard School, for example, the grey stone and brick walls of the church and the tower. In 1834, work on a new church roof led to the opening up of the apse. The left side of the apse contains a slate tabernacle carved in 1513. The two side-altars, on the other hand, are Baroque: the one on the left has twisted columns.

CAMOGLI [22 km]

The (vertical) nature of the town was dictated by the lie of the land, with its tall buildings and its network of steep, narrow streets and flights of steps. The result is one of the most successful examples of coastal architecture in eastern Liguria. Rows of unusually tall, brightly-painted houses following the line of the seafront huddle around the large rock known as the "Isola" (previously separated from the mainland) where the town's two most important monuments now stand. The **church of S. Maria Assunta**, erected in the 12th century, has been extended and rebuilt several times. Its facade in the Neoclassical style dates from the last phase of building work in the 19th century. The black and white cobbled pavement in front of the church dates from the 17th century. The interior, richly decorated with marble and gilt stuccoes, has a frescoed ceiling. Another building of medieval date is the nearby **Castel Dragone** (closed to the public), a single tower dominating its mighty walls. Like the church, the fortress was rebuilt several times. A demanding but beautiful walk (about 1.5 hrs) leads to the tiny peninsula of Punta Chiappa. The path starts at Camogli, heads southeast and follows the Gentile Stream until it enters the town of San Rocco, right in front of the parish church (1863). There is a splendid **view** from the front of the church. The path continues down towards Punta Chiappa from the right of the church. On the way it passes the little **church of S. Nicolò di Capodimonte**, first mentioned in 1141,

The brightly-painted houses of Camogli are a unique feature of the seafront.

Complesso abbaziale
di S. Fruttuoso di Capodimonte

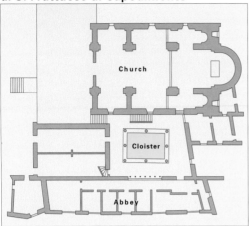

monumental complex of
S. Fruttuoso di Capodimonte*
in the charming little **hamlet
of San Fruttuoso**** has been
restored to its former glory.
We recommend you visit it
by boat (the boat ride from
Camogli takes about
30 minutes). The only
alternative is to walk along
the footpath that begins at
Portofino Vetta (1 hr 15 mins).
When you arrive at San
Fruttuoso by sea, the first
thing you notice is the *tower
of Andrea Doria* (1562),
situated on the cape between
the two inlets of the bay. In
the 8th century, the Bishop of
Taragona, Prosperus, who

which has a beautiful original
Romanesque apse. The marble high
altar is probably as old as the church.
The last section of the walk is very
steep: after Porto Pidocchio, where
boats moor, it ends at Punta Chiappa.
Thanks to restoration work conducted
by the FAI (the Italian Fund for the
Environment) in 1986-88, the splendid

was pursued by the Moors, fled from
Spain, settled here and founded a
chapel to enshrine the holy relics of
St Fructuosus (the first patriarch of
Taragona) and the deacons Augurius
and Eulogius. Benedictine monks
settled here in the 10th century and
built a **church** with a *dome* which was
subsequently incorporated in the

 ## TCI HIGHLIGHTS

THE CRISTO DEGLI ABISSI
(CHRIST OF THE DEPTHS)

"I, a man of the sea, would also have liked
something sacred to turn to, like the crosses on
mountain tops that give courage to the soldiers
of the Alpine regiments (...) In my mind I could
see what the statue should be like, standing
bathed in transparent blue light on the sea floor,
surrounded by the mystical decoration of marine vegetation and flickering fish, in the
solitary silence of the depths: a fluctuating figure, conceived in the water, its arms
stretched high, invoking God and embracing humanity at the same time, slender and
bright, with beautiful human proportions, and deep religious significance". The writer had
taken a dive to ease his mind, troubled by the death of a dear friend, Duilio Marcante, a
pioneer of scuba diving in Italy. He returned to the surface with an idea that was to
become reality on August 22,1954, when the bronze statue of the Savior by Guido Galletti
was gently lowered into the water off San Fruttuoso. It immediately became a symbol of
the close relationship between the people of Camogli and the sea, a source of great
richness, but also of tragedy. The ceremony held each year on the last Sunday of July
commemorates all those who have lost their lives at sea and who spend their lives at sea.
It culminates in the laying of laurel wreaths at the foot of the statue on the sea floor. The
event always attracts a large crowd, many boats and divers. Since the creation of the
Riserva Marina di Portofino (in 1999), only diving in organized groups is permitted.

For further information, please contact The European Diving Center of Santa
Margherita Ligure (tel. and fax 0185293017).

octagonal *bell tower*, and the bottom part of the **cloister**: the upper part was added two centuries later.

In the 13th century, the Doria family financed the building of the **abbey**, obtaining in exchange the right to use the crypt adjoining the lower cloister as a family sepulchre. Between 1275 and 1305, eight tombs of white marble and grey stone were put there, echoing the colors of many of the Tyrrhenian churches of that period. In the 17th century, the upper cloister was remodeled. In 1861, the Dorias purchased the whole complex. In 1933 the two tiers of three-light windows were restored in the abbey. Then, in 1983, the property was handed over to the FAI. San Fruttuoso attracts not only tourists and swimmers, but also a large number of scuba divers. Many come to see the underwater statue known as Cristo degli Abissi (Christ of the Depths).

Waves breaking at Camogli, a picturesque fishing-town on Paradiso Bay.

CHIÀVARI [43 km]

The town's geographical position meant that it had fairly easy access to the Po Valley side of the Apennines. As a result, the town became important as early as the 8th-7th centuries BC. Much later, in the 19th and 20th centuries, the town expanded rapidly.

Every morning (except Sunday), a lively fruit and vegetable market is held in Piazza Mazzini, overlooked by the Neogothic Palazzo di Giustizia (1886). To make room for it, the citadel constructed in 1404 had to be demolished: all that remains is the mighty square tower standing between the palace of justice and the Town Hall behind. The church of S. Giacomo di Rupinaro, the oldest in Chiàvari, was founded in the 7th century. However, the building we see today is the result of restructuring completed in 1637. It has a 18th-century bell tower and a modern (1938) facade.

S. Giovanni Battista ❶, founded in 1332 and remodeled in the 17th century,

Chiavari 1: 17 000 (1 cm = 170 m)

has a modern marble facade (1935). The bell tower was altered in 1557. Inside, in addition to the fine crucifix above the high altar, there are two altar-pieces by Orazio De Ferrari above the second and third altars on the right. Not only is the library here one of the finest in Liguria (it contains 70,000 volumes), but the institution, founded in 1791, also houses three other permanent collections: the **Museo Storico**, including an important collection of relics from the Risorgimento period; the *art gallery*

View of Piazza Mazzini in Chiàvari.

and, at No. 1 Via Ravaschieri, the *Museo Garaventa*, entirely devoted to the work of sculptor Lorenzo Garaventa. Another building converted into a museum is *Palazzo Rocca* ❷, the residence commissioned from Bartolomeo Bianco by the Marquis of Costaguta (1629) and subsequently extended. It is surrounded by a large and very beautiful *park* and houses the **Museo Archeologico per la Preistoria e Protostoria del Tigullio**. The most important exhibits here were found in an Iron-Age necropolis. The Galleria Civica focuses on paintings of the Genoese Baroque School (B. Strozzi, D. Fiasella). The **Cattedrale di Nostra Signora dell'Orto/Cathedral of Nostra Signora dell'Orto** ❸ was built as a sanctuary (1613-33) to

enshrine an image of the Madonna which had become an object of veneration after the plague of 1493. However, the appearance of the church today is the result of building work begun in 1823. At this time the imposing pronaos was added, the interior was divided into a nave with two aisles separated by pillars and it was lavishly decorated with marble and gilt stuccoes. Next to the right side of the cathedral, in a continuation of the facade, is the *Bishop's Palace*, which houses the Museo Diocesano and the Seminary, both of which date from the 19th century.

PORTOFINO [36 km]

Charming enough to move the heart of an officer of the German Wehrmacht who, when ordered to bomb the little town from the air to prevent munitions falling into enemy hands, refused to do so. The view of Portofino, with its tall, narrow houses painted in pastel shades clustered around the little harbor, is one of Italy's most famous coastal landscapes. Perhaps the general public is less aware of its origins. During the Roman Imperial period it was referred to as "Portus Delphini" (Dolphin Harbor). Today, the center of the town still has its Roman grid layout. Portofino should be visited on foot. Via Roma leads down to the sea. On the right is the 14th-century oratory of Nostra Signora Assunta (note the fine carved slate doorway (1555), now used for art exhibitions. The road ends in Piazza Martiri dell'Olivetta, known by the locals as "*la piazzetta*"*. All the way around the harbor are porticoes with shops and restaurants. Behind the square on the left is the *church of S. Martino*, built in the 12th century in the Lombard Romanesque style, although its present appearance dates from the 19th century. The *church of S. Giorgio* was rebuilt after the last war (1950) and occupies a splendid position on the isthmus at the base of the headland with superlative views. It enshrines the relics of St George. Further on is the **castle of S. Giorgio**, a 16th-century adaptation of a medieval fortress. The last stop is the lighthouse at the tip of *Punta del Capo*.

RAPALLO [31 km]

This town has the largest population on the Tigullio Gulf and, thanks to bathing establishments, the marina and an array of other modern tourist facilities, it is one of the most prestigious holiday resorts in eastern Liguria – known as the Levante Riviera. The elegant Art-Deco-style hotels that line the **Lungomare Vittorio Veneto** (the seafront street and promenade) emphasize Rapallo's longstanding importance as a vacation resort. The

The Lungomare Vittorio Veneto in Rapallo.

promenade ends in front of a small **castle** that was built in 1551 and is connected to the mainland by a narrow strip of land. Restored in 1960, it is now used for a range of temporary exhibitions and cultural events. On the far side of *Piazza Garibaldi*, *Via Mazzini* and Via Magenta lead to the **church of S. Stefano**, first documented as early as 1155. The building we see today is the result of major restructuring work carried out in the 17th century. The nearby City Tower dates from 1473, whereas the Bianchi Oratory dates from the 17th century. At the end of Via Mazzini stands the elegant Neoclassical facade of the *parish church of Ss. Gervasio e Protasio*, also of medieval origin (1118) but altered in the 17th-20th centuries. The bell tower (1753-57) has an obvious lean. A good way to complete any visit to Rapallo is to head to the so-called Ponte di Annibale (Hannibal's bridge), which dates from the early Middle Ages.

SANTA MARGHERITA LIGURE [31 km]

The brightly-colored facades of many of the houses are a reminder that this used to be a small fishing village, whereas the elegant hotels in the Art-Deco style date from its early years as a popular holiday resort, between the mid-19th and early 20th centuries. After World War II, although considerable development and rebuilding did take place, it was more restrained here than elsewhere in this zone. The parish church of S. Margherita d'Antiochia was designed by the architect Giovanni Battista Ghiso in the 17th century. Proceeding to the right of the church, we come to the municipal park of Villa Durazzo: one half of the park is laid out in the Italian style, with many exotic species, and the other half as an English wood. Controversy reigns as to whether the **villa***, built shortly after 1560, can be attributed to Galeazzo Alessi. The square building has windows on all four floors and is decorated with rustication and moldings with reliefs. Inside, the riot of marbles, majolica, tapestries, stuccoes, Murano glass and chinoiserie has to be seen to be believed. The picture gallery has works by a number of well-known painters. The park also incorporates the Villa del Nido and Villa S. Giacomo (both 19C). As we leave, in the direction of the sea stands the white facade of the 17th-century church of S. Giacomo di Corte, dramatically poised above the Tigullio Gulf. A flight of steps leads down to the 17th-century oratory of S. Erasmo (St Erasmus is the patron saint of sailors). In the 17th-century church of the Cappuccini, the confessional room contains a statue (**Madonna Enthroned***) from the Provencal School of the 12th century. Opposite the church are the ruins of the castle, which was built in 1550 and, amazingly, only took six months to complete.

BANDIERA ARANCIONE

THE QUALITY LABEL FOR TOURISM AND THE ENVIRONMENT IN ITALY'S INLAND AREAS

The Bandiera Arancione (*Orange Flag*) is a label of quality for the development of tourism in Italy's inland areas. Municipalities with less than 15,000 inhabitants may be awarded it if selected criteria are achieved and maintained: cultural heritage, respect for the environment, hospitality, information and services, and quality local production. The Orange Flag program is run by the Touring Club of Italy. The World Tourism Organisation has chosen the Orange Flag Program as a success in the sphere of environmental tourism. For more information: www.touringclub.it/bandierearancioni

SANTO STÉFANO D'ÀVETO [73 km]

The aim of this mountainous area is to become popular with the Genoese. It has largely succeeded and has been awarded the TCI's Orange Flag. The town, which lies at the foot of Mt Maggiorasca (1,799m) is mostly modern and is dominated by some of the mighty bastions of the Malaspina castle (13C). Opposite the fortress is the bell tower of the old parish church, now an oratory. Above the high altar of the new church, completed in 1929, is an altar-piece known as the Madonna di Guadalupe, which, according to tradition, was fixed to the main mast of Andrea Doria's galley.

SESTRI LEVANTE [51 km]

The Promontorio dell'Isola stretches out to sea, giving the town on which it is built two of the most lovely views in the Levante Riviera. North of the cape, the **Baia delle Favole/Bay of Fairy Tales ❶** has a name coined by one of the world's greatest story-tellers, Hans Christian Andersen, who stayed in Sestri Levante in 1833.

On the other side, and perhaps even more beautiful, is the **Baia del Silenzio/Bay of Silence* ❷**, its beach framed by houses painted in pastel shades. Between the two bays is the narrow isthmus where *Piazza Matteotti* is situated. Overlooking the square is the 17th-century *Palazzo Durazzo*

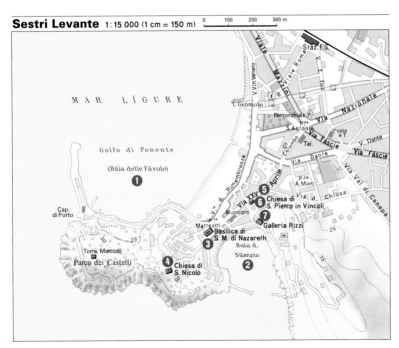

Sestri Levante 1:15 000 (1 cm = 150 m)

Pallavicini, now the Town Hall, and the **Basilica di Santa Maria di Nazareth** ❸, built in 1604-16. Beyond the Neoclassical pronaos on the facade, (1840), the interior is decorated in the Baroque style. Note the 12th-century wooden crucifix, and the paintings by Domenico Fiasella (**Pentecost**) and Lazzaro Tavarone (*Madonna of Our Lady of Mt Carmel and Sts Lawrence and John the Baptist*), in the fourth and second chapels on the left respectively. Left of the church, Via Penisola di Levante climbs up towards the headland, past the rather sad ruins of the oratory of S. Caterina (1578), destroyed by bombs in 1944. A commemorative plaque has been placed next to a statue of the saint. Just beyond it is the apse of the **Chiesa di San Nicolò/Church of S. Nicolò** ❹ dell'Isola, built in 1151. The facade dates from the 15th century, while the bell tower with its pyramid-shaped roof has a belfry with two-light windows. Next to it, in the *Parco del Grand Hotel dei Castelli* is the *Marconi Tower* where Guglielmo Marconi conducted his first radio transmission experiments. Back in Piazza Matteotti, *Via XXV Aprile* ❺ and Via Palestro lead through the town past lovely views to Vico Macelli and the 17th-century *Chiesa di S. Pietro in Vincoli/Church of S. Pietro in Vincoli* ❻.

Despite its rather forlorn state, it contains some good artworks: a wooden sculpture (the *Martyrdom of St Catherine of Alexandria*) in the first chapel on the right and, in the second chapel on the left, *Christ Bound to the Column*. Nearby at No. 8 Via dei Cappuccini, the *Galleria Rizzi* ❼ has an exhibition of painting and sculpture from the 15th-18th centuries. Not far away is the **little town of Moneglia** where, like many towns on the Riviera, in the late 19th century, the town abandoned its traditional seaside activities and became a holiday resort. Luca Cambiaso the painter was born here. He may have painted the *Adoration of the Magi* on the right wall of the *church of S. Giorgio* as a young man. The church was built in 1396 and remodeled in 1704. The Franciscan cloister next-door dates from the 15th century. At the opposite end of town a magnificent **cobbled pavement*** lies in front of the *parish church of S. Croce*, another example of a Baroque remodeling (1726) of a medieval building. The church is named after the Byzantine crucifix kept in the fourth altar on the left, found on the beach after a shipwreck. The painting of the *Blessed Virgin* above the third altar on the right is by A.M. Maragliano. In the sacristy is a *Last Supper* by Luca Cambiaso.

The charming Bay of Silence off Sestri Levante.

LA SPÈZIA

La Spèzia was transformed from a small seaside town into a prosperous city almost overnight in 1808 when Napoleon Bonaparte arrived, declared the gulf a naval base and the town a Maritime Prefecture. New construction methods meant that defensive fortifications could be built on the seaward side, and that the medieval landing-stages, located in naturally protected little bays, could be replaced with larger, modern ones. Later, La Spèzia became the newly-created Kingdom of Italy's main naval base. In the late 19th century, the medieval fabric was largely destroyed to make way for a new arsenal and a new town layout, which is mainly what you see today. In La Spèzia, whether you are visiting its array of interesting museums, climbing up to the imposing castle of S. Giorgio on a sunny day or strolling along its bustling, well-kept seafront, there are unexpected delights in store.

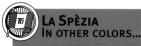

LA SPÈZIA IN OTHER COLORS...
- **ITINERARIES:** pages 87, 88, 93, 97
- **FOOD:** pages 123, 125, 129
- **SHOPPING:** pages 148, 150
- **EVENTS:** pages 157, 160
- **PRACTICAL INFO:** pages 177, 178

Corso Cavour ❶

This long street is the result of the "expansion plan" worked out in 1862, which swept away most of the medieval town. This period of town planning is perhaps what characterizes most the appearance of the town center, which is elegant, tidy but without many memorable landmarks. The most interesting buildings on this long street and the squares which intersect it are the *church of Nostra Signora della Salute* (1900) in Piazza Brin, *Palazzo Crozza* (No. 251), now the municipal library, with the Musei Civici (city museums) behind, and the **church of S. Maria Assunta**, in Piazza Beverini. This 15th-century church was actually founded in the 13th century, and then altered in the 20th century. At the far end of the left aisle is a fine polychrome terracotta figure by Andrea della Robbia depicting the Coronation of the Virgin.

Museo Civico Giovanni Podenzana/ Giovanni Podenzana Civic Museum ❷

Now that the archeological collection has been moved to castle of S. Giorgio, the museum at No. 9 Via Curtatone is divided into two sections: a natural history section (with paleontological and mineralogical collections resulting from research in the hinterland of La Spèzia) and an ethnographical section, which is excellent and comprises costumes, tools and equipment used in everyday life and by the farming community of the area around Luni.

Museo Civico d'Arte Antica, Medievale e Moderna Amedeo Lia/ Civic Museum of Ancient, Medieval and Modern Art ❸

The meticulous restoration of the 17th-century *Paolotti convent*, with the aim of converting it into a suitable showcase for the town and the art it was to house, has resulted in a museum that is worthy of the outstanding collection donated by the collector Amedeo Lia to the town of La Spèzia. This is one of Europe's most important collections of paintings from the 13th to 15th centuries. The 13 rooms also contain liturgical objects from various periods, medieval ivory, fragments from windows, a rare and precious collection of miniatures, medals, rock crystals worked by Milanese craftsmen, Venetian glass, and a large number of archeological artifacts from the Mediterranean area.

Each section contains works of exceptionally high caliber, creating a veritable anthology of the best of the various arts represented.

The paintings make up the largest collection and include several masterpieces by such painters as Paolo di Giovanni Fei (*Annunciation*), who, in the second half of the 14th century, continued the great Sienese tradition of artists like Simone Martini and Lippo Memmi . Some of the other major artists represented in the collection are Giovanni Bellini (*Nativity*), Sebastiano del Piombo (*Birth of*

41

Adonis), Jacopo da Pontormo (**Self-portrait**, the symbol of the museum, painted with tempera on terracotta) and Titian (**Portrait of a Gentleman***). There is also a *Deposition* by Lippo di Benivieni, a *St John* by Pietro Lorenzetti, a *Madonna and Child with Saints*, possibly by Sassetta (Stefano di Giovanni) and a *St Martin and the Poor Man*, that has been attributed to Raphael.

Finally, don't miss the magnificent collection of **bronze figurines*** from the Renaissance, Mannerist and Baroque periods.

Castello San Giorgio/ Castle of S. Giorgio ❹

The first 13th-century fortress was gradually demolished, rebuilt in 1371 and enlarged in the 17th and 18th centuries. The importance of the castle, because of its size and its splendid position dominating the town and the bay, is reflected in the careful restoration work which has recently been completed. The Museo Civico Archeologico Ubaldo Formentini has a very good **archeological section**, famed above all for its 19 precious anthropomorphic sandstone **statue-stelae*** dating from the Bronze and Iron Ages. There are

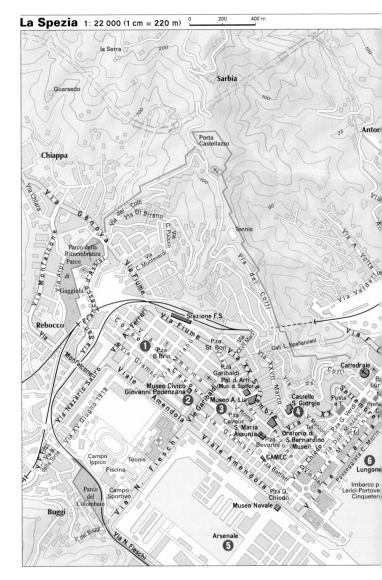

La Spezia 1: 22 000 (1 cm = 220 m)

also remarkable finds from the excavations at Luni, finds from Ligurian necropolises in the La Spèzia area and other objects of various provenance.

La Spèzia, castle of S. Giorgio: statue-stelae from the Lunigiana.

Arsenale/Arsenal ⑤

This was one of the first and most important public works undertaken by the newly-united Italy. In just a few decades, the naval arsenal transformed the social and economic structure of the city, as well as its physical layout. The architect behind the design of the industrial and military complex and the new town plan was Domenico Chiodo. Having been severely damaged by Allied bombing raids, after World War II, the Arsenal was carefully and painstakingly reconstructed. To the left of its monumental entrance is the

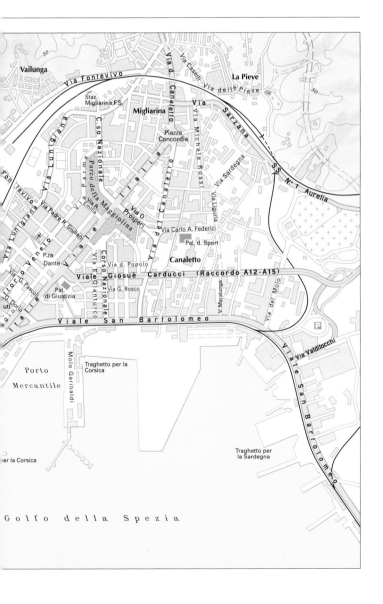

Museo Tecnico Navale della Marina Militare (navy museum). The original nucleus of the collection is amazingly old, consisting of material collected in the 16th century. The prize of the collection are 28 figure-heads from ancient ships.

Naval exhibits and model ships at La Spèzia's naval museum.

Lungomare/Promenade ❻

This extensive pedestrian precinct is laid out with trees and flowers and dotted with benches that are ideal places for leg-weary tourists to relax for a while. The lovely setting is matched by the delightful views out to sea, of the famous bay and, in the distance, the Apuan Alps. The promenade itself runs parallel to the first section of the long *Viale Italia*, bordered with Aleppo pines, palms and oleanders.

On the first Sunday of August every year, the water just in front of the promenade is the setting for a traditional and very colorful seaside festival, the *Palio del Golfo*, an exciting rowing competition between 13 towns overlooking the bay.

At the crossroads with Via Diaz (the continuation of Via del Prione), stands the *Salvador Allende Cultural Center*, where debates and conferences are regularly held. Beyond the jetty is Piazza Europa, the center of the modern town, where the most important public buildings are situated. The *Cathedral of Cristo Re* was inaugurated in 1975 and now dominates the square.

BRUGNATO [27 km]

Immediately after WWII, the town, which has been awarded the TCI's "Orange Flag", was still completely devoted to agriculture and trade. The "scissors-shaped" historic center is accessed through the medieval gates, *Porta Sottana* and *Porta Soprana*. Through the arch of the last gate you can see the Baroque facade of the *oratory of S. Bernardo*. The heart of the town is Piazza S. Pietro, where the ancient *parish church of Ss. Pietro, Lorenzo e Colombano* is situated. It began as a cemetery church near the site of an early Christian necropolis. In the 8th century, it was rebuilt and became part of a Benedictine monastery. The church we see today dates from the 11th-12th centuries and has been altered several times since. The facade, in particular, dates from the 18th century. The adjoining *Bishop's Palace* dates from the previous century and stands on the site of a medieval monastery.

CASTELNUOVO MAGRA [25 km]

This town situated on a ridge has a complex layout, considerable environmental status and buildings with remarkable doorways (especially in Via Dante) and has been awarded the TCI's "Orange Flag". The parish church of *S. Maria Maddalena* contains some remarkable artworks.

The facade dates from the 19th century but the rest of the building is from the late Renaissance. Inside, look for the wooden panel depicting *Calvary* attributed to Pieter Brueghel the Younger, and a *Crucifixion* attributed to Van Dyck. There is an interesting 13th-century castle which was remodeled in the 15th century. A short, steep climb brings us to **Nicola***, where the medieval hill-top structure has been preserved. The focus of the town is its beautiful church square (the present church dates from the 18th century but was founded much earlier) and you can still see some of its original fortifications.

Do not miss the **view*** which stretches from the Apuan Alps with their

The Cinque Terre, terraces covered in vineyards with Manarola in the background.

striations of white marble, across wood-covered hills and olive-groves to the open sea.

CINQUE TERRE

Visiting the Cinque Terre, listed since 1998 as a UNESCO World Heritage Site, means taking a dive into one of the most unspoiled corners of the coast – many would say the country – in terms of history and landscape. Like the exquisite Sciacchetrà *passito* wine made here, the little towns are the result of centuries of hard work under conditions rendered even more difficult by the steepness of the land. Many are of the opinion that the best way to explore the Cinque Terre is to walk its demanding but well-maintained network of footpaths which are highly rewarding in terms of views, smells and sea breezes.

RIOMAGGIORE [13 km from La Spèzia]

The main street lies above the final, covered-over section of the Rivus Major Stream, after which the town is named. Tall, narrow houses stand on either side, forming two compact, parallel terraces. The charm of the town has been further enhanced by recent restoration work, which has removed the structures built above the medieval arches in the mid-1900s. Monuments in the town include the *parish church of S. Giovanni Battista* (1340), with a Neogothic

facade, (but the rose window is original). Riomaggiore lies in the middle of a protected area which, amongst other things, regulates scuba diving activities in the stretch of sea offshore, one of the richest in Italy in terms of marine flora and fish species. At each end of the protected area is a well-known diving location: in the south, Punta di Montenero, and, in the north, Punta del Mesco. The headquarters of the recently created **Parco Nazionale delle Cinque Terre** is in Riomaggiore (*see p. 88*). A panoramic footpath leads to the ruins of the *castle* (15-16C). A more demanding route leads to the *sanctuary of the Madonna di Montenero* (341m), built on a hill above the town overlooking a broad stretch of sea. It can also be reached by car or by using the rack tramway known as the *trenino del vino* (wine train), normally used by local farmers to transport grapes. Recently, an *Environmental Education Center* was established at Torre Guardiola, on the

Via dell'Amore, between Riomaggiore and Manarola.

Montenero promontory. There is a botanical route where you can learn all about the species of the Mediterranean scrubland, a birdwatching hide and an innovative "writing route", which encourages visitors to observe and write about the local wildlife.

One of the most famous walks in the Cinque Terre starts at Riomaggiore: the **Via dell'Amore***, a footpath carved out of the rock in the 1920s. Poised above the sea, it winds its way past geological formations and wonderful views to Manarola (about 30 mins).

MANAROLA [6 km from La Spèzia]

Dramatically situated on a huge black rock with a sheer drop down to the sea, the town spreads gradually down to a tiny port. The perimeter of the houses on the outer edge of the town, unusually striking on account of its shape and colors, corresponds to the original size of the castle, destroyed in 1273. The **church of S. Lorenzo** (or of the Natività di Maria), built in 1338, is a remarkable building and stands in a fine position dominating the town. The Gothic facade has a *rose window* while, inside, there are three good 15th-century artworks: a *low relief of St Lawrence* (formerly situated in the lunette above the door), a triptych and a polyptych. In December, lasting from Christmas until Epiphany, an unusual *nativity scene* is constructed on a hill above Manarola (and illuminated at night) with figures made of recycled material.

CORNIGLIA [33 km from La Spèzia]

This delightful little town, built on the ridge of a promontory about 100m above the sea, has the atmosphere of a hill-town rather than a seaside town, apart from its magnificent view, of course. 365 steps connect the town to the sea and the train station. The layout of the town, the traditions of its inhabitants and their relationship with the neighboring hills have resulted in a

town based on farming, especially growing vines. Wine has been made here for at least 2,000 years. Amphoras with the name "Cornelia" were found during excavations at Pompeii. The *church of S. Pietro*, altered during the Baroque period, has a Gothic door and rose windows.

VERNAZZA [27 km from La Spèzia]

The town, situated at the mouth of the Vernazzola Stream (now covered up) boasts the only little yacht harbor in the Cinque Terre. The medieval town was built around it and is still in place, with fine architectural features testifying to the fact that the town was richer than its neighbors. This was due to the fact that it had easy access to the sea, thanks to which, in Roman times, the excellent local wine could be traded. The view of the town includes two mighty Genoese lookout towers, and

Vernazza: a colorful festival at S. Margherita d'Antiochia.

the charming Ligurian Gothic **church of S. Margherita d'Antiochia**, arranged, unusually, on two levels. Its apse (not the facade) overlooks the town's pleasant main square.

MONTEROSSO AL MARE [34 km from La Spèzia]

There are two parts to Monterosso. The old town, although its appearance has been marred somewhat since the railway was built between the town and its beautiful beach, has the typical atmosphere of other towns in the Cinque Terre, with narrow streets winding up the hill. The seaside resort area of **Fegina**, on the other hand, looks like any other resort, but has a noble and longstanding tradition. For example, it was here that the Montale family from Genoa used to come on holiday. Young Eugenio Montale was later to be awarded the Nobel Prize for Literature (1975). Later, in his poetry, he described his feelings and the places he visited in some of his most beautiful and successful poems. The old town has two fine churches. The *parish church of S. Giovanni Battista*, on the little square, has a typical Gothic facade with horizontal stripes and a magnificent carved rose window. In the lunette above the door, there is a *Baptism of Christ* (18C) and, at the back of the church, an elegant loggia facing out to sea. The fine bell tower was converted from an old lookout tower. The **church of S. Francesco** (1619), situated at the top of the hill next to a Capuchin monastery, contains some good paintings: a *Crucifixion* and a *Mocking of Christ* by Bernardo Castello, *La Veronica* by Bernardo Strozzi, a *Penitent St Jerome* by Luca Cambiaso and a *Pietà*, possibly by the same artist.

The charming coast near Lérici.

LÉRICI [10 km]

Today the town still has the atmosphere which made it a favorite tourist destination during the Romantic period. Its charm lies in the narrow alleys and flights of steps that make up the fabric of the oldest part of the town. The **castle*** guards the town from the promontory. Built by the Pisans (13C), it was enlarged and fortified by the Genoese. When you visit it, you can see that it is one of the most complex and best-preserved examples of military architecture in Liguria. Note the 13th-century *chapel of S. Anastasia,* in the Ligurian Gothic style. Some of the rooms and courtyard of the castle house the **Museo Geopaleontologico**. It takes visitors on a splendid tour through the age of the dinosaurs. The room devoted to seismic simulation shows how earthquakes happen and what effects they can have. The town has two important churches. The **oratory of S. Rocco**, on Corso Marconi, with a 14th-century bell tower and, inside, above the high altar, a fine 16th-century panel of Sts Martin, Cristopher, Sebastian and Roch. In the left aisle is

an original painting on lavagna slate (16C) of the Madonna of Health. The 16th-century **church of S. Francesco**, in Via Cavour, has some remarkable altarpieces, all by painters of the Genoese School. A door in the sacristy leads into the *oratory of S. Bernardino*.

Not far from the town, the road that leads to Tellaro hugs a section of beautiful wild **coastline**. The sea here is rich in marine vegetation. The area has been designated a marine archeological park and contains the remains of a Roman trading ship. Another place only a few kilometers away from Lérici, worth visiting for its *panoramic position*, is **Ameglia***, perched on top of a hill, with tall, narrow houses. Some of the crenellated walls of its ancient fortifications are still visible. At the top of the town is the remarkable Palazzo Comunale (Town Hall).

LÈVANTO [36 km]

The town has a broad beach and buildings which have preserved their noble appearance, uncluttered by concrete additions. *Piazza Cavour* lies above the site of a former cloister belonging to the 17th-century convent of the Clarisse (Poor Clares). A passageway to the left of the town hall leads from the square to Via Vinzoni. Follow this street and keep right to the next street,

The facade of the parish church of S. Andrea in Lèvanto.

Via Guani, with old houses which have only partly been restructured. On the left of the street is an arch. Go through it up the steep flight of steps called the *Salita Madonna della Costa*, a favorite haunt of cats. At the top is the old church of S. Maria della Costa, with a 16th-century high relief of *St George Slaying the Dragon* above the door. Just beyond it is the oratory of the Confraternità di S. Giacomo. From here, the Salita S. Giacomo leads down to *Piazza del Popolo*, with its fine **loggia** from 1256.

Next to *Casa Restani*, with its composite structures, is Via Emanuele Toso, which leads to the **parish church of S. Andrea**, in the 13th-century Gothic style, enlarged in the 15th century. The elegant facade, with its horizontal stripes, has a rose window (18C) and a fresco in the lunette depicting the Coronation of the Virgin. Inside, on the left, note the much-revered "black" crucifix (its color prior to being restored recently). Adjoining the parish church is the *Mostra Permanente della Cultura Materiale*, an

ethnographic exhibition of objects used by the people of Lévanto in the past for work and in everyday life. As you climb up to the castle, notice the best-preserved part of the town walls, including the clock-tower dating from 1265. Having reached the Bonassola road, you can visit the **convent of the Annunziata**, where there is a 16th-century low relief of the *Annunciation* on the facade of the church. It contains **remarkable paintings**. The town of **Bonassola** is composed of elegant villas built on the hillside, which blend into the surrounding landscape and have views of the Mediterranean. The parish church contains many votive offerings made by fishermen saved from shipwrecks and storms at sea, an unusual painting of *The Pious Women below the Cross* (1924), and, in the sacristy, a painting of *St Francis* by Bernardo Strozzi. A famous, easy coastal walk of about 1km leads to the *tiny chapel of the Madonna della Punta*, high on a cliff, which is particularly striking at sunset.

LUNI [33 km]

This was once a flourishing port, and such a wealthy and important town that

it gave its name to the entire area, a name still used today, the Lunigiana. Founded in 177 BC, the town prospered under Rome, and resisted even the most destructive invasions. But, gradually, the port silted up (and became unusable in the 11-12C) and the area was also struck by malaria. Abandoned by its inhabitants, it became a ghost town and eventually fell into ruin and became overgrown.

(boat-houses on the harbor side and shops and houses on the main street), an architectural genre that is probably unique. The two levels are connected by steep, vaulted flights of steps called *capitoli*, with loopholes and embrasures above which meant that they could be defended easily. The monumental entrance to the old town is marked by the old *gate* bearing the Latin inscription "Colonia Januensis 1113",

The church of S. Pietro in Portovènere, dramatically situated on the tip of the promontory.

Today it is an archeological site, famous, in particular for its large **amphitheater** (it could seat 5,000 spectators), situated outside the ancient urban complex. The site also houses the **Museo Archeologico Nazionale*** where many of the artifacts found on the site are exhibited. Some of the material is exhibited on the site at some of the key buildings excavated.

PORTOVÈNERE [13 km]

The spectacular combination of art and nature and the picturesqueness of its colorful houses separated by narrow alleys, is so charming that, even in the summer, when the town is besieged with visitors, the place is still magical. From the promenade beside the small yacht harbor, there is a good view of the older part of the town. It has developed on the promontory in a compact sequence of tall, brightly-painted houses with two entrances

commemorating the fact that the place was fortified by the Genoese in the 12th century. Low down, on the left side of the gate, note the old Genoese wine and grain measures (1606). From here, walk up *Via Capellini*, the town's narrow main street, which ends in a dramatic square with steps leading up to the **church of S. Pietro**, situated right on the tip of the promontory. In ancient times, this was the site of a temple dedicated to Venus Erycina, hence the name of the site and the settlements built here thereafter. This is an unusual building because it comprises an earlier Christian church in black Palmaria marble (6C), the part built by the Genoese in the striped Gothic style (13C) and a massive bell tower also used for defensive purposes. In fact, the church was the focal point of the town's defensive walls. Around the edge of the church is a small Romanesque loggia with graceful arches framing the splendid view of the coastline from the Falesie del Muzzerone to the Scoglio di Ferale and Punta Mesco. Returning to Via Capellini, beyond the steps on the left which lead down to the sea and the cave of *Grotta Arpaia* (dear to Byron), by keeping to the left you come to the **church of S. Lorenzo** (12C). Inside, a 15th-century marble *altarpiece* of the Florentine School contains a painting on parchment of the *Madonna Bianca* (White Virgin). According to the legend, the picture was "brought here by the sea" in 1204 and, on August 17, 1399 was miraculously transformed into its current 14th-century form. Every year, on the same date, a charming candle-lit procession commemorates the event. From the church you can walk up to the castle, an imposing fortress dominating the town, built mainly in the 16th and 17th centuries. Opposite Portovènere are some beautiful **islands****: there are boat trips to **Palmaria**, the largest one, from Portovènere. People go mainly to visit the Grotta Azzurra, which can only be accessed by sea, although the Grotta dei Colombi, which can only be reached with difficulty by land, is also interesting. La Palmaria, like **Tino**, which is much smaller, and **Tinetto**, which is little more than a rock (the two smaller islands are a military area and closed to the public), were colonized by Benedictine monks. On the island of Tino, which can only be visited on September 13, on the festival of St Venerius, a local hermit, you can see the ruins of the abbey of S. Venerio (11C). In 1998, the three islands and the town of Portovènere were designated a UNESCO World Heritage Site.

Crucifixion by Master Guglielmus in Sarzana.

SARZANA [16 km]

Situated in the east of the flood-plain of the Magra River, the town developed rapidly. We recommend you visit it following the old pilgrim route known as the *Strada Francigena*, now the streets of Via Bertoloni and Via Mazzini. The beginning and end of the street are marked by the gates of Porta Parma and the Neoclassical Porta Romana. The town's main squares lie along this thoroughfare, overlooked by important monuments and tower-houses. No. 28 used to belong to the Buonaparte family before they moved to Corsica in 1529. The elegant palazzi on **Piazza Matteotti** date from the 17th and 18th centuries. In the middle stands *La Procellaria*, a war memorial built in 1934. On the southwest side of the square is the 16th-century *Palazzo Comunale* (Town Hall), separating it from the quiet Piazza Luna behind. The **church of S. Andrea** is the result of a radical transformation (1579) of a Romanesque parish church (the lovely two-light window on the facade belongs to the original church). The height of the bell tower was raised in the 14th century. Dedicated to the Assumption, the **cathedral*** forms a lovely backdrop to the piazza named after Sarzana's pope, Nicholas V (1447-55). Built in 1204, it has been altered several times, as you can see from the facade. 14th-century features include the doorway with the embrasure, the finely carved rose window and the merloned bell tower with four tiers of windows. The majestic interior based on classical lines contains several fine artworks: in the chapel to the left of the high altar, the **Crucifixion*** (1138), a fine and extremely early panel painting by the Tuscan Master Guglielmus; in the right

transept, a **Purification** from 1436; in the left transept, a **Coronation** from 1432. The **citadel** was built between 1488 and 1492 on the site of a Pisan fortress that had been destroyed, and was planned by Florentine military architects. It has a regular plan with six round bastions around the edge and is surrounded by a large moat. The **church of S. Francesco**, founded in the 13th century, has been altered several times. Its many fine artworks include the tomb of Guarnerio degli Antelminelli.

Leaving by Porta Romana, a road on the left leads after 2km to the **Sarzanello fortress**, built in about 1322 and restructured in the 15th century and later again by the Genoese.

The Fortezza di Sarzanello, near Sarzana.

VARESE LIGURE [52 km]

This town, with its **Borgo Rotondo*** is probably the most interesting town in the La Spèzia region and has been awarded the TCI's Orange Flag. It is also known for its cheese

production. In *Piazza Marconi*, the mighty walls of the *castle* of the Fieschi family, an interesting example of 15th-century fortified architecture, strike a marked contrast with the elegant Baroque facade of the **church of Ss. Teresa d'Avila e Filippo Neri** (17C), with its identical bell towers. Inside the church, built on a Greek-cross plan with a dome, note the *Madonna and Child with the young St John and St Francis Xavier* on the left-hand altar, by Gregorio De Ferrari. You can see two more paintings by this artist from Savona above the first and second altars in the right aisle of the parish church of S. Giovanni Battista (1648), which can be reached by walking along Via Colombo and then heading down Via della Chiesa. Note also its fine 17th-century wooden choirstalls. Starting again at Piazza Marconi, follow Via Umberto I and Via Garibaldi, the main thoroughfare of the so-called "Borgo Nuovo", to Piazza Mazzini.

The unusual 15C elliptical plan of "Borgo Rotondo".

SAVONA

Some towns become famous tourist destinations regardless of their real merits whereas others, having established themselves in economic or productive sectors, have treasures which nobody even knows exist. Savona is one of these. In fact, Savona keeps its attractions well hidden, revealing them only to people who are really interested and are willing to pay more than a flying visit. A passing visitor is likely to focus on the quays of the port and the industrial complexes (many now abandoned) which have engulfed the seaward side of the old town, making it look rather ugly and off-putting. They conceal the town's considerable artistic and architectural treasures, which can only be discovered by exploring the streets of the old town on foot. Indeed, in the post-war period the productive areas of Savona were at the center of a debate as to whether the city was a trading/port town, a crossroads or a tourist hub. Historically, the city was a port and military fortress, although it has always had a duplicity: on the one hand, it was a seaward looking rival of Genoa, on the other, it looked inland to Piedmont, especially since it is near one of the best points to cross the mountains.

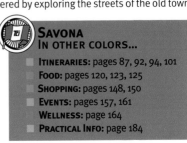

SAVONA
IN OTHER COLORS...

- **ITINERARIES:** pages 87, 92, 94, 101
- **FOOD:** pages 120, 123, 125
- **SHOPPING:** pages 148, 150
- **EVENTS:** pages 157, 161
- **WELLNESS:** page 164
- **PRACTICAL INFO:** page 184

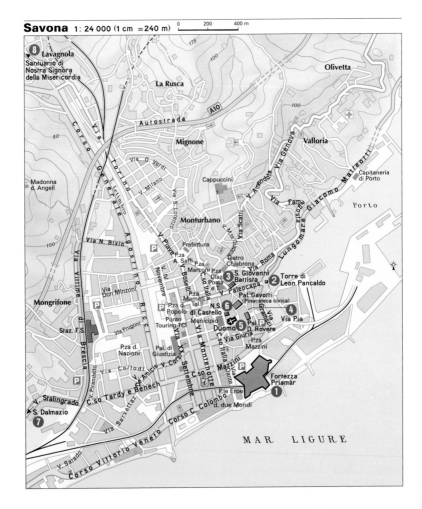

Savona 1: 24 000 (1 cm = 240 m)

Priamàr ❶

This great fortress, begun by the Genoese in 1542 (as a base for its garrison), stands on the hill where the first town of Savona was established, and was then destroyed, together with the old *castrum* and the first cathedral. It was then altered many times, and was recently converted it into a major museum complex. We particularly recommend visiting the castle, since it offers not only a splendid example of

examples of the ancient local pottery tradition dating from the 16th century, whose fame spread far beyond the local area.

Civico Museo Storico-Archeologico. Also located in Palazzo della Loggia, on the floor below the Pinacoteca, the exhibits refer to the original settlement of Savona that was established on this hill. Archeologists have excavated a necropolis dating from the 5th-6th

Savona: Fortezza del Priamàr

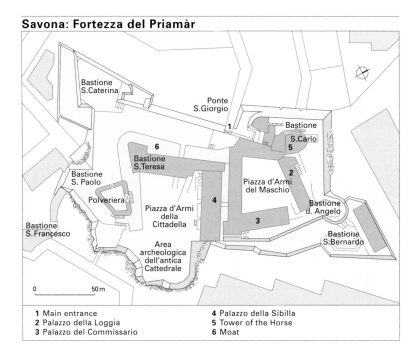

1 Main entrance	**4** Palazzo della Sibilla
2 Palazzo della Loggia	**5** Tower of the Horse
3 Palazzo del Commissario	**6** Moat

military architecture (with magnificent views from the ramparts) but also the excellent museums described below.

Pinacoteca Civica. Situated on the third floor of Palazzo della Loggia, the gallery gives an insight into Ligurian painting from the Middle Ages to the 18th century. Undoubtedly, the most interesting section is the one devoted to art of the 14th and 15th centuries, which includes two splendid **Crucifixions***, respectively by Donato de' Bardi and Giovanni Mazone, who also painted the magnificent polyptych depicting the *Annunciation, Calvary and Saints*. The rooms devoted to 17th- and 18th-century painting contain works by painters whose art is to be found in many of the churches and oratories around Genoa and Savona. The ceramics section has some excellent

centuries AD, and the route includes a visit to the excavations. Other items of interest include some mosaic floors made by North African craftsmen (3-4C AD). There are also artifacts from the Bronze Age, some Etruscan bucchero ware (7-6C BC) and a Greek *skyphos* (5C BC). On the middle floor of Palazzo della Loggia is the **Museo d'Arte Sandro Pertini**, which contains about a hundred paintings collected by this famous politician from Savona and donated to the city by his widow. Finally, by walking through the tunnels underneath the fortress, we reach the **Collezione Renata Cuneo**, located in the S. Bernardo bastion: it contains sculptures by this artist from Savona who produced sculpture for most of the 20th century. Not far away is the *Torre del Brandale*, which towers over the square of the same name, opposite the oldest part of the port. You can still see traces of the tower's medieval origins despite the fact that it has been altered many times over the ages. Built in the 12th century, the interior still contains medieval frescoes, whereas the facade is decorated with a ceramic panel depicting the Madonna della Misericordia (1967), an example of local craftsmanship.

Roman amphora in the Museo Archeologico.

Torre di Leon Pancaldo/ Leon Pancaldo Tower ❷

This small tower looking out to sea, decorated with a statue of the Madonna of Mercy, was erected in the 14th century. It is named after the navigator from Savona who accompanied Magellan on his voyages and died tragically in 1537 on the Rio de la Plata. On the side facing the sea is a couplet dedicated to the Madonna which sounds the same in both Italian and Latin: *In mare irato, in subita procella, invoco Te, nostra benigna stella* (Amid an angry sea, surrounded by misfortune, we invoke Your name, our benign star). Next to it is *Via Paleocapa*, the town's lively, busy main street, whose elegant porticoes on either side shelter any number of shops. The street was laid out at the end of the 19th century with the aim of providing people with a fast way of reaching the new train station from the old town center. The station was then situated on the Letimbro Stream, in the vast flat area next to today's Piazza del Popolo. At Nos. 3 and 5, note *Palazzo dei Pavoni*, with lovely floral decoration on the facade (1912). The 18th-century *church of S. Andrea* (only open in the morning) lies on the same street. Its elegant steps were added when the construction of Via Paleocapa removed part of the rise on which it was situated, lowering the level of the street. The interior, which contains 18th-century frescoes and paintings, is very striking. In the sacristy is an *icon of St Nicholas* from Constantinople. Nearby, the **oratory of Cristo Risorto** is worth a visit. Formerly the Augustinian church of the SS. Annunziata, it was rebuilt in 1604.

Its lavishly decorated interior includes 18th-century frescoes. In the presbytery, a majestic *Triumph of God and Angels* frames the statue of *Christ Resurrected*. Notice the 18th-century organ and two small panels (*Flagellation* and *Crucifixion*) in the northern Gothic style (late 15C). The oratory is famous for its three groups of carved wooden figures used in processions: an *Annunciation* by Maragliano, *Addolorata* by Filippo Martinengo and a *Deposition* by Antonio Brilla.

S. Giovanni Battista ❸

At the other end of Via Paleocapa, at the beginning of Via Mistrangelo, stands this important church built by the Dominicans in 1567, after the church of S. Domenico Vecchio was demolished to build the Priamàr fortress. The facade was redone in the Baroque style in 1735. The interior, divided into a nave and two aisles, contains good artworks dating from the 16th-18th centuries: on the back of the facade is a fresco depicting the *Glory of St Dominic*; in the chapel right of the high altar, a *Madonna and Child*; at the sides of the presbytery, two paintings by Carlo Giuseppe Ratti depicting *Stories*

The port of Savona and the Torre di Leon Pancaldo.

from the life of St Dominic; in the chapel to the left of the high altar, a *Nativity* by Antonio Semino and, on the left, a *Madonna and Child with Saints* by Teramo Piaggio; coming back along the left aisle, a *Virgin Mary, St Mary Magdalene and St Catherine with the image of St Dominic* by Paolo Gerolamo Piola, a 16th-century *wooden crucifix* and, above the baptistery, the *Birth of the Virgin Mary*.

Picturesque houses surround this square in the old town of Savona.

Via Pia ➍

This narrow street, packed with shops of all kinds, yet retaining its monumental dignity, is the hub of Savona's old town. Its medieval origins are still very apparent. Notice the many beautiful slate doorways (15-16C) with carved lintels. No.1, *Palazzo Sormani*, dates from the 16th century and is decorated with frescoes; No.5, *Palazzo Della Rovere-Cassinis*, has the typical lines of the Ligurian Renaissance. Then, beyond the old square of *Piazza della Maddalena*, No. 26 is *Palazzo Pavese Spinola* (16C), which still has a few frescoes of grotesques in the atrium. **Palazzo Della Rovere**, begun in 1495, is now the Police Headquarters at No. 28 Via Pia. From 1673 onwards, it was the convent of the Clarisse (Poor Clares), so that it was given the name of "Palazzo S. Chiara", but it has lost its beautiful interior decoration which was plastered over for religious reasons. At the beginning of the 19th century, it became the Prefecture under Napoleon Bonaparte. Just before the street ends, near the Torre del Brandale, is *Palazzo Sansoni*, with a pleasing black-and-white-striped facade and a 13th-century loggia which has been closed in.

Duomo/Cathedral ➎

A walk along Via Sansoni and Via Vacciuoli brings us to the cathedral dedicated to St Mary of the Assumption, built in 1589-1605 (although the facade is 19C). Inside, against the back of the facade, is a marble **Crucifix*** dating from the late 15th century and a *font* made out of a Byzantine capital, with carved balustrades; it has a remarkable *pulpit of the Evangelists* (1522) and even better carved **wooden choirstalls*** (1500-15). In the chapel to the right of the high altar is a **Madonna and Child Enthroned with Sts Peter and Paul***, a masterpiece by Albertino Piazza, and a 16th-century marble relief depicting the *Presentation of the Virgin*. Notice the harmony of the Mannerist decoration of the fourth chapel on the left, and, near it, the 14th-century low relief of the *Assumption*. The **Museo del Tesoro della Cattedrale** (access from the cathedral or from No. 11 Via Canzoni, on request) contains some important paintings, including the polyptych of the *Assumption and Saints* by Lodovico Brea (1495), a *Madonna and Saints* by Tuccio d'Andria (1487) and an *Adoration of the Magi* by a Flemish artist; it also has some fine gold- and silver-ware on display and some interesting statues made of English alabaster.

Adjoining the church is the 15th-century *cloister*, with 21 statues of saints. From here you can enter the **Cappella Sistina**, built by Pope Sixtus IV (who was from Savona) in 1481-83. However, the interior was charmingly redecorated in the 18th century in the Rococo style. The organ also dates from the 18th century, whereas the *cenotaph of the parents of Sixtus IV* dates from 1483. Below the dome, you can see patches where the original frescoes have been uncovered.

Savona: the ceiling of the Sistine Chapel.

Nostra Signora di Castello ⑥

In Corso Italia, this oratory, which is quite well hidden, contains a **Madonna and Saints****, a splendid monumental late 15ᵗʰ-century polyptych by Vincenzo Foppa, completed by Lodovico Brea. Notice also the tallest existing set of carved figures used in processions, a *Deposition* by Filippo Martinengo (1795). Along with Via Paleocapa, the long, straight Corso Italia, with its elegant shops, is the other main thoroughfare in the area into which Savona expanded in the 19ᵗʰ century. If you walk along it from Piazza Sisto IV towards the sea, in Piazza Giulio II, you come to the former Ospedale S. Paolo (19C). A slight detour brings you to Via Untoria (an important street in medieval times) and the 17ᵗʰ-century church of S. Pietro. Originally a Carmelite church, it has an unusual elliptical facade. Inside, note

Savona: polyptych by Vincenzo Foppa in the church of Nostra Signora di Castello.

the polychrome marble features separating the chapel of the high altar from the choir.

San Dalmazio ⑦

You reach the church by turning right just before the 13ᵗʰ-century *Ponte di S. Martino*, in the old suburb of *Lavagnola*. The parish church is easily recognizable on account of the modern relief of St Dalmatius that adorns the bare facade. In the apse is a lovely polyptych of the **Madonna and Child with Saints*** by Barnaba da Modena (1376) and, on the right of the presbytery another fine 14ᵗʰ-century *polyptych*, by the Provencal Ligurian school.

Nostra Signora della Misericordia ⑧

The sanctuary stands in the village of *Santuario*, 6.5km from Savona. The buildings on this broad square form a delightful scene: on the left, Palazzo Pallavicino and the old hospice; on the right, the new hospice and, at the back, Palazzetto Tursi. The fine **facade** of the sanctuary (1610-11) in the Mannerist style was added by Taddeo Carlone to the original Renaissance church designed by Pace Antonio Sormano in 1536-1540. The frescoed interior contains many fine artworks: in the second chapel on the right, the *Birth of the Virgin* is a masterpiece in the style of Caravaggio; in the third chapel, a *Presentation at the Temple* by Domenichino; the rich marble decoration of the entrance to the crypt is by Giovanni Battista Orsolino; the 17ᵗʰ-century *wooden choirstalls* were enhanced with marquetry work in the 19ᵗʰ century; in the third chapel on the left is a high relief in marble (*Visitation*) within the altar, probably by Gian Lorenzo Bernini. *Palazzetto Tursi* houses the *Museo del Tesoro*, with liturgical gold- and silver-ware, sacred furnishings, wood carvings and votive offerings.

DAY TRIPS

ALÀSSIO [51 km]

This is one of the most exclusive resorts on the west Ligurian Riviera, the undisputed queen of the so-called *Riviera delle Palme* (the term used to describe the coast around Savona). Its long beach of very fine sand fringes the broad bay between Capo Santa Croce and Capo Mele. The original fishing town dates back to the 6th-7th century, when a group of people from Milan fled here after the Lombards invaded the Po Valley. After 1303, it belonged to Albenga, from which it became independent in the 16th century and began to prosper. In the last two decades of the 19th century, it was "discovered" by English tourists, who turned the town into one of the most famous and popular resorts on the riviera. Many of the villas and luxuriant gardens on the hill date from this period.

Tourism is vital for the town's economy even today. All kinds of cultural initiatives and events of various kinds are organized to attract and entertain visitors. Yet, despite the fact that Alàssio is crossed by the Via Aurelia, and has many new buildings erected to cope with the large numbers of tourists, it still has typical features of a Ligurian town. For example, the so-called **budello** (literally, gut), the narrow alley which stretches the length of the town. It is the narrow, busy *Via XX*

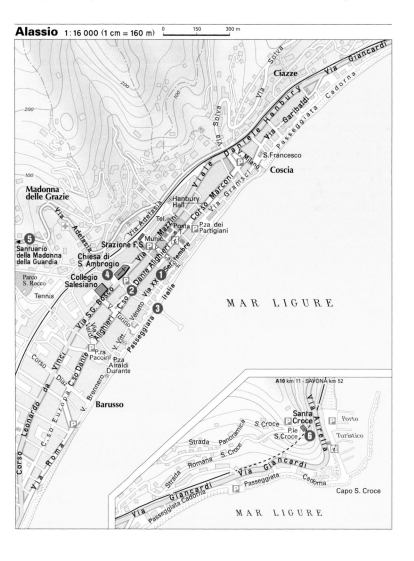

Alassio 1 : 16 000 (1 cm = 160 m)

MAR LIGURE

The coast at Alàssio in an early photograph: the same festive atmosphere then as now.

Settembre ❶, which runs parallel to the beach but is separated from it by a block of houses which look directly onto the beach. This street is the commercial hub of Alàssio and its shops and restaurants stay open until late. Not far away, in Corso Dante Alighieri ❷, is the famous **muretto** (little wall), which was particularly famous in the 1950s and 1960s and is still a popular meeting-place today. The autographs of celebrities from the world of art, culture and show business who have visited Alàssio have been reproduced here in ceramic tiles. The narrow alleys that cross the *budello* towards the sea lead to the *Passeggiata Italia* ❸, the promenade which winds along the part of the shore opposite the old town, with splendid views across the bay. On the Via Aurelia is the **Chiesa di S. Ambrogio/Church of S. Ambrogio** ❹, which was entirely rebuilt during the 15th and 16th centuries above the site of an earlier church. The 19th-century facade still features a Renaissance slate doorway (1511) depicting *St Ambrose, Christ and the Apostles, and the Eternal God.* The bell tower (1507), with its two- and three-light windows, is a good example of the late Romanesque-Gothic style. The interior, divided into a nave and two aisles, is decorated in the Baroque style and contains interesting works from the 16th and 17th centuries.

On Mt. Tirasso, which can be reached from Piazza della Stazione in Alàssio by driving along a tortuous road for 8km, is the **Santuario della Madonna della Guardia/Sanctuary of Madonna della Guardia** ❺, built in the 17th century on the site of a medieval castle. The place has the most incredible **views***, both out to sea and inland towards the Lerrone and Arroscia valleys and the Maritime Alps. From Alàssio, by taking the Solva road, you reach the **Chiesetta di S. Croce/ Church of S. Croce** ❻, originally Romanesque, and built in a panoramic position on the cape of the same name. It was built by the Benedictine abbey on the island of **Gallinara** and provided refuge and support for travelers. It was altered several times and then restored, but the walls, apse and left side of the church are original and date from the 11th century. This is the starting-point of the so-called *passeggiata archeologica* to Albenga, a footpath across the Mediterranean scrubland along the old Roman road. In summer, it's well worth taking a boat trip from Alàssio to **the island of Gallinara***. Since the island is privately owned, you can go round it by boat but landing is not permitted. Now a regional nature reserve (it lies within the municipal territory of Albenga), it has a rich flora with several endemic species, and caves on the south side of the island. In ancient times, Gallinara was settled by a community of hermit monks, the first of which, according to tradition, was St Martin of Tours, who lived here between 356 and 360. Then, in the early 8th century, it was taken over by the Benedictines, who

Scuba diving in the sea off Liguria, which is rich in fish species.

founded an abbey which acquired a considerable amount of land, first along the Ponente Riviera and later in Provence. Today, the remaining ruins of the abbey are incorporated in a villa.

ALBENGA [51 km]

The town dates back to the 6th-4th centuries BC and it was finally conquered by Rome in 181 BC. The grid

tower dating from the 13th century. Inside, the palazzo is decorated with 17th-century frescoes and houses the interesting **Museo Navale Romano**, with amphoras used to transport wine, the remains of a Roman ship that sank off the coast in the 1st century BC, and other archeological finds. On the same side of the square is Palazzo del Municipio (Town Hall), which incorporates (on the corner with Via Ricci)

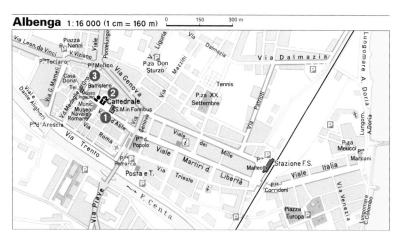

Albenga 1 : 16 000 (1 cm = 160 m)

network of regular blocks we see today is the original town plan, modeled on that of the Roman *castrum* (camp). Between the 11th and 13th centuries, the town flourished. In the Middle Ages, the walls and the main public buildings were erected, making Albenga the best-preserved medieval town in western Liguria today. **Via Enrico d'Aste** ❶ starts from the tree-filled Piazza del Popolo. On the right is the *church of S. Maria in Fontibus*, founded in the early Middle Ages but altered many times over the centuries. At the front of it is the 13th-century *Cazzulini Tower*, the forerunner of an architectural genre that is one of the most obvious and interesting features of the old town. The towers, public buildings and the cathedral denote the important role of civic and religious life in Albenga. These, together with the early-Christian baptistery and other medieval buildings overlooking **Piazza S. Michele** and **Via Bernardo Ricci**, form a charming scene. On the left, at the far end of Piazza S. Michele, at No. 12, stands the massive **Palazzo Peloso Cepolla**, with its late-16th century facade and a corner

the 14th-century tower-house of the Malasemenza family.

The **Cattedrale/Cathedral*** ❷, dedicated to St Michael, was rebuilt in medieval times on the site of a 5th-century early Christian church, and has been altered several times since. The bottom of the center of the facade is 11th-century Romanesque, whereas the two side-doors date from the 13th century. The central doorway dates from 1669. The **bell tower***, rebuilt between 1391 and 1395 using the

Albenga: hunting scene in Palazzo Peloso Cepolla.

Byzantine mosaic in the baptistery in Albenga.

base of a Roman lookout tower, is a remarkable example of the late-Gothic style. The interior of the cathedral, divided into a nave and two aisles, has a monumental 17th-century organ with an original sound-box. In the right aisle is a votive shrine dating from 1456. In the central apse is a 16th-century fresco depicting a *Crucifixion with Saints*. The roof above the nave is decorated with 19th-century frescoes. Restoration work conducted in the 1960s uncovered its 13th-century lines, including the original floor and the remains of the early-medieval apse and the Carolingian crypt, part of which can be seen below the presbytery. **Palazzo Vecchio del Comune** stands next to the baptistery, to the left of the cathedral. These two buildings and the **Municipal Tower** (on the corner of Via Ricci) are all medieval. The tower houses the **Civico Museo Ingauno***, an eclectic collection of objects pertaining to Albenga and the surrounding area, dating from the pre-Roman period to the Middle Ages, including inscriptions, mosaics, sculptures and a particularly interesting Roman pottery section. The **baptistery***, built in the first half of the 5th century, is the only example of late-Roman architecture to survive and is

the most important early-Christian monument in Liguria. You access the baptistery from the loggia of Palazzo Comunale (Town Hall), where a staircase leads down to the level of the 5th-century town, situated just one meter above sea-level. The lower part of the building, which is perfectly preserved and absolutely fascinating, has ten sides while the drum above has only eight. Inside, in the lower part has only eight sides. Behind the arches are alternating rectangular or semi-circular niches. The outsides of the niches are covered by sandstone **screens*** carved with braid motifs which are typical of Lombard art. On the inside, the columns of Corsican granite have re-used Corinthian capitals. One niche contains the remains of a mosaic (5-6C) depicting the Trinity and the Apostles in the form of doves. This is the only extant example of Byzantine art in

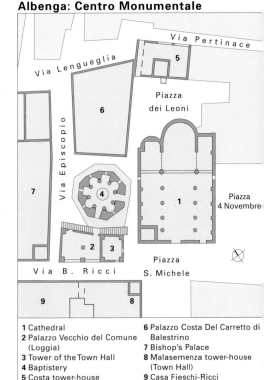

Albenga: Centro Monumentale

Via Pertinace
Via Lengueglia
Via Episcopio
Via B. Ricci

Piazza dei Leoni
Piazza 4 Novembre
Piazza S. Michele

1 Cathedral
2 Palazzo Vecchio del Comune (Loggia)
3 Tower of the Town Hall
4 Baptistery
5 Costa tower-house
6 Palazzo Costa Del Carretto di Balestrino
7 Bishop's Palace
8 Malasemenza tower-house (Town Hall)
9 Casa Fieschi-Ricci

northern Italy outside Ravenna. Another niche contains a Romanesque fresco depicting the Baptism of Christ. Back outside, behind the apse of the cathedral, with its one-light windows and a colonnaded gallery (13C), is **Piazza dei Leoni***. This quiet, charming square is named after the three stone lions brought here from Rome in 1608 by Count Costa, who owned the medieval buildings in this area. The passageway between the left-hand side of the palazzo and the baptistery leads into Via Episcopio, the opposite side of which is occupied by the Bishop's Palace. On the left-hand corner is a 12th-century tower. The palace, decorated with frescoes and furnishings from the 15th century, houses the *Museo Diocesano d'Arte Sacra*, and contains ancient inscriptions and silverware from the cathedral treasury, Flemish tapestries and fine paintings. These include a *Last Supper*, an *Annunciation* and a fine *Martyrdom of St Catherine* by Guido Reni. The left-hand side of the palace is decorated with black and white horizontal stripes and a fresco. It overlooks **Via Ricci*** which, with its double row of medieval houses, is the most historically interesting and picturesque street in Albenga. *Via Medaglie d'Oro* ❸, which began as one of the arteries of the Roman town, has always been one of the town's most important shopping streets. The point where it crosses Via Bernardo Ricci is marked not only by the Torre d'Aste Rolandi Ricci (tower), but the charming Loggia dei Quattro Canti. This has a Gothic arcade overlooking Via Ricci and a Romanesque arcade overlooking Via Medaglie d'Oro. Opposite it is the *Lengueglia-Doria* tower-house (13-14C), restored in 1936. In the southwest section of Via Medaglie d'Oro, turn left into Via Cavour. On one side is the 17th-century main facade of *Palazzo d'Aste*, an important noble residence (with Roman and Renaissance busts adorning the grand staircase). The present building is the result of restructuring which incorporated some medieval houses which can still be seen in Via Ricci. A few kilometers away from Albenga

is **Villanova d'Albenga***, a delightful polygonal town surrounded by walls with towers and gates which, until a few decades ago, were perfectly preserved. Today, the best-preserved section is on the northwest side. The narrow streets of the town are extremely charming, not only because of their strong medieval flavor, but also because of the delightful local custom of decorating doorways and windows with flowers and pot-plants.

Albenga: a view of Piazza dei Leoni with the apse of the cathedral.

ANDORA CASTELLO [65 km]

This is the name usually given to the isolated and beautiful site (a road leads up the short distance from Marina di Andora near the viaduct above the highway) of the impressive ruins of the **Andora castle**. Next to it is the Romanesque-Gothic **church of Ss. Giacomo e Filippo***. Together, they form one of the most important medieval complexes in western Liguria.

The church has stone walls and the facade is decorated with cornices and small Gothic arches. There is a pointed arch over the door and a large five-light window dating from restoration executed in 1901. On the left side of the church is a fine doorway and, at the back, a remarkable apse. Inside, the walls are again of unadorned stone, and the roof is supported by huge round columns and octagonal pillars. In the ruins of the castle, both the Romanesque and Gothic phases are very obvious.

The early-Romanesque *church of S. Nicolò*, which stands at the entrance to the central castle complex, was probably the original church on the site.

CASTELVECCHIO DI ROCCA BARBENA [49 km]

Built on a panoramic rocky spur in a strategic position, this, the oldest feudal town in the Neva valley, has been awarded the TCI's "Orange Flag". The **castle** (12C) became a military fortress in the 18th century.

Andora Castello

Pedestrian entrance from the "Roman road"

Tower-gate

0   20m

Church of Ss. Giacomo e Filippo

Central part of the castle

Church of S. Nicolò

Southwest gate

Vehicle entrance

- ▬ Buildings of medieval date
- ▬ Remains of medieval buildings
- ▬ Buildings of later date
- ═══ Old paths

The concentric circular structure of the town occupies two sides of the fortified rock. This fascinating town is surrounded by defensive walls and has a network of winding narrow streets. If you explore the town on foot, you will notice the typical Ligurian style of the houses, which have terraced roofs with little parapets to collect rainwater, and features more typical of mountain houses such as pitched roofs, hay-drying apparatus and decorated plaster around the windows.

FINALE LIGURE [24 km]

Of the three *borghi* (hamlets) which form the town, once separate entities and now, thanks to ribbon development, a single unit, **Finale Pia** is the oldest. The earliest part of the town focuses on the **Chiesa di**

S. Maria di Pia/Church of S. Maria di Pia ❶, which already existed in 1170 as a chapel, and then, in the 16th century, became the abbey church of the adjoining Benedictine convent. The building has a Rococo facade as the result of being completely rebuilt in the 18th century. However, the fine bell tower has retained its original Romanesque-Gothic lines (13-14C). The interior, decorated in the Baroque style, contains a 15th-century tabernacle (on the left wall) and some 16th-century wooden cabinets (in the sacristy). Behind the church lies the 16th-century *abbey* with terracotta works by the Della Robbia School, including a *Madonna and Child with Sts. Luke and John the Evangelist.* Starting in Piazza di S. Maria, leave Finale Pia on the road which follows the left bank of the Sciusa Stream. In a short time you come to the new part of *Calvisio*. Here, take Vico Bedina which climbs up - to the left just beyond the church - to the interesting **old town**. It comprises an agglomeration of typical houses built of regular stone blocks. Before the town stands the *church of S. Cipriano*, altered in the Baroque period, with a Romanesque bell tower. Continue to climb up the Sciusa valley to the Ponte di Verzi. Beyond the bridge, turn left at the first junction, into *the Ponci valley*. The route along this valley was much used in Roman times, as you can see from the

Castelvecchio di Rocca Barbena is still dominated from above by its medieval castle.

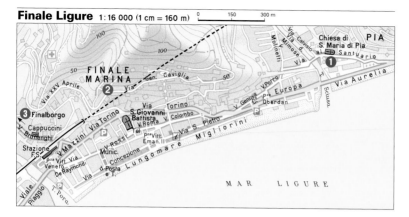

Finale Ligure 1:16 000 (1 cm = 160 m)

five **bridges*** dating from the 2nd century. The ancient town of **Finale Marina** ❷, a popular seaside resort that has developed parallel to the coast, expanded thanks to a prosperous period of marine trading activity. In the second half of the 16th century, it was the area's most important trading hub. The old town center contains several interesting buildings dating from the 16th and 17th centuries, whereas, above the Via Aurelia, you can see the bastions of *Castelfranco*. **Finalborgo***, set slightly back from the coast, is the most interesting of the three parts of Finale Ligure ❸. It was defended by a set of defensive walls (many of which are still well preserved) connected to Castel S. Giovanni, situated above the town, and by the two streams which run close to the town and above which the town gates are situated. Finalborgo is a well-kept, interesting place. Just walking about its streets you can perceive its aura of antiquity. Its streets and squares have plenty of character, and there are many buildings of historic interest, such as the magnificent **bell tower*** of the **church of S. Biagio**, built in the late-Gothic period above the site of one of the towers in the defensive walls. Inside the church is a fine *triptych* (1513), an imaginative marble *pulpit*, and a panel (*Our Lady of the Rosary*) from 1527. Near the 15th-century *Porta Testa*, on Piazza S. Caterina, is the *convent of S. Caterina* (1359), closed down in 1864 and used as a prison until 1965. In the Olivieri Chapel, there are some good frescoes (14-15C). The two cloisters of the convent (15C), are also interesting and have been

converted into the important **Museo Archeologico del Finale**. It contains prehistoric, Roman and medieval material from the surrounding area and a ceramics section.

Leaving Finalborgo, if you drive 4km up the valley of the Aquila Stream you come to the old town of **Perti**. The beautiful *church of S. Eusebio* (late-14C) has a Romanesque crypt and a small belfry on the apex of the roof. From here, a short drive across the hillside leads to the interesting **church of Nostra Signora di Loreto**, known as the "church of five bell towers", an unusual building set among olive groves, dating from the Renaissance period. Near Perti stands **Castel Gavone***, which can also be reached on foot from Finalborgo by

The hinterland of Finale Ligure is popular with rock climbers.

following the 17th-century path known as the Strada Beretta.

The 15th-century Diamanti Tower, the only one which is still perfectly intact, with rusticated walls, still contains original frescoes.

Behind Finale Ligure, in the nearby area of *Orco Feglino*, there are about

30 **climbing walls*** on the local stone, called "Pietra del Finale". This area is an international benchmark for free-climbing enthusiasts. The white

The town of Noli below Ursino castle.

limestone walls of Mt. Cucco, Mt. Rocca di Perti and Mt. Boragni (these are the best-known) offer about 2,000 free-climbing routes, ranging from easy routes for beginners to extreme routes for veterans. Every year, thousands of climbers come here from all over the world to practise their sport.

Driving west from Finale Marina on the Via Aurelia, after 3km, you come to **Borgio Verezzi**, a town with two distinct parts: *Borgio*, which stands on a low hill not far from the coast, and **Verezzi***, situated in a dominant position. The old centers of the two towns have been almost perfectly preserved, with old cobbled streets winding their way past vegetable gardens and olive groves. Verezzi, in particular, which lies at the top of a very winding panoramic road, has an interesting layout that is well-preserved. For more than 30 years, it has hosted a drama festival of international importance. Not far from the town lie the *Grotte di Borgio Verezzi*, natural caves containing extraordinary stalactites and other limestone formations, and a rich deposit dating from the Quaternary period.

NOLI [15 km]

This medieval town, one of the best-preserved in Liguria, is situated on a small bay between Capo Noli and the slopes of Mt. Ursino. There are beautiful views of the town, dominated by the towers and the castle higher up. Ancient Neapolis ("new city" in Greek) was founded at the same time as Varigotti,

further along the coast, during the Byzantine period. Because it had participated in the First Crusade, Noli obtained political and commercial privileges, and became a very prosperous trading port. The Via Aurelia passes through the edge of the town (separating it from the beach) in the form of *Corso Italia*, the promenade crowded with holidaymakers in summer. On one side of it there was once an arcade which acted as a public thoroughfare and a shelter for boats. A section of it still exists in the north of the town, opposite the *porticoes*

Noli: S. Paragorio

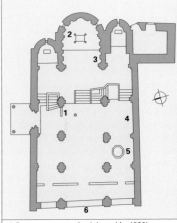

1 Romanesque ambo (altered in 1889)
2 Renaissance tabernacle
3 Bishop's throne
4 Wooden crucifix (12C)
5 Font (altered in 1889)
6 Excavations showing levels of the Imperial age

and the *Loggia della Repubblica*, where you can still see some of the original cobble stones. The porticoes lead into the heart of the old town, criss-crossed by picturesque narrow streets spanned by arches. Immediately on the left is *Palazzo del Comune* (Town Hall), dating from the 14th-15th century, with mullioned windows on the seaward facade and a long double arched loggia on the other. Next to it is a perfectly preserved tower (13C) with Ghibelline merlons. Set among medieval houses and towers is the 13th-century **Cathedral of S. Pietro**, which, below its Baroque transformations, conceals a medieval stone structure. Inside, in the apse, is a polyptych depicting the *Madonna and Child Enthroned, with Angels and Saints* and a fine Roman *sarcophagus* which is now the altar. Further along is *Piazza Morando*, and the tall Canto Tower. From here there is a lovely view of the dramatic ruins of Ursino castle. However, the most important monument in Noli lies beyond Casa Pagliano. The **church of S. Paragorio**** is one of the best surviving examples of Romanesque art in Liguria. The present building, which was completely restored in the late 19th century, probably dates from around the year 1000, but the original church is thought to be 8th century. The sarcophaguses made of local stone, found near the church and now situated along its left side, also date from this period. The church is divided into a nave and two aisles with semi-circular apses on the seaward side. The facade is decorated with the small arches and pilaster strips typical of the Lombard Romanesque style. Inside the church (the entrance is on the left side), you can see a Romanesque *ambo*, a wooden *Crucifix* dating from the same period, the original *bishop's seat* (12C) and some 15th-century frescoes.

By climbing up through the olive groves and terraces of Mt. Ursino, you reach the ruins of the **Ursino castle** or Noli castle, which dates from the 12th century and was altered subsequently. It is situated in a dramatic position overlooking the town and the bay. Imposing sections of the old walls drop down towards the sea.

The small town of **Varigotti***, which, in ancient times, provided coastal access to the territory of Finale, is preceded by white limestone rocks which drop down precipitously to the sea around Capo Noli. Like Noli, this was also used by the Byzantines as a defensive base against the Lombards, and was an important port, situated in the area known today as the Baia dei Saraceni (Saracen Bay). The architecture is typically Ligurian. Its square stone houses with flat terraced roofs look out over a wide sandy beach about 2km long. The *castle*, situated in a

Inside the caves at Toirano.

panoramic position, consists of the ruins of a Byzantine fort and later structural additions. North of the old town, a small footpath leads to a crag with a sheer drop down to the Baia dei Saraceni, site of the **church of S. Lorenzo Vecchio**. This early medieval church was almost destroyed during the Great War but has subsequently been restored.

SASSELLO [27 km]

This pleasant holiday resort, known for its cool summer climate, gentle breezes and delicious *amaretti* (almond biscuits), has been awarded the TCI's "Orange Flag" for quality tourism in the hinterland. The town has many places full of charm, such as *Piazza Concezione*, with the 16th-century church of the same name, and the square in front of the *church of* the *SS. Trinità*. The *Museo Perrando*, on the same street, has a fine collection of paintings and objects associated with the local area. On the edge of the town stands the 18th-century church of *S. Giovanni Battista*. Starting from Via Perrando, a 15-minute walk past some picturesque rustic houses leads up to *Bastia Soprana*, a medieval fortified complex which is now in ruins and heavily overgrown.

In Sassello is the headquarters of the Visitors' Center of the **Parco Naturale Regionale del Bèigua** (Via G.B. Badano 45). The park was created in 1985 and has an area of 18,160m². The mountain after which it is named, which is 1,287m high, is situated 8km from Sassello and is the same distance from the sea. There are plenty of marked footpaths for hikers and the views from the summit are breathtaking. The flora is extremely interesting, raptors are a common sight and, if you're lucky, you may encounter roe deer or wild boar in the woods.

The Grotte di Toirano have some amazing caverns.

TOIRANO [39 km]

Situated between the Varatella and Barescione streams, this ancient town has been awarded the TCI's "Orange Flag". In the oldest part of the town, you can still see traces of the defensive walls and towers, as well as medieval houses and loggias. A charming three-arched stone *bridge* spans the Varatella. The medieval parish **church of S. Martino** was rebuilt in 1609. You can still see its massive 14th-century merloned bell tower which was once part of the town's defensive fortifications. On the main street, which climbs up through the town between ancient houses and interesting shops, is *Palazzo Del Carretto*, with a walled-in medieval portico and Renaissance doorway. The stables have been converted into the *Museo Etnografico della Val Varatella*, a vast ethnographical collection devoted to the cultivation of olives, vines and corn, as well as traditional habits and skills. 1.5km from Toirano, the turn-off to Bardineto leads to the **Grotte di Toirano***, natural caves set in a dramatic landscape of white limestone. The entrance to the *Grotta della Bàsura* (or Grotta della Strega, Witch's Cave) is just beyond the car-park. The cave is very important, not only from the point of view of speleology,

but also because of its prehistoric deposits dating from the Early Paleolithic. Inside the cave, highlights include amazing crystalline formations, and evidence of of human footprints, torches and scratch-marks left by bears. From Grotta della Strega you continue to *Grotta di S. Lucia Inferiore*, which has no prehistoric deposits but which is famous for its stalactites and stalagmites. You emerge on the other side of the mountain below the *Grotta di S. Lucia Superiore*, the end of which opens out onto a sheer drop down to the valley.

ZUCCARELLO [54 km]

This small town with a linear plan, partly surrounded by walls, is in a good state of preservation. The street that winds through the town, with picturesque medieval **porticoes** on either side, connects the two *tower gates* which were once linked to the curtain walls leading down from the castle on the hill. The opposite side of the town was defended by the river and its rocky bank, where some houses still stand today. The *parish church*, altered in the 17th century, has the original **bell tower** built in local stone with two- and three-light windows, the bottom of which dates from the 12th-13th centuries, and the top from the 14th century. A footpath sets off from the north end of the main street to the ruins of the castle (20 min.). In the cathedral there is a famous funerary monument by Jacopo della Quercia (1408).

IMPERIA

I n 1923, Oneglia and Porto Maurizio were combined to form a single administrative unit called Imperia. Almost 80 years on from then, the two parts of Imperia still look like two quite distinct towns. Indeed, the difference is magnified by the very different layouts, which is partly the result of geography. Oneglia, prevalently modern, lies at the mouth of the Impero Stream, while Porto Maurizio, which is full of historical interest, is situated on a hill overlooking the sea. The hinterland is extremely varied in terms of landscape. The terraced hills around the town are covered with an endless expanse of olive groves, the main resource of the area since early medieval times. There are plenty of sites to visit in the surrounding area. Most of these date from the medieval and Baroque periods, sometimes hidden away in picturesque mountain villages and in the towns dotted along the coast. However, the coastal towns are often busy and tend to be dominated by tourism.

IMPERIA
IN OTHER COLORS...

- **ITINERARIES:** pages 86, 100
- **FOOD:** pages 120, 123, 125
- **SHOPPING:** pages 150, 151
- **EVENTS:** pages 156, 159
- **WELLNESS:** pages 164, 165
- **PRACTICAL INFO:** page 177

ONEGLIA

The admiral Andrea Doria and writer Edmondo De Amicis are the town's most famous sons. During the 20th century, a thriving industrial zone boosted the town's traditional resources, based on its port and the cultivation of olives, yet it is still pervaded by a small-town atmosphere.
No. 4 of the centrally located *Piazza Dante* ❶ is overlooked by the eclectic pseudo-medieval facade of the *former Palazzo Comunale* (1890-91). *Palazzo del Tribunale*, in *Piazza De Amicis* ❷, dates from almost the same time (1891-92) and is the birthplace of Edmondo De Amicis. Near the harbor, fish shops and

restaurants are sheltered by the characteristic **porticoes** of *Calata G. B. Cuneo* ❸. Behind them stands the **Collegiata di S. Giovanni Battista/ Collegiate church of S. Giovanni Battista** ❹, begun in 1739. It has a large dome and is divided into a nave and two aisles, separated by pillars. The marble *tabernacle* on the left of the presbytery is by the Gagini family (1516). In the fourth chapel of the left aisle is a late 17th-century *crucifix*, while the first chapel contains a *Madonna of the Rosary*.
The **Museo dell'Olivo***, in the Fratelli Carli olive-oil plant (*see p. 128*), in Via Garessio ❺ sums up 6,000 years of olive cultivation in this area.

Olive-presses in the Museo dell'Olivo at Oneglia.

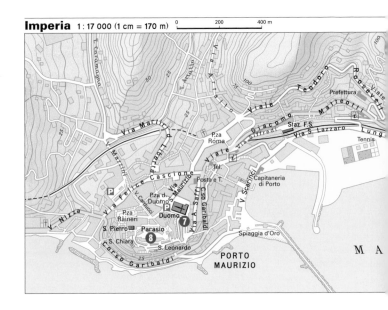

Imperia 1 : 17 000 (1 cm = 170 m)

PORTO MAURIZIO

Apart from the *Palazzo Municipale* (Town Hall, 1932), there is not much else of interest on *Viale Matteotti* **6**, the main road connecting Oneglia to the western part of the town. In Porto Maurizio, on the other hand, there is no shortage of interesting buildings. For example the **Duomo/Cathedral 7**, completed between 1781 and 1838, a building with majestic proportions, designed according to the tenets of the

The naval history museum in Porto Maurizio.

Neoclassical style. The pronaos, with its eight Doric columns, leads into the church proper, built on a central plan. It contains a rich collection of 19th-century paintings in addition to works from the former parish church of S. Maurizio, now

demolished. They include a statue of the *Madonna of Mercy* (1618), in the second chapel on the right, and, in the third chapel on the left, a *crucifix* in typical Genoese style. On Piazza Duomo, which was laid out when the church was built, stand the *Pinacoteca Civica* (art gallery) and, at No. 11, the **Museo Navale Internazionale del Ponente Ligure**. Although the exhibition space available is somewhat limited, the museum has an interesting display of nautical objects, with an excellent section about life on board a ship. The name of the **Parasio* 8**, the old port of Porto Maurizio, comes from the palace of the ruler of Genoa ("Paraxu"). In the late 20th century, after a long period of decline, foreign investment poured into the town to improve its commercial status. Starting in Piazza del Duomo, *Via Acquarone* leads up towards **Palazzo Pagliari** (14-16C), with its portico of pointed arches. Further up, at the top of the hill, is *Piazza Chiesa Vecchia*, named after the church of S. Maurizio, which was demolished in about 1838. The "Paraxu" stood on the same square. The three churches on the seaward side of the Parasio are all decorated in the Baroque style. The 17th-century **oratory of S. Leonardo** contains a painting by Gregorio De Ferrari (*Our Lady of Sorrows with Souls*

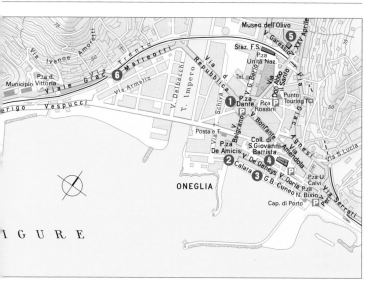

in *Purgatory*) and two by Domenico Bocciardo (*Death of St Joseph* and *Tobias Buries the Dead*).
The house next to the oratory is the birthplace of the titular saint. The **convent of S. Chiara** (14C), on the other hand, is of medieval origin. It was rebuilt in the 18th century. Inside there are several good artworks: a *St Domenico Soriano and the Madonna* and a *Madonna and Child with St Catherine of Bologna*. Behind

the church, the convent has a beautiful **portico*** with spectacular views out to sea. The **church of S. Pietro**, a 17th-century reworking of an earlier church, belonged to a confraternity of merchants. The facade (1789) is very dramatic, with three arches on coupled columns, and a small belfry made from a converted lookout tower. The cycles of paintings (depicting the *Life of St Peter*) inside the church are by Tommaso and Maurizio Carrega.

View of Porto Maurizio and the old port of Parasio.

APRICALE [54 km]

The Latin name for the town, Apricus, means " south-facing". It is also known as the "village of painters" because of the numerous wall paintings which add further interest to the picturesque streets. The town has been awarded the TCI's "Orange Flag". In the scenic **Piazza Vittorio Emanuele*** stands the *parish church of the Purificazione di Maria*, founded in late Middle Ages but rebuilt in the 18th century.

The *oratory of S. Bartolomeo* contains an interesting polyptych (*Madonna and Child with Saints*) of 1544 and

View of Apricale, in the western Ligurian hinterland.

a *St Anthony Abbott*, also from the late 16th century. In the summer, this spot, overlooked by the ruins of the *castle* (which hosts a permanent exhibition about local history and occasional art exhibitions), becomes the setting for tournaments of *pallone elastico*, an ancient sport which is very popular in the hinterland of Imperia.

To the right of the oratory, the interesting *Via Cavour* leads towards the cemetery, and the 13th-century *church of S. Antonio Abate*.

The facade is Baroque but the cycles of paintings inside date from the 15th century.

BORDIGHERA [38 km]

It was Giovanni Ruffini's bestselling novel "Doctor Antonio", translated and published in Edinburgh in 1855, that first attracted British tourists to this town. That was just the beginning of constant influx of visitors which, by the end of the 20th century, had reached enormous proportions. In addition to people attracted to the "town of palms", many botanical scholars and archeologists came here. One of them founded the important **Biblioteca "Clarence Bicknell"**, now a *library and museum*. In addition to the plaster-casts of rock carvings found in the Meraviglie valley and grave-goods from the Roman period, it contains a herbarium and a butterfly collection. The museum also has a permanent exhibition of the *private collection of Pompeo Mariani*.

Elegant hotels in the Art-Deco style grace the walk along *Via Romana* towards the charming old town. On *Piazza del Popolo* stands the 17th-century **church of S. Maria Maddalena**, with a *group of marble figures* above the high altar by the workshop of Domenico Parodi (who used the models of his father Filippo) depicting the titular saint, the *oratory of S. Bartolomeo* and an 18th-century *bell tower*, possibly a converted lookout tower. A few kilometers away lies the delightful little town of **Ceriana****, which looks as if it is built into the rock. With an urban layout similar to that of Pigna di Sanremo (*see p. 76*), the village, mentioned in Roman times, is of great environmental interest as well as having several monuments worthy of mention. The **church of Ss. Pietro e Paolo**, founded in the Romanesque period (12-13C, but rebuilt in the late 15C and early 16C), situated in the lower part of the town, has two early 16th-century *doorways* on one side. One very unusual feature is the wall across the middle of the church, dividing it into two parts, creating separate areas of worship for men and women. Adjoining the church, which was once the parish church of Ceriana, is the **oratory of S. Caterina**, built in 1736-37. *Porta della Pena* (which dates from the 12C and later) stands next to the 17th-century *oratory of the Visitazione*. Beyond the gate, follow the road up to the top of the town, using the bell tower of the Romanesque bell tower,

Claude Monet: Bordighera between the hills and the sea.

with its 17th-century columns, of the *church of S. Andrea* as a reference point. There are lovely views walking down *Via Celio* towards the Baroque **parish church of Ss. Pietro e Paolo** (18C), with twin bell towers on the facade. Inside, both the polyptych (*Sts Peter, Andrew and Paul*) on the right wall and the **altar*** of carved lime-wood in the sacristy date from the 16th century. The altar-piece depicting *St Catherine with St Martha and St Mary Magdalene* dates from 1544.

CERVO [10 km]

Always a very attractive place, especially at night, this little town is perched on a hill that slopes gently down towards the sea. The fact that it is now a popular tourist resort has not changed the appearance of Cervo, which has controlled this stretch of the coast since medieval times. Crucial to this role was its *castle*, situated at the top of the town, documented as early as 1196. Altered several times over the years, it now houses the *Museo Etnografico del Ponente Ligure*. From here, *Via Salineri* winds down towards the splendid **church of S. Giovanni Battista*** (1686-1734), regarded as one of the finest expressions of the Ligurian Baroque style. Designed and begun by Giovanni Battista Marvaldi, its great concave facade decorated with stuccoes faces the sea. The bell tower, added in 1771-74, was designed by Francesco Carrega. Inside, all the 18th-century *altars* and fine *stucco work*, like the wooden seats of the *choir*, date from the 18th century. A niche between the second and third altars in the right aisle contains a group of polychrome wooden statues (*St John the Baptist*) by Marcantonio Poggio, whereas the *crucifix* in the fourth altar of the left aisle is attributed to Maragliano. The nearby *oratory of S. Caterina* was erected in the 13th century. Beyond its fine Gothic doorway, restoration work

 TCI HIGHLIGHTS

ONCE UPON A TIME THERE WAS A PRINCIPALITY

It was so small that the prince was forgotten. On January 20, 1729, the principality of Seborga became the property of Victor Amadeus II of Savoy by means of a deed that was never registered in the archives of the Kingdom of Sardinia, nor in those of the House of Savoy. This apparently unintentional oversight was never rectified, because, from then on, this tiny state, recognized in 1079 by the Holy Roman Empire, was ignored in all further documentation regarding its territory. The Treaty of Aix-la-Chapelle, in 1748, even recorded its *de facto* possession by Genoa, and, the state was totally ignored at the Congress of Vienna (1815) and in the documents establishing the Kingdom of Italy and the Italian Republic. The tiny state finally emerged from oblivion in 1963, when the inhabitants of the "ghost principality" once again claimed independence for the principality which had never formally been denied. First they elected a prince, and then went on to declare a constitution. This was renewed in 1995, concurrent with the re-opening of the mint which had operated between 1666 and 1688. The unit of currency then was the "Luigino", a name chosen for a coin that was worth one quarter of the French "Luigi", whereas the modern currency was expressed in U.S. dollars. However, it must be said that it is hard to imagine a future for the coins and stamps of Seborga, except as collectors' items or souvenirs. While the minute state eagerly awaits the arrival of casinos and tax reductions, its main resources to date are still the cultivation of mimosa and broom. The 17th-century *parish church of S. Martino*, which overlooks the square of the same name, is worth visiting.

S. Giovanni Battista, Cervo's parish church, with its elegant 18C facade looking out to sea.

A spectacular **bridge** (15C) spans the Nervia Stream, linking the districts of Borgo and Terra. The latter, which is older, has an interesting semi-circular plan, and was laid out in this way for defensive purposes. The Baroque *parish church of S. Antonio Abate* contains a polyptych (*St Devota*) dated 1515. Opposite the church, the *monument to the olive-mill* commemorates the discovery of Pier Vincenzo Mela, who, in the early 18th century, invented a way of washing olive residues. The walk up towards the majestic ruins of the **castle**, which was damaged in an earthquake in 1887, is like taking a step back into the Middle Ages.

PIGNA [59 km]

The urban layout is similar to the homonymous district in Sanremo. However, tradition has it that the name of the town (*pigna* means pine-cone) derives from the coniferous forests which once surrounded it. Below the town, the grand ruins of the **church of S. Tommaso** (12C) are situated in the town's original location. Later it began to develop higher up, on a hill which provided better defense. Our first stop is the 15th-century *Loggia della Piazza Vecchia*, which was rebuilt after damage incurred during WWII, and is important from an environmental point of view. Next is the **parish church of S. Michele*** (1450), rebuilt on lines which reflect the transition from the Gothic to the Renaissance style. On the facade, above the pseudo-porch with a low relief (*St Michael and the Dragon*) in the lunette, is a magnificent **rose window**. Rays of divine salvation radiate out from the central figure of the Lamb of God to earthly creatures, symbolized by floral motifs in the early Renaissance style. The Twelve Apostles are depicted in the window. Inside the church, which has round and octagonal columns, is a 15th-century *crucifix* and, in the presbytery, the monumental **polyptych of S. Michele*** (1500) divided into 36 sections. In the cemetery, notice the frescoes (the **Passion***, 1482) in the little *church of S. Bernardo*. The frescoes were removed from the walls, carefully restored and, a few years ago, put back in place on a glass-fiber surface. Before leaving the town, it's worth walking up to **Piazza Castello***.

carried out in about 1959 removed the post-16th century additions, restoring the building to its original medieval lines. As you continue down towards the sea, look out for the slate doorway of *Palazzo Morchio* (16C), now the Town Hall, and the broad 18th-century portico of *Palazzo Viale*. The *frescoes* of the *piano nobile* are attributed to Francesco Carrega.

DOLCEÀCQUA [48 km]

This curious place-name (meaning sweet water) comes from the name of the Roman-Ligurian estate in this area but, coincidentally, the town also produces one of Italy's best wines. However, the delicious Rossese wine is just one of many reasons for visiting the town, which has been awarded the TCI's "Orange Flag" for quality tourism in the hinterland. We begin in the cemetery, with the *church of S. Giorgio*, the original Romanesque features of which are still visible on the facade and at the base of the bell tower. The cemetery has splendid views of the town, dominated by its castle, built in the 12th-14th centuries by the Doria family.

Pigna, the church of S. Bernardo: detail of a fresco depicting the Passion.

SANREMO [48 km]

Sanremo, known as the Riviera dei Fiori (Flower Riviera), alluding to its natural beauty, was one of the favorite destinations of the Victorian *bourgeoisie* throughout the Belle Époque. It was the rich subjects of Her Majesty the Queen of England, with their passion for wildlife and gardens, who laid the foundations of the flower industry which was to make Sanremo famous all over the world. Its beaches are popular, yet no-one bothers to visit the lovely green hinterland of Sanremo, a region which, despite the wildness of the landscape, has been inhabited since ancient times. There is plenty of evidence of this, in terms of medieval and modern reminders, in the multitude of small mountain villages, some perched on ridges, others hanging on the sides of steep gorges, like something out of a fairytale. It is no coincidence that they inspired some people to write tender love-stories and others to speculate about witchcraft. It took about 50 years, at the turn of the 19th century, to remove the Baroque additions and restore the **Cathedral of S. Siro ①** to its original Romanesque lines. They were crafted by the legendary master stonemasons from Como, who built the church (13C) above the ruins of an earlier place of worship. The fact that there was no clay in the local area for making bricks made it logical to use the yellow limestone from the quarries at Verezzo. This gives the facade a very somber appearance, somewhat attenuated by the protruding structure around the main doorway. The sides of the building have two doorways with pseudo-porches and pointed lunettes decorated with low reliefs. The one on the right (*Madonna Enthroned with two Saints*) dates from the 15th century, while the one of the left (*Easter Lamb*) dates from the 12th century. The nave and two aisles are separated by columns and octagonal pillars, culminating in three apses which were extended in the 17th century. In the right-hand aisle is a black **crucifix★** (15C). Above the high altar is a grand *crucifix* (1722 or 1727) and there is a 16th-century panel (*St Sirus with Sts Peter, Paul, John the Baptist and Romulus of Genoa*) on the wall at the back of the choir. Finally, note the *pulpit* and the *holy water stoups* in Brescia marble, carved in 1950 by Dante Ruffini. To the left of the cathedral stands the **Battistero/Baptistery ②**, which was converted in 1576-1624 from a medieval church dedicated to St John the Baptist. Inside is a painting depicting *St Mary Magdalene Receiving Communion*.

Sanremo: Cattedrale di S.Siro

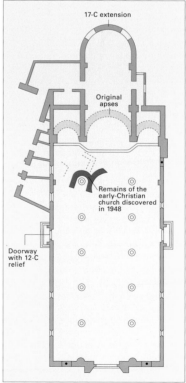

17-C extension

Original apses

Remains of the early-Christian church discovered in 1948

Doorway with 12-C relief

The medieval borgo of Dolceàcqua

Dominated by the ruins of the castle built by the Doria, the little town of Dolceàcqua occupies both sides of this section of the Nervia Stream, with two bridges connecting them. The Ponte Vecchio is a daring 15th-century construction with a single arch (33m wide) spanning the river. The oldest part of Dolceàcqua, Terra, is situated on the left bank of the river. This medieval town was built on an interesting plan of concentric circles, for defensive purposes. The church of S. Antonio Abate was built in the

CHURCH OF S. GIORGIO

15C HUMP-BACKED BRIDGE

15th century near the south side of the walls. It was remodeled in the Baroque period. An ancient passageway reserved for the Doria family still runs between the church and the adjoining palace. On the opposite side of the river is the western part of the town, called Borgo. Of later date, the plan here is linear, following the line of the river. By the entrance to the town on this side stands the church of S. Giorgio, the first collegiate church of Dolceàcqua.

Castello Doria, built for defensive purposes in the 12th century, was gradually made larger by adding structures to the original round tower. In fact, in the 15th century, a bastion and the square side-towers were added. In the two following centuries, it was further enhanced, but the emphasis now began to shift towards its role as a noble residence. When the castle surrendered in 1754, having incurred serious damage, it was dealt the final blow by an earthquake in 1887.

PALAZZO DORIA

CHURCH OF S. ANTONIO ABATE

From the left bank, the locals could reach the "Pontagno", a flat area on the riverbed used for meetings of the townsfolk and the local authorities.

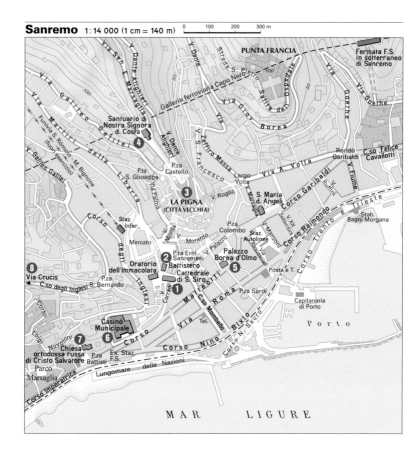

Sanremo 1 : 14 000 (1 cm = 140 m)

0   100   200   300 m

MAR   LIGURE

Opposite the cathedral is the **oratory of the Immacolata Concezione**, erected in the 15th-16th centuries and altered again after 1667. It contains eight paintings by various artists depicting *Stories from the Life of the Virgin* and some very fine polychrome marble decoration.

The name **La Pigna*** ❸ is very old and derives from the particular urban layout devised for the lie of the land here, where the houses cling to the hillside in a series of concentric rings, creating a maze of narrow alleyways, steep flights of steps and covered passageways. A scenario which, despite the undeniable degradation of the district and the debatable wisdom of local development, has retained a certain charm. This is obvious as you walk through *Porta S. Stefano* (1321), beyond which the steps of *Rivolte S. Sebastiano* climb up towards Piazzetta dei Dolori. From here, Via del Pretorio and Via della Palma lead to the *church of S. Giuseppe*, erected in

Sanremo's casino is one of the town's most famous places.

1666-84. The nearby gate of Porta S. Giuseppe, or Porta della Tana, with its rounded arch, dates from the 16th century. A broad avenue leads to the **Santuario di Nostra Signora della Costa/Sanctuary of Nostra Signora della Costa** ④. The original church, which was replaced by the present one in the 17th century, dates from 1361. Inside, as well as the ponderous marble and stucco decoration, note the frescoes in the dome

The palazzo, which has two *doorways* opening onto *Corso Matteotti* and *Via Cavour*, decorated with late 17th-century sculpture (*Madonna and Child* and *St John the Baptist*), is now the **Museo Civico**. The display is divided into three sections: an *archeological collection*, with finds dating from the prehistoric, protohistoric and Roman periods, a *collection of relics of the volunteers who accompanied Garibaldi on his mission*

A view of Sanremo and the surrounding sea.

(*Assumption*), painted in the 18th century, and the three wooden *statues* by Maragliano. The same sculptor also created the four statues at the high altar, where there is a *Madonna and Child*. According to tradition, painters attempting to create the face of the Virgin Mary used to paint kneeling, almost as if they felt embarrassed by her gentle gaze. Damage caused by a naval bombardment was responsible for the Rococo makeover of the *church of S. Maria degli Angeli*, situated at the corner of *Piazza Colombo* and *Corso Garibaldi*. Its impressive interior is divided into a nave and two aisles. In the third chapel of the left aisle there is a wooden *crucifix* (16C). The lines of **Palazzo Borea d'Olmo** ⑤ are a mixture of the Mannerist and Baroque styles. In 1814 it managed to avoid an unusual episode of looting. With considerable difficulty, the owners succeeded in driving back a crowd which had come to take away the furnishings collected by Pope Pius VII.

and an *art gallery* with paintings (17-19C). The Art-Deco style rooms of the **Casinò Municipale** ⑥, built in 1904-06, contain reminders of the Belle Époque – sadly ruined by the appalling taste of the end of the second millennium. A little further on, in Corso Nuvoloni, are the unmistakable domes of the *Chiesa Ortodossa Russa di Cristo Salvatore/Russian Orthodox church of Cristo Salvatore, S. Caterina Martire e S. Serafim di Sarov* ⑦. Building the church was the idea of the Empress of Russia, Maria Alexandrovna, who spent the winter of 1874-75 in Sanremo. It was consecrated in 1913. Life-size bronze high reliefs of the **Stations of the Cross** ⑧ were erected in 1990 at No. 374 *Corso degli Inglesi*, where there are interesting mansions in eclectic and Art-Deco styles.

TAGGIA [20 km]

This little town on the Argentina Stream is not only famous for its delicious *Taggiasca* olives. Inside its 16th-century

The Russian Orthodox church designed by A.V. Ščusev.

walls, the streets are knee-deep in history and features of outstanding artistic and architectural importance. Before you even enter the town, the **monastery of S. Domenico*** is a good example. After it was completed in 1490, it became a benchmark for the very lively local school of painting. As a result, the church, which was restored in 1935 to its original Gothic lines, contains an extraordinary treasure of paintings. First and foremost, there are works by Lodovico Brea, who painted the polyptychs in the right aisle, in the first (*Annunciation*), second (**Madonna of the Rosary***), and the third chapels (*St Catherine of Siena and Sts Agatha and Lucy*, a triptych), above the high altar (*Madonna of Mercy with Saints*) and above the altar on the left of the presbytery (*Baptism of Christ and Saints*). Notice also the remarkable *organ doors* on the back of the facade and the *frescoes* that decorate the refectory and the chapterhouse, and the cusped triptych (*St Domenic and the Doctors of the Church* at the bottom and the *Madonna and Child with*

Four Saints at the top) in the fourth chapel on the right (1478). The monastery is arranged around a 15th-century **cloister** with black stone columns (15C) and the remains of frescoes in the lunettes (*Stories from the Life of St Domenic*) dated 1611-13. The fine paintings once included a splendid **Epiphany*** (1528-35) attributed to Parmigianino, which has sadly been lost. The abbey was also famous for its school of Lombard engravers, who were responsible for the 16th-century reliefs above the main door (*Pietà*) and the left door (*Madonna of Mercy*) of the church.

Our visit to the town begins at *Porta dell'Orso*. Following Via Lercari (the *low relief* above the doorway of No. 10 is attributed to the Gagini) we come to Piazza Farini. The 17th-century *Palazzo Lercari* (No. 5) overlooks the square. On nearby Via Curlo, No. 3 is *Palazzo Curlo-Spinola* which dates from the first half of the 18th century. In nearby Piazza Gastaldi, the **parish church of Ss. Giacomo e Filippo** dates from 1675-89. Inside the church, in the third chapel on the right, there is a painting (*Sts Anthony Abbot and Paul the Hermit*) by Luca Cambiaso and, in the Chapel of the Body of Christ, a *Resurrection* by his father Giovanni Cambiaso (assisted by Luca). Note also the altar-piece (1510) depicting the *Crucifix with the Madonna and Saints* in the first chapel on the right. "Pantan" is the local nickname for the centrally located **Via Soleri**, which passes under the vaults of *Palazzo Lombardi*. As we walk towards *Piazza della SS. Trinità*, we pass noble mansions with porticoes and family crests on either side. The first building we come to is the

The river that flows through the Argentina valley.

orange marble facade of the *oratory of Ss. Sebastiano e Fabiano*. Other buildings on the square include the *oratory of the SS. Trinità*, the *church of S. Caterina* and, on the right, the remains of a bastion. From here it is only a short distance to the imposing 16-arch **medieval bridge***: the last two are Romanesque, whereas the others are later (15-19C). On the far side of the stream, near *Villa Curlo* (17-18C) a footpath sets off in the direction of the sea to the **church of S. Martino** (about a 10-minute walk). The church is of early foundation but was reworked several times. Its frescoes date from various periods. Back on the other side of the bridge, turn right towards the **church of S. Maria del**

Madonna of the Rosary by Lodovico Brea in the monastery of S. Domenico near Taggia.

Canneto. It has an elegant cusped *bell tower* and a doorway dating from 1467, recovered from the no longer extant church of S. Anna. It contains *frescoes*. Beyond the gate of *Porta del Colletto*, the buildings facing onto **Via S. Dalmazzo** have beautifully carved slate doorways. Go through *Porta Barbarasa*, under the *Clavesana Tower* (12-13C) and walk up towards the district of S. Lucia, the original nucleus of the town, with a *church* of the same name. Go back down to Via S. Dalmazzo, and walk out of the old town through the gate of *Porta Pretoria* (or Porta Parasio, built in 1541). Our visit ends with a walk past the bastions of Ciazzo and dell'Orso.

TRIORA [46 km]

About a dozen unfortunate women were burned at the stake following the famous trials for witchcraft held in 1587-89, which earned the town the name of the "town of witches". Despite the damage inflicted in 1944, the village has preserved its original urban layout, including an elaborate system of defense and an ancient water supply, based on fountains which provided constant fresh water to every level of the town. As you climb up towards the town, on the right, you pass the *church of the Madonna delle Grazie* (12-13C) and the ruins of the *Forte della Colombara* (or *Forte del Poggio*). Further on, a road on the left leads to the little 15th-century **church of S. Bernardino***, with a portico on one side supported by four pillars. The cycles of paintings inside also date from the 15th century (*Passion, Apostles, Last Judgement*). Near the church are the ruins of the *Sella fortress*. In the centrally located Corso Italia, No. 1 is the **Museo Etnografico e della Stregoneria**, which has a whole room devoted to witchcraft. A little further on, the **collegiate church of the Assunta** has preserved its original Romanesque Gothic doorway and the base of the bell tower. Inside, in addition to the precious **Baptism of Christ*** from 1397, there are two panels (*Pietà* and *St James*) dating from the early 15th century. The nearby **oratory of S. Giovanni Battista** (1694) has a marble doorway and holy water stoup. It contains an 18th-century wooden *statue* of St John the Baptist and a painting (*Madonna and Saints*) by Luca Cambiaso and his assistants. The apse rests on pillars which can easily be seen from the road below the church, with its medieval houses. The road leads to *Porta Sottana*, preceded by a *fountain* of the same name (1480). Back in Piazza della Collegiata, *Via Cima* goes to the *church of S. Dalmazio*, which has been engulfed by the surrounding houses. Not much remains of the homonymous *fort*, or the nearby *Cabotina*, where

The ancient town of Realdo is set in wild mountain landscape.

witchcraft is supposed to have been practiced.

Back in Piazza della Collegiata, *Via Dietro la Colla* climbs up to the *Soprana Fountain*, the oldest in Triora, situated near the round-arched *Porta Soprana* gate. The climb ends opposite the ruins of the **castle**, built by the Genoese in the 12th-13th centuries. Outside the town stands a *bell tower* covered with an onion dome, faced with polychrome tiles. It belongs to the *church of S. Agostino* (1616, altered in the 18C).

Continuing along the opposite side of the valley, the town of **Realdo**** suddenly appears, spectacularly situated on a rocky spur with a sheer drop down to the valley. **Molini di Triora** was named after the mills situated along the Argentina and Capriolo streams (there were 23 of them

in the late Middle Ages). This town at the bottom of the valley used to be in the municipality of Triora but it became a separate town in 1903. The layout of the village is relatively modern. The **parish church of S. Lorenzo** (1486), which was rebuilt in the Baroque style in the 18th century, still has a Gothic doorway and bell tower. Inside is a polyptych (*St Mary Magdalene with Sts Martha and Catherine*), painted in 1540, and a wooden *St Lawrence* from 1925. The 15th-century **Sanctuary of Nostra Signora della Montà** has cycles of paintings from the same period (*Madonna*, *Crucifixion*, *Evangelists* and *Founders of Religious Orders*). From the front of the church there is a lovely view over the town.

VENTIMÌGLIA [43 km]

The border-town of Ventimìglia is the heir of Roman Albintimilium and the even older Albium Intemelium. Travelers passing through must look beyond the huge square of now deserted customs offices and the maze of railway lines below and raise their eyes towards the rocky spur on which the medieval town was built. This is the first stop on a transnational journey into the past with

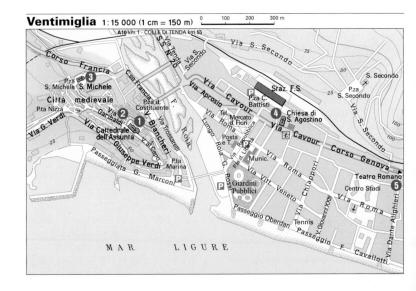

a pause at the caves of Balzi Rossi, where the relics of Paleolithic Man were discovered in 1892, and then, once we have crossed the border, to the Trophée des Alpes, that great symbol of the *Pax Romana*. Inland lie the valleys of the Roia and the Nervia, where the landscape is mountainous but you can still smell the sea. The **Cattedrale dell'Assunta/ Cathedral of the Assunta*** ❶ was built on the site of a Carolingian church and has been enlarged and transformed several times. The right side and facade of the cathedral are Romanesque (11C). In 1222, a Gothic pseudo-porch was added. The top of the bell tower (12C) is Baroque and was altered in the 19th century, while the apses and the tiburium date from the 13th century. The chapels in the left aisle, which, although they break up the architectural uniformity of the church, lighten the interior, date from the 16th century. Inside, there is an *Assumption* by Giovanni Carlone in the first chapel on the left, and look for the Byzantine *dosseret* (5-6C)now used as a holy water stoup. In the *crypt* you can see part of the early medieval church (8-10C). Behind the cathedral is the **baptistery**: built on an octagonal plan, it was constructed at the same time as the cathedral (11C; ceiling from the 16C). It contains a magnificent sunken *baptismal font*, datable to the 12th–13th century, and, in a niche, a bowl bearing the date 1100. Many of the buildings on **Via Garibaldi** ❷, the main street of the medieval town, are worthy of note. First, on the left, we encounter the *Vescovado* (bishop's palace), facing the 15th-century **Loggia del Parlamento** or *Loggia dei Mercanti*. Part of the portico, with a motif of double pointed arches supported by low rectangular pillars, was demolished in the 19th century to make room for the *Teatro Civico* (city theater). This Neoclassical building is currently the seat of the **Civica Biblioteca Aprosiana**, the oldest library in Liguria (1648) with an extremely important collection of manuscripts and incunabulae. If we proceed along Via Garibaldi, on the left there are noble palazzi dating from the 16th century, many of which were restructured in the 19th century, with hanging gardens at the back, level with the *piano nobile*, as was the Genoese custom. On the right, is the Baroque

facade of the *oratory of the Neri*, which contains frescoes by Maurizio and Tommaso Carrega (1784-86). A little further up, on the left, is the deconsecrated *church of S. Francesco*, the side of which stands on the street leading to the imposing gate of *Porta Nizza*. First a monastery (16C), then a fortress under the House of Savoy, the *Forte dell'Annunziata*, at No. 41 Via Verdi, is now used for

Ventimiglia: Cattedrale dell'Assunta

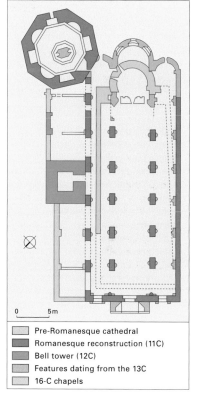

```
0        5m
```

	Pre-Romanesque cathedral
	Romanesque reconstruction (11C)
	Bell tower (12C)
	Features dating from the 13C
	16-C chapels

exhibitions. The fortress now houses the **Museo Archeologico "Girolamo Rossi"**. In addition to material from excavations of the Roman town of Albintimilium, there are archeological collections put together in the late 19th and early 20th centuries, with grave-goods, ancient glass, sculptures and a fine collection of inscriptions. There is a demanding but satisfying walk from Porta Nizza to **Forte S. Paolo**. The fort was built by the Genoese in 1222 and remodeled several times that followed (the rectangular plan is oriented according to the points of the

necessary after the earthquake of 1564, then, in 1885, the facade was restored. In the *crypt* you can see re-used Roman architectural features and a milestone from the time of Caracalla.

The Roman theater at Ventimìglia and a detail of the mosaic depicting Arion in the bath complex.

compass). Another walk leads to *Porta Canarda*, which incorporated a huge 13th-century tower and was restructured in 1880. You can walk or drive to the ruins of **Castel d'Appio**, built on a site that was already fortified in Neolithic times, and later became the site of a Roman *castrum* (camp). Local tradition associates it with the name of the Consul Appius Claudius, who defeated the local tribes in 185 BC. Features surviving from the fortress built in the 13th century by the Genoese include two pentagonal towers and a large water cistern. **S. Michele** ❸ is a Romanesque church standing on a square overlooking the Roia valley. Erected in about 1100 on the site of a 10th-century chapel, it was first remodeled at the end of the 12th century (the apse, the bell tower and the nave date from this period). More building work was

The modern part of Ventimìglia is a hive of commercial activity, thanks to the French who come here to shop at weekends. The *Chiesa di Sant'Agostino/ Neogothic church of S. Agostino* ❹ contains a precious 15th-century *crucifix* and a panel depicting *St Augustine with Sts John the Baptist and Anthony the Abbott*. The town's Roman **theater** is small (it has a diameter of 21m) but very well preserved, and is the most interesting building on the archeological site of Albintimilium, just east of the modern town ❺. The arena, built in the late 2nd century using blocks of stone from La Turbie, has two points of access: the entrance on the right is almost intact. A short distance from Ventimìglia, the

Villa Hanbury was given to the State in 1960.

Giardini Hanbury** cover an area of 18 hectares sloping gently down towards the sea. The two brothers who created the gardens, Thomas and Daniel Hanbury, were two of the many Englishmen who, in the 19th century, fell in love with this stretch of the coast. Around their villa, they laid out a magnificent garden with medicinal and ornamental plants. In 1960, it was handed over to the State. Now, half of this large botanical garden is devoted to typical Mediterranean scrubland, and the flowers traditionally grown in Liguria. The other half is planted with an interesting collection of exotic plants (including agaves and aloes), which grow well here because of the mild climate and the situation of the garden, which is sheltered from the cold north winds. There are species from the Australian jungle and succulents from desert habitats all over the world. The garden contains aromatic, sweet-smelling varieties such as thyme, jasmine and the genus Salvia, the ornamental varieties of which bloom even in the depths of winter. The Via Aurelia runs through the lower part of the

The limestone cliff of Balzi Rossi overlooking the coast between France and Grimaldi in Ventimìglia.

garden. A plaque left by Thomas Hanbury recalls famous travelers who passed this way, including Dante, Niccolò Machiavelli and Pope Pius VII. Another "must" near Ventimìglia is **Balzi Rossi***, a stone's throw from the Franco-Italian border, where we take a dive into prehistory. This promontory, a few hundred meters from the border, is famous because of the extraordinary prehistoric finds made in these caves. Some of them are on display at the **Museo Preistorico dei Balzi Rossi**. The entrance to the museum is on the square opposite the pass of the Ponte San Ludovico. The fossilized remains of animals that thrive in warm climates (elephants, hippopotamus and rhinos) were found in the oldest deposits, while fossils of marmots and reindeer prove

that these animals lived here during the Würm glaciation. The human remains date mainly from the Upper Paleolithic, when the caves were used for burials. The *triple grave* discovered in 1892 inside the *Barma Grande cave*, containing the remains of an adult and two adolescents with rich grave-goods, is the most important exhibit. It is now displayed in a modern, functional building (1993). A walkway leads from the museum to the caves, which contain the only examples of *rock carvings* of that type from the Upper Paleolithic in northern Italy. **La Turbie** is another thing altogether. The huge monument built by Augustus to celebrate the pacification of the Alps must have been visible form afar. In fact, you can clearly see what is left of the **Trophée des Alpes*** from Roquebrune. It was built and dedicated in 5 BC. Originally the monument was 50m high and 36m wide. Above the base was a Doric colonnade with statues of the generals who had been active in the campaigns fought in the Alps. Above it was a decorated dome and, on the top, a marble sculpture of the emperor with two prisoners. The

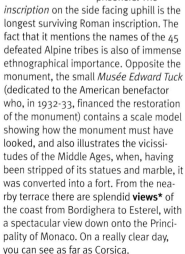

inscription on the side facing uphill is the longest surviving Roman inscription. The fact that it mentions the names of the 45 defeated Alpine tribes is also of immense ethnographical importance. Opposite the monument, the small *Musée Edward Tuck* (dedicated to the American benefactor who, in 1932-33, financed the restoration of the monument) contains a scale model showing how the monument must have looked, and also illustrates the vicissitudes of the Middle Ages, when, having been stripped of its statues and marble, it was converted into a fort. From the nearby terrace there are splendid **views*** of the coast from Bordighera to Esterel, with a spectacular view down onto the Principality of Monaco. On a really clear day, you can see as far as Corsica.

BEACHES

PARKS

MARINE PROTECTED AREAS

CHILDREN

CINEMA

SPORT

WALKING

HISTORICAL ITINERARIES

BIKING ROUTES

The mention of Liguria normally brings to mind images of the sea, cliffs rising up out of the water and charming inlets and bays. In short, it recalls vacations. Tourists can enjoy thin beaches, perhaps sandy or pebbly, and often trapped between sheer cliffs jutting into the sea as well as lush Mediterranean scrubland and two marine protected areas. Liguria is a land with plenty to explore, offering far more than its renowned seaside stretches. It abounds with hidden hamlets where time seems to have stood still, preserving a superb harmony between history and nature. The great parks and nature reserves are excellent destinations for outings and hikes. The watercourses and splendid sea are superb locations for water sports. The undulating cart tracks, inland forestry roads and rewarding circuits not far from the seaside resorts make this a paradise for cyclists. The mild climate – temperate in winter and fresh in summer – makes Liguria an excellent tourist destination in any season. Still, the best time begins in early spring

Itineraries

because the vegetation has started to blossom and the days are already warm; even at that time of the year, you are likely to find good enough days to enjoy a dip in the sea. Finally, spring often allows you to explore places of rare beauty away from the high-season crowds.

Highlights

- Two pearls of the sea: the Portofino and Cinque Terre marine protected areas.
- The Genoa aquarium: a journey through the wonders of the sea, exploring carefully reconstructed ecosystems and watching stunning sea creatures.
- Apricale, Pigna, Dolceàcqua, Sassello, Torriglia... hamlets where history, culture and nature come together.
- Liguria: an open-air gym.

Inside

Italy's two main mountain ranges are the Alps and the Apennines, and Liguria is where they meet, resulting in a narrow region that hugs the coast amid a mountainous embrace. These are the elements that characterize the Riviera, perhaps seeming a little narrow for those more akin to open spaces, but charming nonetheless. As such, Liguria's beaches are often thin and pebbly, trapped between rocky cliffs that fall sharply into the sea. Yet, this landscape is precisely where the beauty of this coastline lies, especially when the sheer cliffs are broken by little bays and gulfs, although all too often these have been turned into harbors or jetties. The climate is mild thanks to the warm and humid winds that arrive from the sea and the mountainous barrier that blocks the cold northern winds. Finally, the region can also boast two marine protected areas: Portofino and Cinque Terre.

Balzi Rossi beach (Province of Imperia)

Near France, along the Via Aurelia road, you find a lighthouse with a path that leads to a splendid, rocky stretch of coast. At the foot of one of these cliffs lies a series of caves and shelters that has been used since prehistoric times. You reach the beach from road to the Museo Preistorico. After passing the privately-managed beach – also called Egg Beach after the oval-shaped rocks – you need to continue until you come to a number of large, flat rocks that are ideal for lying in the sun. This is also a good scuba-diving spot.

Calandre beach (Province of Imperia)

This beach is 2km from the center of Ventimìglia and can be reached on foot along a lovely, clearly marked path that cuts through the Mediterranean scrubland. The sea is not too deep here and the beach is sandy. The clean water and relative lack of people make this beach especially attractive.

Tre Ponti beach (Province of Imperia)

This beach has sandstone sand, with a shallow, sandy seabed. There are toilets and places to eat nearby. The excellent waves ensure this beach is favored by surfers, even in winter. You can reach the beach from the paths leading off Via Aurelia and Via Tre Ponti. If you come on public transport, get off along Via Aurelia and then use the steps opposite the final station of the trolleybus in the La Brezza area (150m).

Capo Verde seaside
(Province of Imperia)

This beach lies on the eastern side of Sanremo. To get there, you need to leave your car or bike on Via Aurelia near the roadman's house (parking is limited and it is easy to pick up a fine). You then need to jump over the guardrail and head down the steep path to the reef: 150m of relatively well preserved rocky beach, with small, crystal clear inlets that are filled with sea grass. The hidden nature of this beach means it is popular with nudists. There is no sand, only rocks and gravel. The only real downside is the purification plant.

Riva Ligure beach (Province of Imperia)

Over the last few years, the main Italian environmental group, Legambiente, has organized the "Clean Beaches" initiative on the last Sunday in May. The aim is to clean up as many of Italy's beaches as possible. Riva Ligure has a lovely reef with a shallow, pebbly seabed. The only facilities available for bathers are the showers.

Arma di Taggia fortress
(Province of Imperia)

From the Arma di Taggia seaside road, you can easily reach a public beach with toilets and places to eat. This is a popular beach that is sandy with fairly shallow water. Umbrellas, sun beds and showers are all available.

Balzi Rossi beach.

Bergeggi isle (Province of Savona)

An ideal place for diving, you can get there by dinghy or boat, mooring at the little jetty on the northern side of the island. Along the coast, you can go to Punta delle Grotte (Cave Point) from Via Aurelia. In the various underwater caves (35m underwater), scuba divers can see stalactites and stalagmites. The zone is a regional reserve and it might become a national marine protected area.

Torre beach (Province of Savona)

This sandy and rocky inlet lies between Celle Ligure and the Albisola Superiore municipality. If you come from Albissola Marina, you can park along Via Aurelia, at the exit of the tunnel after Celle Ligure. Buses also stop along Via Aurelia near the beach. About 50m after the tunnel, on the right, a small gap in the fence leads to a path (about 200m) that heads down, after some steps, to the small Torre beach. It is protected by a high cliff and the crystal clear water is refreshed by a freshwater spring. The inlet also has a small cliff with a hole in it – cut by the sea – that is known as the *Buco del Prete* or Priest's Hole. The beach has a bathing establishment.

Santa Margherita beaches
(Province of Genoa)

This public beach with some places to eat lies before Santa Margherita Lìgure – near the petrol station and after Hotel Miramare – if you head along the SS227 road. The beaches near Covo (a local nightclub) have no facilities, but there is parking.

Pozzetto beach (Province of Genoa)

This beach is about 3km from Rapallo, following the SS Aurelia road towards Zoagli. It is hard to find a beach in this part of Liguria that is not crowded. Pozzetto has a bar and sun beds, but a small section of the beach is still free.

Cinque Terre beaches
(Province of La Spèzia)

The two villages on the edges of Cinque Terre (Monterosso to the west and Riomaggiore to the east) are the only two beaches that can easily be reached by car. The others can be reached by boat (from Genoa or La Spèzia) or on foot, following the "Azzurro Trail". Monterosso has a lovely sandy beach. A little before Punta Linà lies the Frate (or friar) reef. The point itself has a small natural tunnel, *Pertuso del Diavolo*, just on the water line, making it accessible for small boats. The beaches between Vernazza, Manarola and Corniglia lie along an impervious path. The Guvano beach deserves a mention alone as it is one of the most beautiful in the Cinque Terre park. You can reach it by following the very taxing path or, from the Corniglia station, by heading through a tunnel (although you must pay a toll).

Canneto beach (Province of La Spèzia)

This splendid beach is perhaps the most beautiful one in the province, although it is hard to reach, lying alone a little before Riomaggiore, between Punta Castagna and Punta del Cavo. Various little streams run over the overhanging rocks, with one forming a little waterfall that doubles as a natural shower! Unfortunately, it can only be reached via the sea.

Pozzale beach (Province of La Spèzia)

On the western side of Palmaria island lies the lovely Pozzale beach. It can only be reached via the sea, with water taxis heading there from La Spèzia and Portovènere. Although a military camp and a small bar/restaurant back onto the beach, the place has an uninhabited feel. Many private boats moor here in summer, but the beach remains one of the loveliest and cleanest in the zone.

Palmaria island (Province of La Spèzia)

Also on the island, but this time facing Portovènere, you find an amazingly beautiful beach that is washed by the current that constantly flows through the Portovènere Channel. The beach is a mixture of rocks and gravel.

Punta Corvo beach
(Province of La Spèzia)

After Lérici, near Tellaro, you find a lovely little inlet by the Montemarcello headland, dividing Liguria from Versilia. The beach, which is still quite wild, can be reached from the sea (in summer, tourist boats leave from Bocca di Magra) or from the land along a lovely, but quite difficult path that consists of hundreds of natural steps near a sheer drop into the sea.

PARCO NAZIONALE DELLE CINQUE TERRE

PROVINCE OF LA SPÈZIA

AREA: 3860 HECTARES. FROM THE TRAMONTI ZONE, THE PARK SPREADS EAST TO THE LA SPÈZIA MUNICIPALITY AND WEST TO THE MONTEROSSO MUNICIPALITY.

HEADQUARTERS: VIA TELEMACO SIGNORINI 118, RIOMAGGIORE TEL. 018776031.

VISITORS' CENTER: C/O THE CORNIGLIA TRAIN STATION - TEL. 0187812523, MONTEROSSO - TEL. 0187817059, RIOMAGGIORE - TEL. 0187920633, VERNAZZA - TEL. 0187812533, MANAROLA - TEL. 01877760511.

WEBSITE: WWW.PARCONAZIONALE5TERRE.IT

EMAIL: INFO@PARCONAZIONALE5TERRE.IT

Between Sestri Levante and La Spèzia the coastline is wild and rugged, with soaring cliffs and steep slopes that plunge into the sea. Despite the inhospitable landscape, this stretch has long been inhabited and cultivated. The charming hamlets of the Cinque Terre – Monterosso, Vernazza, Corniglia, Manarola and Riomaggiore – are spaced almost equidistant from each other, trapped between the sea and mountains, and enclosed by narrow, steep valleys. Cinque Terre literally means *five lands*, hence lands refers to the hamlets or, in the Middle Ages, to five country estates.

The Parco delle Cinque Terre, created in 1995, is a combination of rocks, shades of green, sky blue and the ever-present sea that only ever slips out of sight in the narrow village streets. Man's presence in these parts is evident, but it certainly doesn't reduce the pristine nature of the landscape. Indeed, man is trapped in a narrow band, with steep cliffs and small pebbly beaches broken by needle-like headlands and rocky outcrops dominating the view. Behind the hamlets rises a mountain chain that blocks out the cold northern winds, but draws up the warm sea vapors causing fog in the middle reaches and rain higher up.

Five lands and many colors

The rocks in the park were commonly used to build dry walls, creating a color contrast with the dominant, natural shades of the area. Around Riomaggiore, the rocks are striped with thin bands, around Manarola, gray marl with nuances of green and red, around Corniglia, dark clay and then, in the Vernazza and Monterosso area, sandstone. The geology is complex, which is to be expected in this border zone between the Alps and the Apennines that was molded by enormous pressures that created the many folds in the mountains and the great slabs of rock that stick out into the sea like the pages of a book.

Variety everywhere

The diversity of the landscape, the different geological layers, the change in altitude (from sea level up to 700m on the ridge) and the various micro-

The Ligurian coast from Riomaggiore to Punta Mesco.

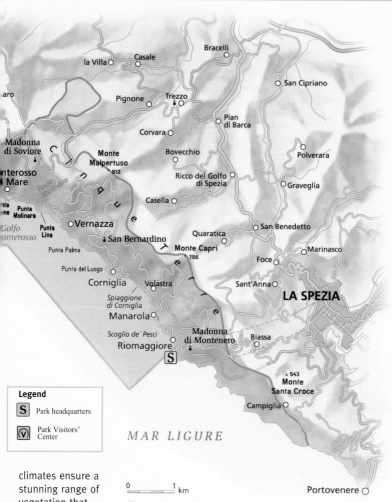

Legend

S Park headquarters

V Park Visitors' Center

MAR LIGURE

0 _____ 1 km

climates ensure a stunning range of vegetation that surprises many visitors. A botanical survey carried out in the area revealed over 1,000 species, with half being typically Mediterranean and the other half being rare, endemic mountainous species. Around the sea line, you find sea fennel and *Daucus gingidium*, a relative of the caper that also has a cultivated past. The rocky areas where the salty air is still common are home to silver ragwort, limonium, rue and other species including the rare *Santolina ligustica* (an endemic species known in Italian as *crespolina ligure*). The large cracks in the rocks often have tree spurge, while the areas where the terrain permits it are covered in Mediterranean scrubland, including lentisk, myrtle, terebinth,

Calicotome villosa, strawberry tree, *Phillyrea* and juniper. These areas might also have smilax, madder and honeysuckle. The abundance of aromatic plants makes this stretch as enjoyable to smell as to look at. At the hotter times of the year, the fragrances are quite intense: wafts of broom mingle with rosemary, oregano, sage, time, fresh mint or the lavender that is grown on the terraced land. The sheer delight of such smells can make one quite hungry! As you head higher up, holm oak, strawberry trees, cluster-pines and Aleppo pines are mixed with an array of cork-oaks, chestnuts, elms and hop-hornbeams.

The colored houses of Vernazza.

flying down from the mountain ridges. The list of mammals includes the dormouse, weasel, mole, beech-marten, badger, fox and wild boar. Wonderfully colored frogs and salamanders live in the brooks. In short, the list of animals might not include some of the bigger mammals, but the more attentive spotter has plenty to look out for and enjoy.

Animals still abound

The Parco Nazionale delle Cinque Terre is also an ideal land for a number of animals. Butterflies and insect pollinators are commonly seen in hot weather. Similar conditions are also a good time to see a lizard or a snake warming itself on a rock or dashing away as it becomes aware that it is being watched. The herring-gull, the peregrine falcon and the raven are often visible soaring or gliding in the skies near the cliffs that rise out of the sea. There are also plenty of sea birds, including the rare Audouin's gull. The blackcap and the whitethroat nest in the Mediterranean scrubland. Of course, bird-watching is also about listening for sounds, and you can often hear the rhythmic tapping of the green woodpecker or the trill of the nuthatch in the woods. Quails and partridges can also be seen

Prestigious recognition

In 1997, the Parco Nazionale delle Cinque Terre became a UNESCO World Heritage Site because of its environmental and cultural heritage. It was chosen because it "is a cultural landscape of great scenic and cultural value. The layout and disposition of the small towns and the shaping of the surrounding landscape, overcoming the disadvantages of a steep, uneven terrain, encapsulate the continuous history of human settlement in this region over the past millennium." In short, the park was included in the list precisely because of the way humans have interacted with the landscape - often out of necessity - resulting in the creation of something that is both truly beautiful and captures thousands of years of tradition and labor. It is man and nature together.

TCI HIGHLIGHTS

NOT MORE THAN ONE...

Only a few bushes blossom in late autumn, but among this group the strawberry tree (*Arbutus unedo*) sticks out. It is commonly found along all the Italian coast, but it is its size that marks it out, sometimes growing to over 8m high and 4-5m wide. The solid, shiny evergreen leaves of this bush tend to dominate, making the flowers resemble shy, pale little trumpet-flowers. The fruit, when ripe, looks rather like cherries, but more wrinkled and slightly more pinkish purple. The flesh is edible, although not often eaten. Indeed, even Carolus Linnaeus called it *unedo*, from the Latin for "I'll only eat one"!

PARCO NAZIONALE REGIONALE DI ANTOLA

PROVINCE OF GENOA

AREA: 4837 HECTARES. BUSALLA, CROCEFIESCHI, FASCIA, RONCO SCRIVIA, RONDANINA, TORRIGLIA, VALBREVENNA, SAVIGNONE.

HEADQUARTERS: VILLA BORZINO, VIA XXV APRILE 17, BUSALLA (GE) - TEL. 0109761014.

VISITORS' CENTER: IN TORRIGLIETTA, VIA N.S. DELLA PROVVIDENZA 3, TORRIGLIA (GE) - TEL. 010944175/931.

Pietra castle in the Vobbia valley, an old manor house on a cliff rising 150m.

WEBSITE: WWW.PARKS.IT/PARCO.ANTOLA
EMAIL: BUSALLA@PARCOANTOLA.IT

Antola (1,597m) lies in the heart of the Ligurian Apennines, between the Scrivia, Tebbia and Borbera valleys, and is one of the most hiked mountains for walkers from the Genoa area. The summit is no jagged peak, but rather a gentle, meadowy area that rises up above thick woods and offers wide-open views of the Ligurian gulf and the western Alps. Well-trodden cattle-tracks mark the route to the top, as they have done for centuries since they were originally created by workers from the Ligurian coast making their way across the mountains to the Po Valley in search of seasonal work. In spring, the grassy summit breaks out into a melee of splendid flowers and butterflies. Yet, amid all this natural beauty, the real call of the park lies in the traces of a thousand-year old peasant tradition that is now in radical decline. The old cattle-tracks and transhumance routes are dotted with chapels, fountains, ruined hay-barns and stone houses. The valleys are home to small villages – generally abandoned –, mills and long stretches of terraced land. Some traces of man are invariably tied to major events in history, such as the remnants of the medieval castles that once stood in commanding positions, like the Fieschi castle at Torriglia, to control the main transit routes and defend the valleys. The most spectacular one is the Pietra castle in the Vobbia valley, set between two rocky rises.

PARCO NATURALE REGIONALE DELL'ÀVETO

PROVINCE OF GENOA

AREA: 3018 HECTARES. BORZONASCA, MEZZANEGO, S. STÉFANO D'ÀVETO.

HEADQUARTERS: VIA MARRÈ 75/A, BORZONASCA (GE) - TEL. 0185340311.

VISITORS' CENTERS: VARIOUS CENTERS OPENING SOON, SEE THE WEBSITE FOR MORE INFORMATION.

WEBSITE: WWW.PARKS.IT/PARCO.AVETO
EMAIL: PARCOAVETO@LIBERO.IT

The upper Aveto valley lies quite close to the truly Mediterranean Levante Riviera, but despite the geographical proximity, the appearance of the valley is notably more Nordic because of the sizeable mountains that enclose it,

TCI HIGHLIGHTS

THE MINES OF THE GRAVEGLIA VALLEY

The Graveglia valley lies inland from Chiàvari. This winding valley has long been a mining center, especially from the mid-19th to the mid-20th century. Manganese was the main element mined, with the Gambatesa mine having the largest deposit in Europe. These days, the mine tunnels can be toured using the same little train as the miners that goes a few kilometers into the mine. Before getting on, each visitor is given a coat, hardhat and light.

Information: Gambatesa
(Botasi), 16040 Ne (GE)
Tel. 0185338876
Website: www.minieragambatesa.it
Email: info@minieragambatesa.it

something special to the fauna, especially since it returned here of its own accord from the Central Apennines in the early 1980s. The area is not all wood and rock, with plenty of vast pastures that are home to stone *casoni* or huts where shepherds once lived in the summer while they looked after the herds they had taken to the summer grazing areas. Cattle are still bred in this area, with the milk used to make a famous local cheese.
Plenty of snow falls in winter, turning the roads into ideal cross-country skiing trails.
The park actually covers more than just the Aveto valley, taking in the maritime side of these mountains, including the lovely Mt Zatta beech wood and the higher reaches of the Graveglia valley, which is famous for its mines.
Finally, the park has many historical rural settlements and a number of old religious buildings, such the Abbey of Borzone.

such as the imposing Maggiorasca (1,799m), the highest summit in the Ligurian Apennines, or the basalt Mt Penna (1,735m), a pyramid-shaped mountain that, from the summit on a clear day, offers views reaching as far as Corsica, the Apuan Alps and, northwards, Monte Rosa.
The fir and beech woods hide tiny glacial lakes and flowers normally only found much higher up or much further north: these are, though, just a couple of the hints of the area's climatic past. Glacial remnants are visible here and there, such as the Alpine cliff fern found on Mt delle Lame (and more normally seen in Greenland) or the inundated clubmoss, only found around Lake Riondo in the Agoraie reserve. For scientists, the area is of interest for endemic species like a type of primrose called *Primula marginata*, the Bertoloni sandwort and gravel fescue. The animal life is also rich, with amphibians like the newt, Italian cave salamander and the European frog, insects like the lovely Apollo butterfly, numerous birds and an array of small and medium-sized mammals. The return of the wolf adds

PARCO NATURALE REGIONALE DI BEIGUA

PROVINCES OF GENOA AND SAVONA

AREA: 8715 HECTARES. SOME OF THE MUNICIPALITIES TOUCHED BY THE PARK ARE ARENZANO, COGOLETO, GENOVA, MASONE, ROSSIGLIONE, SASSELLO, STELLA AND VARAZZE.

HEADQUARTERS: VIA G. MARCONI 165, ARENZANO (GE), TEL. 0108590300.

VISITORS' CENTERS: PALAZZO GERVINO, VIA G.B. BADANO 45, SASSELLO (SV), TEL. 019724020.

WEBSITE: WWW.PARKS.IT/PARCO.BEIGUA
EMAIL: INFO@PARCOBEIGUA.IT

The Beigua massif (1,287m) is a gigantic ophiolite ridge that lies behind Varazze, Cogoleto and Arenzano, creating a sort of balcony over the sea. It is a rather unusual massif and the point where the Alpine/Apennine watershed reaches its closest point to the sea: a mere 5km separate the summit of Mt Reisa (1,183m), on the eastern side of the massif, from the beach at Arenzano. The view from the meadows around the summit – lying along the Alta Via dei Monti Liguri hiking trails – is vast, taking in the Alps, the Mediterranean, Corsica and the Tuscan islands. The watershed marks the border between two distinct worlds: to the south, the slopes are harsh and rocky, cut by little rivers that form gullies, little lakes and small waterfalls; to the north, the slopes are much gentler, covered with beech trees and chestnuts. The peaks are home to some interesting, unusual flora. The skies are home to birds-of-prey, while the woods have some roe-deer and wild boars. The plentiful water and timber means man has inhabited this area since prehistoric times and, in pre-industrial times, these resources underpinned metal, glass and paper working.

WEBSITE: WWW.PARKS.IT/PARCO.MONTEMARCELLO-MAGRA
EMAIL: INFO@PARCOMAGRA.IT

The park is the result of the amalgamation of the Montemarcello protected area with the Magra River park. These areas might be geographically close (hence the creation of the park), but they are very different in most other ways: one is a rocky headland on the La Spèzia Gulf, the other is a river running along a plain. The higher areas of the Caprione headland, covered in Mediterranean scrubland with pine woods, are ideal for panoramic views. Lower down, the cliffs plunge into the sea, forming small inlets and beaches. On the other side, towards the Magra plain, the slopes are covered in broad-leaved woods. The headland is home to numerous, interesting medieval

The Magra River before flowing into the Tyrrhenian. The river basin borders on Lunigiana, once inhabited by the Apuan Liguri tribe.

PARCO NATURALE REGIONALE DI MONTEMARCELLO-MAGRA

PROVINCES OF LA SPÈZIA

AREA: 2726 HECTARES. SOME OF THE MUNICIPALITIES TOUCHED BY THE PARK ARE AMEGLIA, BAVERINO, BOLANO, CARRO, CORRADANO LÉRICI, PIGNONE, ROCCHETTA VARA, SARZANA AND TELLARO VEZZANO LIGURE.

HEADQUARTERS: VIA PACI 2, SARZANA (SP) TEL. 0187691071.

VISITORS' CENTERS: ENVIRONMENTAL EDUCATION CENTER, CASTELLO DORIA-MALASPINA, 19020 CALICE AL CORNOVIGLIO (SP) - TEL. 0187936309.

hamlets, such as Tellaro, located on a cliff above the sea, Montemarcello, high and panoramic, and Ameglia, built around a castle. Historically, this zone is the area where the Romans founded the settlement of Luni. On the Magra plain, along the river, you find some wetlands that are favored by water birds. Indeed, bird-watchers should look out for herons, grebes and bitterns. The park also includes the lower section of the Vara River, which flows into the Magra. The Vara flows through a valley bearing its name that is home to some rare amphibians.

PARCO NATURALE REGIONALE PIANA CRIXIA

PROVINCES OF SAVONA

AREA: 794 HECTARES.

HEADQUARTERS: VIA PACI 2 - SARZANA (SP), TEL. 0187691071.

VISITORS' CENTERS: PIANA CRIXIA TOWN HALL (SV), VIA G. CHIARLONE 47 - TEL. 019570021.

WEBSITE: WWW.PARKS.IT/PARCO.PIANA.CRIXIA

EMAIL: PIANACRIXIA@LIBERO.IT

The green lizard is an agile, fast climber that is perfectly at home in this habitat.

The Piana Crixia territory lies on the southern border of the Langhe (a hilly zone). It is a mix of undulating hills and harsher zones where the streams have washed away the soil, leaving a clayey layer that is prone to form gullies. The gray of the gullies, formed of numerous furrows and ridges that are continually being eroded, creates a stunning contrast with the warm colors of the surrounding forests and fields. The gullies, though, are not the only interesting item in the park created by erosion: there is the amazing Pietra del Collo, a giant mound shaped like a mushroom near Borgo.

🎯 TCI HIGHLIGHTS

THE PIANA CRIXIA MUSHROOM

The famous stone mushroom of Piana Crixia, about 15m high, consists of a mass of ophiolite that sits on a column of conglomerate rock (sedimentary rock made by pebbles of different dimensions joined by thinner material). The shape was formed naturally by erosion, rather like some of the "earth pyramids" (created by the erosion of morraine) found in various Alpine areas. The column survived because it was protected from above by the ophiolite, but the surrounding land was washed away by rainwater.

PARCO NATURALE REGIONALE DI PORTOFINO

PROVINCE OF GENOA

AREA: 1056 HECTARES. SOME OF THE MUNICIPALITIES TOUCHED BY THE PARK ARE CAMOGLI, CHIÀVARI, PORTOFINO, RAPALLO, RECCO AND S. MARGHERITA LÌGURE.

HEADQUARTERS: PORTOFINO PARK AUTHORITY, VIALE RAINUSSO 1, 16038 SANTA MARGHERITA LÌGURE (GE). TEL. 0185289479.

VISITORS' CENTERS: FOR INFORMATION, CONTACT THE PARK AUTHORITY.

WEBSITE: WWW.PARKS.IT/PARCO.PORTOFINO

EMAIL: ENTEPARCO.PORTOFINO@LIBERO.IT

The famous Portofino headland is a sizeable mountain that juts over 3km into the Mediterranean sea. The part that reaches furthest into the water is a mix of hard rock that is not easily eroded by the waves, thus creating a steep cliff that plunges deep into an incredibly blue sea. The great beauty of this area is precisely due to the combination of rocks penetrating into the sea and the mix of Mediterranean scrubland and broad-leaved trees that, from the northern slope, face onto the sea. Typically middle European vegetation – including hornbeam and manna-ash – lives in close contact with plants more commonly found in North Africa, such as tree spurge and diss. The latter, known locally as *lisca*, consists of tufts of wiry stalks that can reach over 2m. Diss is quite common on the headland and was once used for weaving rope and for covering hay. The headland is also home to an array of interesting insects, with the most notable being *Charaxes jasius* (sometimes known as the two-tailed pasha) a colorful butterfly with yellow streaks that is, unfortunately, in danger of extinction in Italy. The range of landscapes ensures the bird life is varied with clearing birds, sea birds, scrubland birds and pinewood birds, amongst others.

PARCO NATURALE REGIONALE DI PORTOVÈNERE

PROVINCE OF LA SPÈZIA

AREA: 247 HECTARES.

HEADQUARTERS: C/O TOWN HALL, VIA GARIBALDI 11, PORTOVÈNERE (SP), TEL. 018779481.

VISITORS' CENTERS: FOR INFORMATION, CONTACT THE PARK AUTHORITY.

WEBSITE: WWW.PARKS.IT/PARCO.PORTO.VENERE

EMAIL: ATECNICA@TIN.I

The Parco Regionale di Portovènere (established in 2001) is one of the most prized areas in the far eastern section of Liguria. It consists of a land section, with a high coastline, rich Mediterranean vegetation and numerous sea-level caves, and a sea

TCI HIGHLIGHTS

CAREFUL OF THE EYE

The scientific name of the Sardinian warbler is *Sylvia melanocephala*, that is, "Sylvia with the black head". This is definitely quite accurate, giving a good description of this Silvia with gray plumage and a back head that contrasts with the white throat. The common Italian name, *occhiocotto*, literally means cooked eye and is also closely linked to the bird's physical appearance: the bright red ring around the eye. It favors sun-drenched woods and glades with thick undergrowth and scrubland. The Sardinian warbler is a typically Mediterranean bird that is found all along the coast and on the islands. The fast, rattling song of this warbler is one of those sounds people commonly associate with the Mediterranean.

section, which includes the Portovene Archipelago (Palmaria, Tino and Tinetto). The Portovènere area is a UNESCO World Heritage Site both because of the natural beauty and the various artistic and historical features, such as the prehistoric Grotta dei Colombi (a sea-level cave), the church of San Pietro and the Portovènere castle. The area received UNESCO recognition in conjunction with Cinque Terre.

This gorgonian, *Paramuricea clavata*, loses all its wonderful color if it is taken from the water.

AREA MARINA PROTETTA DI PORTOFINO

PROVINCE OF GENOA

YEAR OF FOUNDATION: 1999.

MUNICIPALITIES: CAMOGLI, PORTOFINO AND SANTA MARGHERITA LÌGURE.

AREA: 346 HECTARES.

MORPHOLOGY: ROCKY HEADLAND LYING BETWEEN PARADISO BAY AND THE TIGULLIO GULF.

OFFICES: VILLA CARMAGNOLA, VIALE RAINUSSO 14, SANTA MARGHERITA LÌGURE, TEL. 0185289469.

WEBSITE: WWW.RISERVAPORTOFINO.IT

Standing like a square fortress, the 610m high rocky headland of Portofino juts out over 3km into the Ligurian Sea, separating Paradiso Bay, to the west, from the Tigullio Gulf to the east. The perimeter is over 13km with the western part of the headland rising towards the spur at Punta Chiappa. In contrast, the southern section is more fragmented, made up of numerous bays and inlets, including the famous San Fruttuoso Bay. Heading eastwards, past the small San Giorgio peninsula, the coast is less steep and the trees and plants reach down to the sea, surrounding the bays in greenery.

Around the headland

The difference between the two sides of the headland is evident in the rock structure. The southern coast is made of the so-called Portofino pudding stone, a mix of pebbles, sand and clay, while heading towards Camogli and Rapallo, the layered limestone of Mt Antola is evident.

The view as you approach from the sea is a combination of rocks and plants. The vegetation closest to the sea, like sea fennel, thrives on the salt of the air, above is sedum, limonium and then strawberry trees and heather. Gradually these give way to pinewoods of maritime and rare Aleppo pines interspersed with lighter green patches: olive trees marking the presence of man. The depth contour has an initial shelf, 10-20m deep, followed by a sharp decline reaching a depth of 50m before becoming a muddy-sandy seabed mixed with pebbles. It is an area rich in cracks, roofs, ledges and caves, making it ideal for marine fauna, as well as having currents that ensure continually changing water. This is particularly true when there are the strong south-west and sirocco winds; however, these winds may cause sea conditions that prevent scuba diving on the southern side.

Scuba-diving sites

The Park Authority has set up 18 dive spots and there are also 2 areas (Isuela and Altare) that are particularly rich in natural terms. The shallowest reefs are surrounded by brown, red or green algae that shelter many invertebrates such as actinia and sea anemones. The deeper rocky shelf has many species typical of pre-coralligenous areas, such as white gorgonian and both single specimens and colonies of stony coral. There are also numerous other species typical of a so-called coralligenous environment where creator species, primarily coralline algae, battle with destructors (sponges, mollusks and crustaceans). At this depth, loved by scuba divers for the beauty, richness and variety of species. Red coral, although difficult to spot due to its size, is also abundant. There are over 150 colorful types of sponges; some are part of an experimental breeding program run by researchers from the University of Genoa, long active on Mt Portofino. In recent years, the number and type of fish has increased substantially: evidence of the success of the protective measures in place in an area as popular as Portofino.

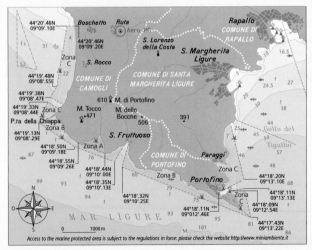

Access to the marine protected area is subject to the regulations in force: please check the website http://www.miniambiente.it

AREA MARINA PROTETTA DELLE CINQUE TERRE

PROVINCE OF LA SPÈZIA

YEAR OF FOUNDATION: 1997.

MUNICIPALITIES: LÈVANTO, MONTEROSSO AL MARE, RIOMAGGIORE, VERNAZZA.

AREA: 346 HECTARES.

MORPHOLOGY: HEADLANDS, INLETS AND THE MOUNTAINOUS SLOPES OF THE LEVANTE RIVIERA.

OFFICES: CINQUE TERRE PARK AUTHORITY, VIA T. SIGNORINI 118, RIOMAGGIORE (LA SPÈZIA), TEL. 018776031.

WEBSITE: WWW.AREAMARINAPROTETTA5TERRE.IT

This coastal stretch, lying at the centre of the Levante Riviera and visible from the Portofino headland, rises rapidly from sea level to 700-800m.

Amid scents and smells

The part of the Cinque Terre above water is not, however, merely a story about man. One of the many paths in this area leads you from the beaches and cliffs by the sea, where the vegetation thrives on the salty conditions, to a scrubland of flowers and herbs. You can see euphorbia, myrtle, mastic trees, rock roses, thyme, rosemary, sage, broom, heather and, further up, a mix of holm-oak and rare Aleppo pines. In places, cork trees stand hidden among the pines that were planted to replace the woods that once stood there. Yet, no matter how much you dwell on the colors of the flowers and enjoy the lovely fragrances of the herbs, your gaze will ultimately be drawn back towards the sea. It is truly beautiful whether calm or when the choppy water gives the air a salty taste and the waves break noisily against the coast, leaving white foam on the rocks and beaches.

Hidden Cinque Terre

When the water is calm and clear, you might even be able to make out the different depths from the viewpoints high above the sea. The cliffs plunge 15-18m below the surface of the sea before giving way to sand, pebbles (a peculiarity of the Cinque Terre), and large isolated rocks or a new rocky level. Between Punta Mesco, where a series of terraces drop

Access to the marine protected area is subject to the regulations in force: please check the website http://www.miniambiente.it

This rugged stretch of land is characterized by cliffs and sheer drops broken by occasional inlets, bays and pebbly beaches. It is also the place in Liguria where the evidence of man's labor, over the centuries, is most clearly visible. The unique landscape of these 'five lands', marked by terraces and little dry walls, led to them being included in UNESCO's list of World Heritage Sites. Their value has also been recognized within Italy by the creation, one after the other, of a national park and a marine protected area. The combined efforts of these two should ensure the overall protection of the area.

sharply to a depth of 60m, and the Fegina beach, sloping from 5-8m to 20-25m, lies the largest *Posidonia oceanica* meadow in the area. The Cinque Terre seabed is relatively small, so numerous species share a very limited area. As a result, there are species that are fairly unusual in other parts of the Mediterranean, such as, the gorgonian *Eunicella verrucosa* and the Mediterranean cowrie *Luria lurida*. The steep walls of Punta Mesco, the most important part of the protected area, are home to the rare *Gerardia savaglia*, more commonly called black coral, numerous colonies of red gorgonians that can be found at a mere 15-20m below the surface, and numerous other species that like the semi-shade.

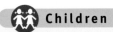

ACQUARIO DI GENOVA/ GENOA AQUARIUM

NEAR THE OLD PORT (PORTO ANTICO) AND SPINOLA BRIDGE

TEL. 0102345678,

WEBSITE: WWW.ACQUARIO.GE.IT

OPEN: ALL YEAR (OPENINGS HOURS ON WEBSITE)

ADMISSION: ADULTS € 15, CHILDREN (4-12 YEARS) € 9 AND DISABLED PEOPLE € 13.

HOW TO GET THERE:

BY CAR: A7 MILANO-GENOVA HIGHWAY, GENOVA OVEST EXIT.

BY TRAIN: GENOVA PORTA PRINCIPE OR GENOVA BRIGNOLE STATIONS, THEN THE BUS.

The Genoa Aquarium, designed by Renzo Piano and Peter Chermayeff and built in 1992, looks like a ship ready to set sail. It is easy to reach (only 10

minutes on foot from the Genova Principe train station) and has good access for disabled people. It is located in the heart of the old port area and is one of the most popular outings in Italy. The aquarium covers most ocean and sea environments in the world, faithfully rebuilding numerous ecosystems. It is one of the largest aquariums in Europe, often attracting visitors because of the giant tanks that one can explore from various angles. You need at least two hours to visit it, but the numerous rest areas, toilets and snack bars make it a good day out

for children as well. The visitors route takes you through two levels and the Great Blue Ship (Grande Nave Blu), an exhibition area that was opened in 1998, adding 2,700m² to original 10,000m². This new area is used to recreate some interesting environments, including one of Madagascar. The aquarium has over 6,000 animals and 600 different species, as well as plenty of vegetal species. The animals, housed in over 70 tanks, include various jellyfish and other invertebrates, fish, seals, sharks, dolphins and numerous other animals that are carefully looked after by a series of biology experts and vets. The tanks themselves are interesting, with some shaped unusually (like the cylindrical jellyfish tank), others extremely large and others designed so that visitors can actually touch the animals: the one with the rays is very popular among children, who seem unable to believe it that they are actually allowed to touch the animals. Some of the tanks are enticing merely for the names: Neptune grass, ancient pier, moluccan islands, mangroves, central American forest, giant Japanese spidercrabs, waves on the reef and the flooded forest.

There never seems to be enough time for the dolphin tank, as they play and jump endlessly. In 2002, one of the dolphins, Bonnie, become a mom for the second time, causing the number of visitors to increase yet again (roughly 1.2 million annually). In the same year, the Genoa Aquarium became home to numerous homeless animals following the closure of the Marseilles aquarium. Some of these new arrivals, like the guitar-fish, were added to the new Mediterranean reef touch tank, an open display area that is designed to spread awareness about the problems linked to conserving and managing the eco-systems in our seas. In 2002, the 10th anniversary of the aquarium was celebrated by adding yet another display area, this time dedicated to the smallest birds in the world, namely hummingbirds. These birds are housed in a reconstruction of a lush rain forest and it costs a little more to see them (€ 2 for adults; € 1 for children). To help raise public awareness about marvelous but scary creatures like the shark, the aquarium has recently renewed the tank housing this sea predator. One of the elements the tank tries to highlight is that of the roughly 400 known species of shark, only 4 are known to attack man without provocation. Thus, to create a more realistic picture of sharks, the tank has a scenic backdrop that includes well made fiberglass rock and special lighting. Two sawfish swim with three species of shark (bull, gray, angel) and amberjack, gilthead, short sunfish and grouper. In short, the aquarium is an excellent, diverse outing.

TRENO GENOVA-CASELLA/ GENOA-CASELLA TRAIN

VIA ALLA STAZIONE PER CASELLA 15, GENOA, TEL. 010837321,
WEBSITE: WWW.FERROVIAGENOVACASELLA.IT
OPEN: ALL YEAR
OPENING HOURS: LEAVING FROM GENOA AT 6.35AM DURING THE WEEK AND 9.08AM ON SUNDAYS AND HOLIDAYS; SOME TRAINS HAVE SEASONABLE TIMETABLES AND DO NOT RUN AROUND CHRISTMAS. SEE THE WEBSITE FOR FURTHER DETAILS.
PRICE: SINGLE TICKET € 2.
HOW TO GET THERE:
BY CAR: GENOVA EST EXIT, RIGHT AT THE SECOND SET OF TRAFFIC LIGHTS (TOWARDS THE CENTER, ON VIA MONTALDO), AT THE END OF THE UPHILL, FOLLOW THE SIGNS FOR THE TRAIN.
BY TRAIN: GENOVA PORTA PRINCIPE STATION AND 39 (BARRED) BUS, OR GENOVA BRIGNOLE AND BUS 33, ABOUT 20 MINUTES.

The three valley railway line (Valbisagno, Valpolcevera and Valle Scrivia), used by the Genoa-Casella train, runs across some spectacular sections that overlook the eastern section of Liguria and the stunning Portofino headland. The landscape also makes the trip of interest for children. There is a panoramic walk from Trensasco and Campi that takes you back to Genoa, while other paths head to the forts or the Creto fields. The station at Sartorella is immersed in chestnut trees and has a pergola with some tables that are ideal for a picnic on a nice day.
If you head up to Sant'Olcese Chiesa, you could add a culinary stop to the tour and taste the famous salami. The next stretch is quite winding, reaching Sant'Olcese Tullo where there is a botanical trail that was one of the first environmental education structures in the province. When you reach Casella, you could hire a mountain bike to discover the surrounding area (you could also take your bike on the train, but you must book in advance). At times, this route can be done on a historic train with the oldest electric locomotive still in use in Italy. It was built by Tecnomasio Italiano Brown Boveri way back in 1924 and the carriages are also from a similar period (1929). On 6 January, there is the Treno della Befana (Epiphany Train).

WHALE WATCH – LIGURIA

CONSORZIO LIGURIA VIAMARE, VIA SOTTORIPA 7/8, GENOA, TEL. 010265712,
WWW.LIGURIAVIAMARE.IT

Seeing a whale or a dolphin from a distance can turn even the most disinterested person into someone who understands the importance of protecting the habitat that these animals live in, feed in and reproduce in. It is also best to remember that humans are the "guests" in their environment and so when we find ourselves near them, we must behave in a way that does not cause them even the slightest disturbance or stress. To find a dolphin in the wild – and not in captivity – it might be necessary to spend a number of hours searching for the animal, thus it is important to embark prepared, both mentally and in terms of what one takes (correct clothing, equipment etc.). Furthermore, whale watching outings are cancelled in bad weather. The ideal conditions are when the sea is calm and there is no wind. This said, the Ligurian Sea is alive with whales and dolphins, meaning that the best way to see them is patient perseverance. Dolphins and whales live underwater and only come to the surface to breath. They key signs for spotting these animals are sprays of water, the fins and the splashing. It can take some training for one's eyes to get used to spotting the slightest movement. It is also important not to look only in one place, but to keep your eyes gazing out across the sea, both nearby and far away. Each species behaves in a specific way when a boat comes near and so it is important to understand which species you are dealing with before getting too close. Furthermore, it is not only the boat's crew that has to behave properly, but everyone: if you behave properly, the chances are much greater that the animals will trust you and swim beside the boat for hours. The golden rules for watching sea mammals are:
1. Cause as little disruption to the animals as possible.
2. Be patient so that you can recognize the signs that the animal is around.

WHALE WATCH – BLU WEST

VIA SCARNINCIO 12, IMPERIA,
TEL. 0183769364,
WWW.WHALEWATCH.IT
SEE THE WEBSITE FOR THE TIMETABLE, COSTS AND DEPARTURE POINTS

Corsara is a boat that was specifically designed for watching marine animals, especially whales and dolphins, but it is also excellent as a scientific vessel (especially as it is an ideal observation platform). The trips start from Imperia or Andora and head into the International Sea Mammal Sanctuary to watch whales and dolphins in the triangular stretch of sea that runs from Sardinia to the French Riviera then east to the Tuscan coast. Numerous sea mammals live in these waters, including the giant rorqual (the largest group of baleen whales, including the blue whale) that thrive on the plentiful supply of tiny shrimps (krill). This whole area is protected and was designed specifically to protect such sea mammals. The list of what you might see includes dolphins, sperm whales, Risso's dolphins and giant rorquals that can grow up to 24m long. It is a truly thrilling experience for both children and adults alike to see the spray of a whale or a dolphin swimming gracefully by the side of the boat. For such trips, it is best to wear sporty clothes and take a windbreaker on board. You should also remember to put some sun cream, a pair of binoculars and the camera in your bag. Since patience is required, it is best to be properly equipped.

GROTTE DI TOIRANO / TOIRANO CAVES

PIAZZALE GROTTE, TOIRANO (SAVONA), TEL. 018298062, WWW.TOIRANOGROTTE.IT

ENTRANCE: NORMAL € 11, CHILDREN AND REDUCED € 5, GROUPS OF 20 OR MORE AND OVER 70S, € 7.

FOR THE OPENING HOURS AND TO BOOK A NIGHT EXCURSION, SEE THE WEBSITE.

HOW TO GET THERE:

BY CAR: A10 HIGHWAY, PIETRA LIGURE EXIT, HEAD TOWARDS LOANO, BORGHETTO SANTO SPIRITO, SP ROAD TO BARDINETO/CALIZZANO.

BY TRAIN: LOANO STATION AND THEN AN SAR BUS (FOR TIMETABLE INFO: TEL. 018221544).

If you head up the Varatella valley, a little beyond Toirano, you come to a limestone massif of gray dolomites, marked by a series of gullies that have over 150 natural caves, which are still being studied by international researchers. The Toirano caves, opened to the public in 1953, are one of the major attractions of the western section of Liguria, recording over 110,000 visitors a year who come not only to see the numerous natural features (stalactites, stalagmites and spectacular crystal formations) but also the traces from prehistory. The great chamber of the Grotta della Strega (witch's cave) was, for thousands of years, a den for the great cave bear, as can be seen from the fossils, prints and claw marks. The cave was also used by Stone Age man (recent studies suggest in the period 12-12.5 thousand years ago), who left behind foot, hand and knee imprints as well as some clay items that seem to have been of ritualistic importance. The cave is also known as Grotta della Basura and became known thanks to the exploratory work of Father Nicolò Morelli Canonico of Pietra Ligure.

To access the other chambers, you need to head down a 120m tunnel located at the end of the chamber. The whole trip in the cave is about 1.3km and you exit on the opposite side to the entrance. You can get back to the entrance along an external path. As always when exploring caves, it is important to wear suitable clothing.

VISIONARIUM 3D

VIA DORIA, OLD CENTER, DOLCEÀCQUA (IMPERIA) TEL. 0184206638, WWW.VISIONARIUM-3D.COM

OPEN: ALL YEAR.

PRICE: € 3.50.

HOW TO GET THERE:

BY CAR: A10 GENOVA-VENTIMÌGLIA HIGHWAY, BORDIGHERA EXIT; TAKE THE VIA AURELIA ROAD TOWARDS FRANCE AND, AFTER VALLECROSIA, TAKE THE SP ROAD THROUGH THE NERVIA VALLEY.

BY TRAIN: TRAIN STATION IN VENTIMÌGLIA, ON THE BUS ROUTE.

It would be unfair to simply call it cinema as it is more like a multisensory cinematic experience. Visionarium 3D in Dolceàcqua, a lovely medieval hamlet that is a short drive inland from Ventimìglia, is a unique projection room where they show nature and travel documentaries with... very special effects. To see the 3D images and Omnimax (complete image) you need to wear special glasses. The whole experience seems real, with light effects mixing with environmental elements (e.g. wind, water, lightening, the sounds of nature and, even, some smells) to create something more than just a "watching experience". The auditorium can only hold 50 people and is in an old 16th-century building that was once used as stables.

The inventor of the Visionarium is the nature photographer Eugenio Andrighetto, who works with experts from various sectors to create the documentaries (film, texts, music, exploration, research) that are shown in the special "cinema".

Poetic Liguria

Genoa is a mysterious, coy city of a thousand different facets. The coastline along the Levante and Ponente (or eastern and western) Rivieras is marked by inlets, little bays and beaches. The landscape abounds with woods, trails, inland hills and even mountains. All of these elements have been used by the cinema in films, but for many years, the typical cinematic picture of the region was at the mercy of Lombard filmmakers who spent

holidays along the Ligurian coast, starting in the post-war years. Certain stereotypes arose and developed, including the temptations of beach life, the dangers of the criminal world around the ports, the worldly, fashionable casinos and the inevitable Sanremo music festival (*see p. 156*). Yet, despite this, overall cinema has managed to portray the region's numerous different aspects, rather than merely focusing on the seaside element. The trails, valleys and inland trade and communication routes recall Neorealist scenes and dark melodramas. Similarly, the regional capital is a web of alleys, jetties, smells and foods in a reserved city filled with reticent inhabitants. It is a mix of melancholy, pride and unconditional love for the sea that the cinema is still learning to understand and explore.

From the Tigullio Gulf to Sanremo: the beach set

The Ligurian coast, like Versilia in Tuscany or the Amalfi coast, has long been synonymous with holidays and light-heartedness, yet cinema has not always portrayed such an image, often seeing things in a more complex light. *Racconti d'estate* (*Love on the Riviera*, 1958) by Gianni Franciolini, is based on an idea by Alberto Moravia, a Ligurian poet, and set along the Tigullio Gulf. One summer's day, on the beach at Rapallo, the lives of various characters become interwoven. The film gives a mischievous, yet effective portrait of the setting and, in many ways, it was like a preview of the cinematic thread of the seaside that ran through so many films in the 1960s and then again in the 1980s.

The little harbor, the colorful buildings situated below the mountain, the sun and the sea of Portofino are the backdrop for the bleak melodrama *The barefoot contessa* (*La Contessa Scalza*; the photo shows an original poster for the Italian version) by Joseph L. Mankiewicz. The radiance of the nature and the image of cheerfulness and luxury conveyed by the setting grate with the tragic rise and fall of the Hollywood diva played by Ava Gardner, a role with clear autobiographical links.

The film starts at the star's funeral and then explores her adventurous existence through a series of flashbacks. The cast is filled with leading names, including a brilliant performance by a regretful Humphrey Bogart as the Pygmalion director. Yet, the star is undoubtedly Gardner, with her lovely eyes that carry a tormenting mixture of sensuality, fragility and oblivious desperation.

Portofino is also used in *Souvenir d'Italie* (*It happened in Rome*, 1957) by Antonio Pietrangeli, a refined, intelligent filmmaker who tells the story, in this "minor" film, of three foreign hitchhikers in Italy. Michelangelo Antonioni's *Al di là delle nuvole* (*Beyond the clouds*, 1995), with John Malkovich and Sophie Marceau, is also set in Portofino. The lovely sequences that convey the brilliance of Portofino and the castle are tied to the rediscovered marital bliss in Mike Newell's *Enchanted April* (*Un incantevole aprile*, 1991). *Preludio d'amore* (*Shamed*, 1947) is set along the stunning Riviera between Portofino and Nervi (and the delightful sea is even described in the film as "smooth as silk"). It was directed by Giovanni Paolucci, who tended to make documentaries, and has some Ligurians in the leading roles, namely Vittorio

comedy about a prostitute on holiday with her young daughter who falls victim to the backbiting of the small town. The Alàssio seafront was used for the glum final scenes of Vittorio De Sica's *I bambini ci guardano* (*The children are watching us* or *The little martyr*, 1944), an interesting portrait of some problems of a young child. Finally, a curious piece of info: Alfred Hitchcock is said to have filmed some rather adventurous scenes from his first film, *The Pleasure Garden*, in 1925, in Sanremo, the Genoa port and Lake Como. However, as often happens with the early days of cinema, films legends become interwoven with reality in an inseparable way!

The road, valleys and rivers of the hinterland

Gianni Franciolini filmed *Fari nella nebbia* (1942) on the inland Ligurian roads. This melodrama about truck drivers included some of the best

From left, Andrea Checchi, Gina Lollobrigida and Lamberto Maggiorani, partisans fighting against the Nazis in *Attention! Bandits!*

Gassman, Lauro Gazzolo and Claudio Gora. The cinematography of Piero Portalupi helps to render the atmosphere of the places. The western side of the Ligurian Riviera, between Spotorno, Varigotti and Finale Ligure, was where Alberto Lattuada set *La spiaggia* (*Riviera*, 1953), with Martine Carol and Raf Vallone, a bitter-sweet

known actors of the day. The film was quite significant at the time because of the humble backgrounds of the protagonists and the gloomy, sensual atmosphere – a feature not often found in cinema of the Fascist era – that recalls French cinema of the 1930s. *Achtung! Banditi!* (*Attention! Bandits!*, 1951), the first film Carlo Lizzani directed, featuring Gina Lollobrigida, Andrea Checchi and Lamberto Maggiorani, tells the story of the partisan war in the valleys west of Genoa and the factories of the Polcevera valley between the pebbly river bank of the Polcevera, Pontedecimo and Trasta. Although the story is fictional it is loosely based on actual events from the Nazi occupation of northern Italy, exploring one of the key dilemmas of that period, namely whether it was better to fight for the occupying ally (the Nazis) or join the partisan Resistance.

Emblematic of the spirit of cinema in the post-war period, the film was made by a cooperative (Cooperativa Spettatori Produttori Cinematografici), which was a unique event in the history of Italian cinema. The extras were local workers and people and the children were recruited directly from district schools. It is even said that some people, who did not realize they were on a film set, became quite alarmed during the scenes in which the partisans fought the Germans and, fearing a Nazi return, "warned their fellow citizens of the danger".

Genoa, a spectacular city between the mountains and the sea

This rather beautiful city, tucked tightly between the sea and the mountains, has not, unfortunately, received as much interest from the big screen as one might have guessed – or the city might have merited.

Via Fieschi appears in *Sissignora* (*Yes, Madam*), an A-list film from 1941 by Ferdinando Maria Poggioli, with Irma and Emma Gramatica playing two stern high-society ladies and Maria Denis as a humble, unlucky domestic servant. The film is seen as an early precursor to Neorealism for the actual scenes shot on location and the relatively unbiased examination of the class issue.

Luigi Comencini's *La Tratta delle Bianche* (*Girls Marked Danger* or *Ship of Condemned Women*, 1952) was a gloomy melodrama with elements of social criticism. The cast included a local actress, Eleonora Rossi Drago, and the Lido di Albaro was the setting for the dance marathon that drew so much from American cinema noir of the 1940s and that was a precursor – to some degree – to the successful *They shoot horses, don't they?* (*Non si Uccidono così anche i Cavalli?*, 1969) by Sydney Pollack.

Perdonami (1953) by Mario Costa, with Raf Vallone, Antonella Lualdi, Marisa Allasio and Tamara Lees, is a sanguine drama of jealousy filmed in the dry docks of Sestri Ponente. It explores a complex love situation where the brother of a murdered man unknowingly falls in love with the murderer's sister.

The old center, with its dark, narrow lanes, was the setting for Anna Negri's debut film, *In principio erano le mutande* (*In the Beginning there was Underwear*, Australia, 1999; in the photo, the poster from the Italian version), with Teresa Saponangelo, Stefania Rocca and Bebo Storti. It tells of the work, loves and sexual experiences of a restless girl living in a multiethnic Genoa. The film is set in a block of council flats, amid the alleys and markets, and is essentially about the emotional education of a imaginative and confused girl who learns through various experiences with the bizarre side of humanity. The melting pot that is so evident in the old center helps to create to the lively, sparkling atmosphere of this spirited, youthful comedy that is at its best in exploring the solidarity between the female protagonists.

In short, Genoa has featured in numerous films, but it is far from overplaying its part.

Sport

Liguria, an open-air gym

Sea and mountains, rivers and rocks, beaches and reefs: Liguria has a wondrous variety of landscapes and so lends itself to just about any type of sport. To begin with, take **water sports**. There are over 60 active yacht clubs, including the Yacht Club Italiano, which is the oldest such nautical association in Italy (1879). This prestigious yacht club, with centers in Genoa (near the little Duca degli Abruzzi harbor) and *Portofino*, even took part in the America's Cup in 1987. The range of options for **scuba divers** is also notable; of course, the area has a natural advantage since the coastline drops off rapidly, ensuring one can reach substantial depths while remaining relatively near the shoreline. Beautiful sea floors, like the ones off the *Cinque Terre* and the *Portofino headland*, make diving an even more attractive option (*see p. 96/97*). **Rowing** is another popular sport, with regattas held at *Sanremo, Savona, Genoa/Pra, Santa Margherita Lìgure, La Spèzia, Sarzana* and *Lake Osiglia*. *Savona* is a good destination for **power-boating** and a world offshore championship is held there. *Genoa* and *Andora* are probably the best places in the region for **waterskiing**. Places like *Argentina, Orba, Teiro* and *Vara* are all stretches of river that are good for **kayaking** and – where possible – **canyoneering**, in which the participants take on rapids and often get thrown around by the currents. **Bungee jumping** is another option: the spring into nothingness from the Loreto bridge – the jumping platform is open for the summer season from April to October – in the *Triora* municipality takes 8 seemingly endless seconds! The *Argentina* gully also has good cliff faces for **free climbing**. There is also a climbing wall at Finale Ligure with over 1,500 routes as well as options in *Albenga, Sestri Levante* (Lastre di Riva and Punta Manara), *Cogoleto*

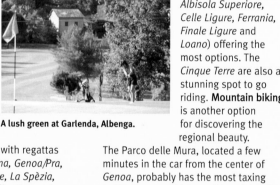

A lush green at Garlenda, Albenga.

(the Sciarborasca district) and *Muzzerone*. For those who prefer artificial walls, there are two fully equipped gyms in Cogoleto and Genoa (*Bòrzoli*).

There are fewer options for the more traditional **mountaineering**, but Pietravecchia and Toraggio are good tests, even for more skilled mountaineers. *Mònesi* and *Alberola* both have a few **ski runs**, while *Colla Melosa, Calizzano* and *Santo Stéfano d'Àveto* have a few **cross-country skiing** trails. In compensation for the lack of skiing, the mild climate means that the **horse-riding routes** are an option most of the year, with the provinces of Genoa (*Genoa,*  *Busalla, Campo Ligure, Carasco* and *Rapallo*) and Savona (*Albenga, Albisola Superiore, Celle Ligure, Ferrania, Finale Ligure* and *Loano*) offering the most options. The *Cinque Terre* are also a stunning spot to go riding. **Mountain biking** is another option for discovering the regional beauty.

The Parco delle Mura, located a few minutes in the car from the center of *Genoa*, probably has the most taxing trail in Genoa, which would explain why it is the venue for the MTB Genoa Cup that is part of the Italian national championship. The park also has two **exercise trails** and an **archery** field. For those who prefer shooting with guns, the best ranges are in *Rapallo, Genoa, Sanremo, Savona, Chiàvari* and *La Spèzia*. *Rapallo* is also home to one of the three 18-hole **golf courses** in the region (along with *Garlenda* and *Sanremo*). *Arenzano* and *Lérici* have 9-hole courses, with all the courses open 12 months a year thanks, once again, to the mild climate. The summer is, though, the only time really for the various beach activities, especially **beach volleyball** and **beach soccer**. A recent addition is **water polo** in the sea, which looks like it has a fairly assured future in a region that has contributed so significantly to Italian **"pool" water** successes.

Walking in Liguria

When the sea and mountains chase each other for hundreds of kilometers, as in Liguria, it is not hard to imagine that it is an ideal area for outdoor pursuits. The entire system of trails and paths hinges on the **Alta Via dei Monti Liguri**, a marked itinerary that is over 400km and runs right across the Ligurian mountains from Ventimìglia to (Imperial Feuds Route) was a key one and deserves a mention here, although the trail is not completely marked. It starts in Genoa and works its way through the former enclaves of the Vobbia and Borbera valleys, crossing lands owned by Emperor Maximilian that had been granted to Ludovic the Moor in 1495. One of the best ways to explore this area is the Genoa-Casella railway line, a tourist line that has

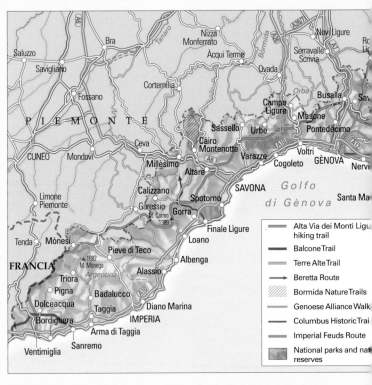

the Vara valley. It works its way along the watershed between the Apennines and the Alps, offering spectacular views both inland towards the Po Valley and the Alpine peaks and towards the Ligurian Riviera. It is an ideal way to learn more about the thousand faces of the hinterland, including those that have been written about by authors like Riccardo Bacchelli.

The Alta Via passes through three major regional parks (Alpi Liguri, Bèigua, Àveto) and is dotted with refuge huts. Many other trails cross the Alta Via, often following the old communication routes between the coast and the Po Valley. Perhaps the most famous of these historical routes are the Salt Routes. The **Via dei Feudi Imperiali** managed to survive while many others were discontinued. One of the other key historical routes is the so-called **Strada Beretta** (Beretta Route), a path running along ridges that connected Finale Ligure with Alessandrino and Milan. It was created in 1666 by the engineer Gaspare Beretta to improve links between Spanish Lombardy and the Marquisate of Finale. Much of the route can still be done on foot, starting from Finalborgo and heading to the Bormida valley.

This part of Oltregiogo is also home to the **Sentieri Bormida Natura**, which cover a series of protected areas, including Bric Tana, Langhe di Piana Crixia, Adelasia, Mt Camulera and Rocchetta Cairo. The **Sentiero Terre Alte** is a three-stage trail that links the Alta Via to the coast at Borghetto Santo Spirito and is an ideal route for exploring the landscape of the Loano area. The ridge where the Alta Via runs might be a little too far inland for some, but there is also a series of coastal trails that are not only fairly easy to do, but also combine lovely landscapes with more historical and cultural elements. The following routes meet these criteria: the

Sentiero Verdeazzurro, created by the local branches of the Italian Union of Chambers of Commerce, runs across the Levante Riviera, with 10 stages covering 140km; the **Sentiero CAI 1** delle Cinque Terre is set in a new national park; the **Sentiero Balcone**, located along the edge of the Ponente Riviera, links Sanremo to

the French border in 7 stages before joining with Balcone Trail (GR51) in France that continues to Marseilles; and the **Sentiero Arcobaleno**, also in western Liguria, links Ventimìglia to Ospedaletti. There are also a number of other cultural itineraries, especially in the Fontanabuona valley: the **Itinerario dei Sette Passi** covers the main historical routes; the **Itinerario dei Feudi Fliscani** follows the old road to Torriglia; and the **Sentieri della Valsangiacomo** is a series of trails linked to a museum project that follow the old cattle tracks between the quarries and the ports. Christopher Columbus was the spark for the **Sentiero Storico Colombiano**, which follows the old cattle track from Fontanabuona to Nervi that might have been used by the great navigator's ancestors. The regional capital is the setting for the **Percorso Genovese del Cammino dell'Alleanza**, created by the Italian Hiking Association (FEI). It works its way around the Bisagno valley, taking in the Parco delle Mura. FEI helped to create another trail around the Magra River in the Parco Regionale Montemarcello-Magra. Various parks and reserves in Liguria have also created theme itineraries, including the **Itinerari Naturalistici Autoguidati** (self-drive nature trails) in the Parco di Portofino. These three trails explore the various natural and human aspects of Mt Portofino, a sort of dividing line between continental and Mediterranean Europe. There are also a couple of other interesting nature trails, namely the **Sentiero Brugneto**, in the Parco Naturale del Monte Àntola, and the **Sentiero Botanico di Ciaé** at Sant'Olcese, near Genoa. Canyoneering, canoeing and kayaking are rapidly growing in Liguria, largely because of the terrain. The best options are the Argentina Stream in the western part of Imperia, the Orba in the Savona section of Oltregiogo, the Lavagna in the Fontanabuona valley and the Vara River in the La Spèzia area.

TCI HIGHLIGHTS

For more info: Associazione Alta Via dei Monti Liguri, located at Centro Studi Unioncamere, Via San Lorenzo 15/1, Genoa - Tel. 01024852205, www.altaviadeimontiliguri.it; **Italian Hiking Association (FEI)**, Via La Spèzia 58r, Genoa - Tel. 010463261; **Sentieri della Fontanabuona**, Comunità Montana Fontanabuona, Piazza Cavagnari 7, Cicagna - Tel. 018597181, www.fontanabuona.com; **Sentieri del Parco di Portofino**, Portofino Park Authority, Viale Rainusso 1, Santa Margherita Lìgure - Tel. 0185289479, www.parks.it/parco.portofino

The hamlets of silence

Inland, away from main transit routes, the hills rapidly become mountains, creating a land of silence that is home to numerous hamlets and villages. It does not, though, take long to reach such places, often a mere few bends along an old salt route and you come to a land filled with little curiosities. In these parts, history and popular culture are intertwined, but nature remains king, leaving a landscape that is often breathtaking.

Ceriana lies not far from Sanremo, at the end of a road that climbs a bare mountain. The hamlet itself appears as you round a bend, slightly breaking the continuum of nature. Built in the Middle Ages around the ruins of a Roman villa, the hamlet follows the shape of the mountain, with houses, churches and functioning mills enclosed by a ring of walls. The maze of streets is like a treasure chest of things to discover, often containing unexpectedly good popular art. Yet, the real fascination is the whole, since it is one of the best preserved examples of this way of life. This is one example, but right across the region, from the western edge to the east, you find small towns and villages that exalt the truly Ligurian concept of the "slow journey", allowing time to take in the landscape, history, culture, traditional trades, food and wines. This itinerary is slightly "virtual" in that it jumps from valley to valley. **Dolceàcqua**, with its single-arch Medieval bridge, straddles the Nervia Stream, although the initial appearance seems to be of an undivided village lying at the foot of an old castle. The wine cellars are alive with the smell of Rossese, a noble wine. The surrounding area is home to a myriad of small towns that are worth visiting. **Apricale** lies on a hill covered in olive trees and topped by a castle, with old houses, narrow streets and ancient flights of steps. **Pigna** has numerous narrow streets and passageways. **Realdo** is an age-old mountain settlement located on a cliff. **Triora** is the town of witches (a theme explored in a local museum) that still has some magic to cast on anyone who visits. **Bussana Vecchia** was regenerated by artists from across the world following a devastating earthquake in the late 19th century. **Calizzano** lies in a green basin surrounded by gentle mountains and beech trees. The houses here are placed in an orderly fashion, as was typical of fortified hamlets. The chestnut groves have some superb mushrooms, especially

prized *porcini*. **Bardineto** lies in a strategic position in the same valley at a crossroads leading to Piedmont or the Riviera. A few bends further south takes you to **Castelvecchio di Rocca Barbena**, a feudal hamlet with concentric rings of houses around a cliff with a castle.

The Bèigua massif dominates the landscape between the provinces of Savona and Genoa. **Sassello** stands like a sentinel for this mass. Immersed in greenery, the hamlet itself is a delightful mix of 17th-century buildings, medieval structures and old industrial ruins, but the true delight probably lies in the taste: this is the home for a smooth almond liqueur and wonderful mushrooms. From Genoa, one can take a rather special form a transport to reach the hinterland: the Casella train (*see p. 99*) heads into the

heart of the Ligurian Apennines, through the Bisogno valley, past breathtaking scenery and into the Scrivia valley. As the name might suggest, the final stop on the line is **Casella**, a town set in a lush green valley. On the lovely main piazza, you should note the 17th-century Palazzo dei Fieschi. **Torriglia**, 770m above sea level, is the capital of the zone known as "Swiss Liguria". Not far way lies **Pèntema**, an enchanting village with its series of bare stone buildings. There are dozens of districts in the Brevenna valley, turning it into a sort of open-air museum for local architecture. Each little town is like a monument to the hardships of Ligurian peasant life. Perhaps the best of all these towns is **Senàrega**.

The Fontanabuona, Graveglia and Àveto valleys lie behind the Tigullio Gulf and are home to a series of roads that lead to forgotten hamlets. **Santo Stéfano d'Àveto** has a lovely old town center with a 13th-century castle and stands like a sentry for Mt Maggiorasca. **Cicagna** in Fontanabuona is one of the most renowned centers for slate. It is also worth making the effort to see the rural houses of **Favale di Màlvaro**

and the old town center with its mill. The Graveglia valley is dotted with well preserved villages amidst woods and is known as the "valley of mills". The La Spèzia hinterland is a truly green land with some interesting historical elements. Yet, this land is not only about the past, with various places combining past, present and future. **Varese Ligure**, in the Vara valley, is home to Borgo Rotondo, where the innermost part has houses with porticoes that face on to the circular piazza, and the Fieschi castle. Varese Ligure (the first European municipality to receive ISO 140001 certification for the environment) is also the capital of the "organic valley", where cheese, meat and other products must be produced using organic methods. **Brugnato** is quite close to the highway exit and has various features from the past. The feudal town of **Càlice al Cornoviglio** – one of the must see stops on the Alta Via dei Monti Liguri – is dominated by a castle (16C). The final stop is **Vezzano Ligure**, located on a mountain top near La Spèzia. It overlooks the Magra valley, which stretches into a plain that extends south towards the Tuscan border.

The hamlets of silence

FINALE LIGURE

The route is located inland from Finale, in a relatively wild region dotted with historical traces. From the Finale Pia bridge, head up along the Sciusa Stream along the road to Vezzi Portio. After 2.1 km, turn right to Verzi along the small asphalt road through olive groves. Continue to the hairpin bend and then head left, along the dirt road through the Ponci valley (look for the "Via Iulia Augusta" road sign, 3 km). After passing the Idolo di Pen menhir – it was worshiped as a god by the ancient Liguri tribes – you come to a wild, deep and narrow section of the Ponci – or bridges – valley. The first bridge you come to is the Fairies' bridge, after which you enter the Punci rian (valley floor). You then need to look out for a signed crossroads (4.5 km), where you must head left, traveling parallel to the small stream as far as the Sordo bridge (collapsed) and then the well-kept Muto bridge. Soon after you reach a crossroads (5.1 km), where you must go left along a rutted trail, look out for the rocks that jut out as well as the traces left by ancient Roman carts. The route climbs up to the Roman caves. The stretch to reach the Acqua bridge, near Ca' du Puncin, is easier. Continue on a broad track along an uphill stretch in the wood on the way to Colla di Magnone. The meadow is cut by a pathway to the right, which you must follow. When you reach the gate, turn left along the trail leading to the Bric dei Monti summit (elev. 406 m, 8.8 km). When you get there, you need to head back about 100 m and, after a bend, you'll see e a trail on your left. This is where an exciting long and winding downhill road starts; following the main trail, you come to a dirt road that climbs up to the SP 45 road. When you reach the asphalt road, head right and then

ROUTE: 23 KM: FINALE PIA - PONCI VALLEY - CA' DU PUNCIN (ACQUA BRIDGE) - COLLA DI MAGNONE - BRIC DEI MONTI - BRIC DEI CROVI - SAN GIACOMO CHURCH - ARMA DELLE MANIE – CROSSROADS OF THE MUTO BRIDGE - FINALE PIA. MIXED ROUTE, MAINLY DIRT ROADS, MULE TRACKS AND PATHWAYS, WELL BEATEN AND MARKED.

DIFFICULTY: THE TECHNICAL PARTS ARE SITUATED ONLY ON THE MULE TRACK IN THE PONCI VALLEY, WITH STRETCHES OF EMERGING ROCKS. SOME SUDDEN SPURTS CALL FOR DUE ATTENTION. THE OVERALL RISE IS 501 M.

BIKE SERVICE: SPORT E NATURA, VIA BRUNENGHI 59, FINALE LIGURE; TEL. 019690007. RIVIERA OUTDOOR, VIA NICOTERA 3/5, FINALE LIGURE; TEL. 0196898024

TOURIST INFORMATION: IAT FINALE LIGURE, VIA S. PIETRO 14, FINALMARINA; TEL. 019692581. ASSOCIAZIONE ALBERGHI E TURISMO, VIA SACCONE 1, FINALMARINA; TEL. 019692615.

left onto a steep dirt road. Then head right, near the panoramic crossroads, onto a wide trail that climbs up to Bric dei Crovi. At the crossroads on the summit crest, keep right and climb up for a short stretch before starting a new descent along a track that is almost like a tunnel through the undergrowth. At the end, follow the dirt road to Mount Capo Noli, keeping right to get back onto the SP 45 road. Then a dirt path leads you to the church of San Giacomo, where you continue on an asphalt road up to Arma delle Manie, a vast cavern once inhabited by Stone-Age man (16.5 km). From this spot, continue straight onto the dirt road, which then switches to a mule track that leads you back on a downhill stretch to the Muto bridge crossroads (18.1 km). You can then return to Finale Pia along the same route.

GIOVO

ROUTE: 36 KM: SAN PIETRO D'OLBA - VARA INFERIORE - VARA SUPERIORE - ACQUABIANCA - PIAMPALUDO - ALBEROLA - LA CARTA - SAN PIETRO D'OLBA.

DIFFICULTY: THIS ROUTE REQUIRES SOME TRAINING; THE MORE CHALLENGING STRETCHES ARE THE UPHILL CLIMBS BETWEEN VARA INFERIORE AND SUPERIORE AND BETWEEN THE CROSSROADS OF ALBEROLA AND PIAMPALUDO .

BIKE SERVICE: ZANINI, VIA PESCETTO 31, ALBISOLA SUPERIORE; TEL. 019486932. FORMULA UNO BICI, CORSO FERRARI 65, ALBISOLA SUPERIORE; TEL. 019489022.

BIKE RENTAL: RIFUGIO SCIVERNA, HAML. OF MADDALENA, SASSELLO; TEL. 019720081. OPEN FROM MARCH 15 TO NOVEMBER 15. GUIDED TOURS WITH AMI LEADERS, CLAUDIO MERLO, TEL. 3495782693. VANESSA CURTO, TEL. 3478434459.

TOURIST INFORMATION:

COMUNITÀ MONTANA GIOVO, CORSO ITALIA 3, SAVONA; TEL. 019841871. WWW.COMUNITAMONTANAGIOVO.IT
ENTE PARCO DEL BEIGUA, CORSO ITALIA 3, SAVONA TEL. 01984187300. WWW.PARKS.IT.
CENTRO VISITE "PALAZZO GERVINO" - IAT SASSELLO VIA G.B. BADANO 45, SASSELLO; TEL. 019724020.

The tour develops in the vicinity of the Parco Naturale Regionale del Beigua, winding through the woods of the former Selva dell'Orba, which was inhabited in prehistoric times and favored by the Lombards as a hunting ground. This is a truly beautiful route, working its way through a pristine environment filled with woods, glades and breathtaking views of the gorges along the Orba River. There are also traces of the more recent past, in old farm dwellings and simple, dry stone structures where chestnuts were once kept. The route starts from the square in front of the church of **San Pietro d'Olba**, an old village with traces of the distant past. After the bridge on the way to Vara Inferiore, keep right and head up the steep section to reach Vara Superiore. The route then heads towards Acquabianca, initially on a panoramic stretch and then down a steep descent on a narrow road overlooking the valley. From Acquabianca, which is one of the hamlets in the Urbe municipality, keep left, heading towards Martina d'Olba. Then, take another left and, after a 2.5 km slope, you come to a bridge where you need to turn left once more. This takes you to the crossroads for Alberola. As you close in on Piampaludo, the wood thins out, giving way to the shrub vegetation typical of wet, swampy areas. From Alberola, ride down the La Carta pass, where you find a small chapel dedicated to St Michael. According to tradition, the chapel was built by Queen Theodolinda at the end of the 6th century. Continuing cycling, keeping right, until you reach **San Pietro d'Olba**.

Riding amid olive groves.

ROUTE: 45 KM: MONTEMARCELLO - ZANEGO - SERRA - PUGLIOLA - PITELLI - BONAMINI - BACCANO - MONTI - LIMONE - SAN VENERIO - CAROZZO - VEZZANO LIGURE - FORNOLA - SENATO - AMEGLIA - MONTEMARCELLO. ALL ON ASPHALT ROADS.

DIFFICULTY: THERE ARE NO TOUGH CLIMBS, BUT IT IS A VARIED ITINERARY AS FAR AS ALTITUDE IS CONCERNED, WITH CONSTANT UP AND DOWNHILL STRETCHES. THE MOST GRUELING CLIMB RUNS FROM LIMONE TO VEZZANO SUPERIORE (6.5 KM, 230 M RISE).

BIKE SERVICE: EUROBIKES DI ARPESELLA, VIA PROVINCIALE 87, ROMITO (SP); TEL. 0187989477.

TOURIST INFORMATION

APT CINQUE TERRE E GOLFO DEI POETI, VIALE MAZZINI 47 C.P. 345, LA SPEZIA; TEL. 0187770900.
WWW.APTCINQUETERRE.SP.IT
INFORMATION OFFICES VIA BIAGGINI 6, LERICI; TEL. 0187967346; VIA NUOVA 48, MONTEMARCELLO; TEL. 0187691071.
ENTE PARCO DI MONTEMARCELLO-MAGRA, VIA PACI 2, I SARZANA; TEL. 0187691071.
WWW.PARKS.IT/PARCO.MONTEMARCELLO.MAGRA

MAGRA - LA SPEZIA

A suggestive itinerary between the Golfo dei Poeti and the Magra River. The route starts in **Montemarcello** and you need to follow Via Nuova to Lerici. The trail heads through the olive groves and Mediterranean scrubland, before climbing up through a wood of holm-oak and cluster pines. The next section is downhill, across the cultivated terraces between Figarole and Zanego. From here, the route heads up again – briefly – before coming to a downhill along which you can enjoy a sweeping view of the bay below, between Tellaro and Maralunga. Continue on to Serra and, after passing the stone arch that goes over the provincial road, take the SS 331 road. You only stay on the SS road briefly, before turning left onto Via Militare. The road then climbs up towards Pugliola, offering a view of the Lerici Gulf and the castle. After passing Solaro, you come to the Tre Strade crossroads, where you should turn right towards Pitelli. At this point, you leave the coast and head inland. Continue along the ridge on Via Fostella, passing the villages of Pietralba and Bonamini. After reaching Baccano, turn left onto the SP 19 road. On the next stretch, you should look out for Villa Picedi (18C), the parish church of Ss. Stefano and Margherita and the houses of Monti di Arcola, before descending towards Termo. Here, you need to turn left onto the SS 1 Aurelia road for 2 km. Pass Termo, Melara and Limone, and then turn right to San Venerio. Once in the village, turn left onto Via San Rocco, skirting around the church. At Carozzo, go into the town and ride on the paved Via Vespucci until you reach the SP 16 road. There, you need to turn right and continue until reaching Vezzano Superiore, which has a pentagonal tower. Continue along the SP 16 road until you reach Fornola, where you come to the SP 10 road. Keep right and pass under the freeway loop. Turn left onto the SS 1 road and then turn right on the SS 331 road. Once you've reached Romito Magra, leave the road and make a detour (left) on the SS 432 road, skirting the hamlet of Senato. At Cafaggio, leave the main road and go right along Via Camisano, until you reach Ameglia. The final section takes you back to **Montemarcello**.

VALLE ARGENTINA

Argentina Stream, although the actual route only starts after passing under the imposing viaduct that supports highway. The SS 548 road narrows and, after approximately 7 km, reaches what was once the Badalucco landed estate, scene of a bloody battle between Romans and Liguri in 181 BC. Today it is a peaceful village that looks out onto the old Santa Lucia bridge with its two imposing stone arches that have watched the silver stream flow gently by since 1555. From Badalucco, the road rises gently, and in the 15 km before Molini di Triora, the environment gradually changes: the olive-covered hills give way to chestnut-covered mountains. After 14.3 km, turn right to Molini di Triora, where the Argentina Stream and its tributaries once drove the 23 mills that account for the village's name (literally, Triora mills). At this point, you need to turn back, following a downhill to the crossroads, where you turn right. Moneghetti is where the uphill proper starts. The bridge over the Argentina is situated at 430 m and the real uphill climbs starts 2 km ahead, at around 450 m. For 8.5 km, the road climbs up to 1,080 m, up to the crossroads on your left (before the Langan hill) to the Sanctuary of San Giovanni dei Prati and the hill crossing of Mount Ceppo (1,505 m above sea level). The topmost point of the route is a good time to take a short break, regain some vital salts, put on a windbreaker and get ready to enjoy the long downhill. After a little more than 7 km, you come to a crossroads where you should turn left towards the Oxentina valley. After passing Vignai, continue riding up to the junction on the SS 548 road, returning into the Argentina valley. Next, you need to turn right onto a downhill stretch and keep going until you reach **Taggia** (6.2 km). The final, short stretch follows the stretch that you started on.

ROUTE: 67 KM: TAGGIA - BADALUCCO - MOLINI DI TRIORA - MONEGHETTI - MOUNT CEPPO PASS- BADALUCCO CROSSROADS - TAGGIA. ENTIRELY ON ASPHALT ROAD.

DIFFICULTY: THIS ITINERARY REQUIRES GOOD PHYSICAL CONDITIONS AND YOUR BEING USED TO STAYING ON A SADDLE ALSO ON UPHILL STRETCHES. THERE ARE NO TOO TOUGH SLOPES, BUT THE OVERALL RISE IS APPROXIMATELY 1,400 M. MOST OF THE UPHILL STRETCH IS SPREAD OVER THE 15 KM BETWEEN THE CROSSROADS FOR MOLINI DI TRIORA AND THE PASS OF MOUNT CEPPO (1,075 M RISE).

BIKE SERVICE: GROSSO SPORT, VIA AURELIA PONENTE 145, ARMA DI TAGGIA; TEL. 0184448830. WWW.GROSSOSPORT.IT

TOURIST INFORMATION

APT RIVIERA DEI FIORI VILLA BOSELLI, VIA BOSELLI, ARMA DI TAGGIA; TEL. 018443733; PALAZZO RIVIERA, LARGO NUVOLONI 1, SANREMO; TEL. 0184571571.

PRO LOCO TRIORA, CORSO ITALIA 1, TRIORA; TEL. 018494487. WWW.COMUNE.TRIORA.IM.IT

The Argentina valley is a magnificent green area named after the silver torrent that runs from the Maritime Alps to the Riviera dei Fiori and the blue sea at Arma di Taggia. The itinerary starts from Taggia. The slightly sloped road runs up the

The ancient Badalucco bridge.

113

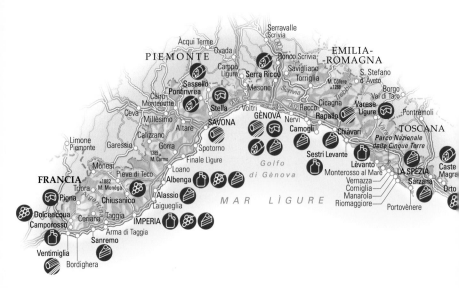

L iguria is a narrow region between mountains and cliffs. The protective barrier formed by the Apennines to the north cuts out many of the cold northern winds, ensuring a mild climate that allows, within a few kilometers, Mediterranean scrubland, vineyards, olive groves and woods to thrive. Still, as fascinating as this land might be, it has never been easy to cultivate, with farmers often taking refuge on slender terraces. In short, this is a relatively small region dominated by sea and mountains. Despite this, Ligurian cuisine is filled with a surprising array of choices. It would not be hard to argue that this cuisine is one of the most complete in the Mediterranean, especially because of the wise use of just about everything the locals could get: from simple anchovies to wild grasses, from the prized Taggiasca olives to the fragrant basil and wild mountain fruits. Genoese cuisine is a melting pot of local raw materials and items shipped in from other cultures. Yet, all these elements are skillfully combined, taking the fruits of local farming and the wares of

PASTA

HAMS AND SALAMI

CHEESE

OIL

WINE

CAKES

Food

generations of sea trading to form wonderful dishes. The fish and vegetables are notable, sometimes eaten alone and sometimes in tasty soups or quiches. The wine might be slightly less well known, but there is certainly no lack of quality wines that fit superbly with the array of local delicacies.

Highlights

- Recco is the local culinary capital, home to the famous cheese *focaccia* and *trofie* pasta that is combined with that most Ligurian of sauces...pesto.

- The *Torta Pasqualina* or Easter Cake is the best known quiche, made with vegetables, cheese and eggs.

- In 1997, Ligurian extra-virgin olive oil received PDO recognition from the EU.

- Amaretti di Sassello and Baci di Alàssio are two sweet delights that also make excellent gifts from Liguria.

Inside

Liguria, the taste of the sea and the mountains

In terms of Italian geography, Liguria is unique. For the first 250km, starting from the east, the zone is characterized by the Apennines, running practically down to the shore. Beyond this, lies the deep sea, with its abundant supply of fish, ranging from species like anchovies, sardines and mackerels to great ocean fish. The coast is steep, sometimes even precipitous, but the slopes have been molded by years and years of human toil to create terraces for vineyards and vegetable gardens. As you head inland, green is the dominant color, although olive groves soon give way to chestnuts and a surprising number of cultivated fields. All of this is compactly laid out, sometimes so much so that one can take it all in from one panoramic spot. The condensed nature of this region is reflected in the local cuisine, which is dominated by Mediterranean products. Olive oil and Taggiasca olives abound, as do vegetables and basil, a key ingredient in the famed pesto that is the region's most famous sauce. The remaining Mediterranean products include mussels from La Spèzia and salted anchovies. All this Mediterranean goodness, though, is combined with products and flavors from inland, such as the cheese from Santo Stéfano d'Àveto, the salami from Valpolcevera, the white beans from Pigna and Conio, and the Gabbiana chestnut from the Bormida valley. Vineyards are another constant. Cinque Terre is home to the now famed Sciacchetrà passito (raisin wine), but there are also some excellent whites, with the Vermentino and Rossese di Dolceàcqua. In terms of what is actually eaten, the specialties tend to be fish, a reminder, like the dried cod, of the ancient fishing customs of the area. There are, though, some exceptional vegetable dishes, including the well-known torta pasqualina or Easter cake, that are made special and unrepeatable by the effect of the excellent climate on local produce. The inland areas also have specialties that are worth trying, from stuffed pastas dishes to goat stews. Genoa is like a microcosm of all the best of Ligurian food: from focaccia bread, often purchased from a street vendor, to trenette pasta with pesto, which has become rather like a regional cuisine flagship. The city also has classic Mediterranean dishes like rabbit with olives and pine nuts or the magnificent *cappon magro* salad that uses vegetables and fish but is as sumptuous as a meat dish fit for a king. Of course, this is a port city and so one should not be surprised to find more exotic foods. In a similar line, the cuisine of this slender region has also been influenced by the surrounding regions. As such, along the sizeable border with Piedmont, once one has crossed the watershed, the aromas of Langa, white truffles and superb boiled meat dishes abound. To the west, from Imperia on, the influence of France can be felt in the delightful smelling dishes from Provence. To the east, from Chiàvari, one might notice the influence of Emilia and then, from Lunigiana, the strong flavors of Tuscany.

Street stalls in Genoa and Liguria

Good quality food, bought from a stall or vendor by the roadside, has a long tradition in these parts. In the past, workers at the port would head down to the *sciamadde*, that is, small shops with wood-fired ovens, where bakers would cook or fry, in a copper pan, a sort of cross between a pizza and a pancake (called *faìna* locally) made with chickpea flour, extra-virgin olive oil, salt and pepper. It was a simple, tasty dish, especially when accompanied with a glass of white Vermentino wine. This tradition of street food is not limited to Genoa, with the Savona area being known for a version made with wheat flour. In Imperia it is called *frisciolata* and in Nice in France, *socca*. Another local delight is the *fugassa* or Ligurian focaccia made with wheat meal and flavored with olive oil and sea salt or stuffed with cheese, pesto, onions or olives. There are also the fried *panissa*, a polenta made with chickpea flour and fried in oil, *frisciu*, a type of pancake, *sgabei*, small, fried focaccia, and a vegetable quiche with zucchinis.

Appetizers

Bianchetti (Gianchetti in dialect)
These are made with anchovy and sardine fry, which are now protected by quotas. They are normally boiled and then served either cold or warm in a salad with olive oil and a few drops of lemon. They are also an excellent addition to an omelet or pancake.

Cappon magro
Almost exclusively made in Genoa. It is made with various vegetables (cauliflower, green beans, celery, carrots, potatoes, beetroot and oyster-plant), a large fish (weever, hake or umbrine) and other ingredients (lobster, shrimps, oysters, etc). The sauce is made with anchovies, garlic, pine nuts, capers, hard-boiled egg yolks, olives, parsley, oil and vinegar.

Torta pasqualina
This is clearly the best known savory pie and is associated with Easter. The filling is made with boiled Swiss chards mixed with milk curds, parmesan cheese and various other ingredients. This is then enclosed in layers of pastry, although before actually closing the pie, four or more little holes are made in the filling and then an egg is placed each hole. There is another version that use artichokes cooked with oil, onion, parsley and marjoram.

Starters

Minestrone alla genovese
This is a classic vegetable soup with plenty of pesto added in. Various types of pasta or fresh, homemade *tagliatelle* are also added in.

Pansoti
A stuffed pasta with a leaning filling. A clove of crushed garlic is added to the dough made of flour, water and white wine. The stuffing is made with borage, Swiss chards, herbs, ricotta, parmesan and egg. The only sauce "allowed" with this pasta is a walnut one.

Ravioli
Generally served with a meat sauce, the identifying feature of Ligurian ravioli is the use of milk curds and wild vegetable in the filling. Recently, fish ravioli has also become popular. It is made by sieving a stew of baby octopus, shrimps, bass and other types of fish and then adding in bread crumbs, borage and other boiled and chopped vegetable, eggs and goat's-milk cheese.

Trenette al pesto
This is Genoa's best known dish. In the most classic version, the pasta is boiled with potato slices and green beans. The *trenette* pasta are also made with whole meal flour; in this case they are dark and referred to as *avvantaggiate*.

Trofie
These are gnocchi made with water and flour. They are very small, and look rather like the curl on a corkscrew. They are boiled and eaten with pesto.

Main course and side dishes

Cima ripiena
This famous Ligurian dish consists of a piece of veal stuffed with minced meat from the same animal that is fried along with brain and sweetbread. An egg, peas, cheese and fresh marjoram add flavor. It is then tied together, boiled, allowed to cool and then served in slices.

Coniglio in umido/Stewed rabbit
This stewed rabbit dish is a classic. The rabbit is cooked in a mixture of oil, butter, garlic rosemary, onion, white wine, black olives and pine nuts.

Stoccafisso accomodato/Dried-cod
This is the most traditional dried-cod dish from Liguria. It is cooked on a base of oil, anchovies, herbs and spices. Later on, olives, pine nuts and potatoes are added. A variant of this dish from the Sanremo area, called *brand de cujun*, is simply the French *brandade*. After being boiled, the cod is cut into pieces and then combined with boiled potatoes and onions before being dressed with oil, garlic and parsley.

Tomaxelle
These veal rolls are stuffed with chopped udders, veal, marjoram, cheese, pine nuts, mushrooms and egg. They are tied together with yarn and boiled in white wine, tomato, meat sauce and broth.

Verdure ripiene/Stuffed vegetables
This is another classic. The stuffing is made with a pulp of carefully chosen vegetables (zucchinis, onions, eggplants) mixed with egg, bread crumbs, crushed garlic, parsley and other herbs, such as marjoram. In a common variant, boiled potatoes and dried mushrooms are added.

FOOD

PASTA

Liguria is synonymous with dried pasta, as opposed to fresh pasta. Local pasta has a documented tradition dating back hundreds of years, including some notary documents from 1244 now conserved in the National Archives in Genoa. In 1574, the Corporation of Pasta Makers was established in Genoa complete with its own statute (*Capitoli dell'Arte dei Fidelari*), making it older than similar ones established in Naples (1579) and Palermo (1605). The first "fine pasta house" opened in Genoa in 1740 and, in Savona, the oldest pasta house in Italy opened in 1794, using methods that are very similar to those employed today. This Ligurian pasta supremacy lasted throughout the 19th century, although as late as 1950, it was common to hear pasta being described as "the pasta in the Genoa style", alongside the "the pasta in the Naples style".

While dried pasta might be the king here, this does not mean the fresh pasta tradition is laughable. Indeed, there are trofie, trenette, piccagge, *lisce* or *avvantaggiate* (made with whole meal flour), which can all be eaten with pesto or a filling Genoese meat sauce, *u toccu*, made with veal and brain. Finally, ravioli and pansoti are also often associated with Ligurian cuisine.

Bricchetti

A short, fresh pasta that is normally used in vegetable soups. In the local dialect, *bricchetti* means matchstick and this is a fairly good description of the pasta. This pasta is often added to vegetable – especially with Savoy cabbage and some lard – and fish soups.

Corzetti

Typical of eastern Liguria, this fresh pasta is disk-shaped (roughly 60mm in diameter). Plenty of egg is used to make the dough. The pasta is cut using a wooden cutter that has various shapes sculpted on it that leave impressions on this relatively thick pasta. It is allowed to dry for a couple of days before being cooked. In the past, each family had its own cutter with a special marking and, indeed, for the nobility, these cutters became a sort of culinary coat-of-arms. These cutters, which are still made by local artisans, are traditionally sculpted from pear, apple, beech or maple wood – all woods that have no tannins that would alter the taste. *Corzetti* pasta can be eaten with pesto as well as with walnut, mushroom and *u toccu* (a type of meat sauce) sauces.

Mandilli de sea

The origins of this name are Arabic, meaning a small silk cloth. The name is apt since the sheets of this lasagna-like pasta are not dissimilar to silk cloths. The sheets of pasta are quite large (about 20cm per side), but they are so thin they are, like silk, almost transparent. In the most traditional form, the dough was made by mixing and kneading eggs, flour and some wine. The pasta was then boiled in a large, wide dish before being eaten with pesto or the local Genoese meat sauce.

Pansoti

This ravioli, with a lean filling, is typical of the territory once ruled by the Republic of Genoa, especially Camogli, Recco and Rapallo. The pasta is shaped like a right-angled triangle, with the filled section accounting for the name, which basically means pot-bellied. The filling consists of ricotta (in the past, *prescinseua* was used), grated cheese (pecorino or parmesan are the most common options), marjoram, eggs, nutmeg and the so-called *preboggion*, a mixture of wild herbs that includes borage, sweet acacia and anise. The best sauce to eat with the pasta is walnut.

Penne di Natale

This is a dried, tubular pasta with a diagonal-cut at the end. *Penne di Natale* is longer than traditional penne, which is associated with Naples. The Ligurian version, literally meaning Christmas penne, gets its name from being the traditional first course on the Christmas menu in these parts. The pasta is cooked in a

TCI HIGHLIGHTS

GENOA'S PESTO AND BASIL

Pesto is the most famous traditional Ligurian sauce and it is used for pasta dishes – trofie, trenette – and the local vegetable soup. Traditionally, pesto is made by mixing the basil leaves – from the Genoa area – with grated cheese (parmesan and Sardinian pecorino, in proportions of two to one), garlic, pine nuts and coarse salt. This is then diluted slightly with some extra-virgin olive oil, which should be from Liguria, of course. The only tool allowed to be used is a marble mortar and a wooden pestle. The wonderful result owes much to the basil that is grown along the Ligurian coast: it is a special variety, now safeguarded by Protected Denomination of Origin (PDO) status, that has quite small, oval leaves that are slightly convex in shape and a light

green. This basil has a delicate smell, without the mint nuances that are common in most varieties. The most famous zone for producing it is the land inland from Genoa, especially the Prà area, which is now the heart of a "basil park". There are a number of other olive oil based sauces, such as a garlic sauce, a pine nut one and a walnut one.

beef or capon (a rooster that has been castrated, normally when it is somewhere between 6 and 20 weeks old) broth and then seasoned with veal tripe, sausage with a chicken giblet and pine nut sauce, and cardoons that have been boiled and then stir-fried in butter.

Piccagge

This is a long, fresh pasta with a rectangular cross-section. This pasta is really the Ligurian equivalent of the more famous tagliatelle: long strips of semolina pasta served with pesto or a meat sauce. The name means strings or ribbons. One fairly common variant sees the addition of some chestnut flour, although the pasta is then usually called *matte* or *bastarde*.

Ravioli

A square, fresh pasta that is filled. Over the years, ravioli have become the symbol of Genoese cuisine. The key feature of Ligurian ravioli is the filling: a mixture of herbs

(prickly lettuce and borage) with cheese and meat. Once again, the ideal sauce to accompany ravioli is a meat sauce, although it is common to serve ravioli with a simple bit of butter and parmesan cheese. In Lèvanto, the ravioli is filled with vegetable fried in oil. This variant is called *gattafin*, which comes from the 14th-century word *gattafura*, once a synonym for ravioli.

Scucuzzun

A type of pasta from Genoa that is used for vegetable soups. The dough is made with semolina and then rubbed between ones hands to create tiny balls that are a mere few millimeters thick. There is a definite similarity to Arabian couscous, and some people even believe this explains its origin. Experts of Ligurian cuisine believe it is best eaten in a cold soup.

Trenette

This fresh or dried pasta is long, with a square cross-section and is not unlike the best known Italian pasta, namely

FOOD

spaghetti. Along with trofie and ravioli, trenette are one of the symbols of Ligurian cuisine. The dough is made with flour, eggs, water and salt. It is then rolled thinly and cut into very narrow strips. The result is a fairly rough, porous pasta, making it ideal for soaking up sauces. The most popular sauce to go with this pasta is pesto, although the truly traditionally version envisages this pasta being boiled and served with potatoes and beans.

Trofie

This is a short, fresh pasta. This pasta is so well-known that it is made by all the main pasta houses as well as

Trofie are traditionally eaten with pesto, especially local pesto made with Ligurian basil.

most of the small, artisan pasta makers across the whole of Italy - and not just Liguria. Originally from the eastern section of the Ligurian Riviera (more precisely, Recco), trofie is perhaps best described as squiggly little pieces of pasta made from a dough of flour, salt and water. The name is said to come from the local word, *strufuggiâ* (to rub) in reference to the hand movement needed to form the shape. It is also quite common to roll the little pasta rods around a thin piece of iron. Like trenette, trofie pasta is normally eaten with pesto and cooked and then strained with beans and potatoes.

GENOVA/GENOA

Il Primo Piatto
Via Lomellini 68/r, Tel. 0102465431
Via Pal. Fortezza 51-53/r,
Tel. 0106459729
Fresh, homemade pasta, including pansoti, trofie, corsetti and testaroli.

You can also buy sauces made with pine nuts and walnuts, pesto, stuffed veal rolls and various pies.

Pastificio Gemma
Via Monticelli 20/r, Tel. 0108393570
Fresh pasta made with a machine and then finished by hand: pansoti, ravioli, trofie, trenette and corzetti. You can also buy various products, including walnut sauce and pesto.

RAPALLO
Pastificio Malatesta
Corso C. Colombo 30, Tel. 018551236
This pasta house makes the expected range of pastas - pansoti, trofie (also with chestnut flour), trenette and ravioli – as well as focaccia, vegetable quiches, rice pies, torta pasqualina, pesto and walnut sauce.

SANTA MARGHERITA LÌGURE
Pestarino
Via Palestro 5, Tel. 0185281890
Via Palestro 10, Tel. 0185287061
You can buy various types of pasta here (pansoti, trofie, and trenette) as well as pesto, walnut sauce, torta pasqualina with artichokes and other Ligurian specialties, including hams and cheeses.

IMPERIA

VENTIMÌGLIA
Boutique della Pasta
Via Cavour 93/b, Tel. 0184351718
This pasta house produces fresh pasta, most of it by hand. The range of pasta includes trofie, orecchiette, ravioli and lasagna. There is also a deli: sweet and savory cakes, meat, walnut and mushroom sauces and pesto.

SAVONA

Pastificio Savona
Via Nazario Sauro 14,
Tel. 019851516
This artisan pasta house makes a range of pasta, including pansoti, trofie and ravioli with various fillings. You can also buy some of their own sauces, such as walnut or meat sauce and pesto.

HAMS AND SALAMI

This small, seafaring region shaped like a narrow arch running from east to west and from the Alps to the Apennines does not have much free space for rearing animals and thus has limited supplies of meat for producing salamis and the like. In the hinterland, where the only open views are those looking seaward, man has carved the landscape into a series of steep terraces covered in vineyards and olive groves. Pastures are not common. Local producers have tended to focus on specialized or niche products, such as the Sant'Olcese salami or the "new" Prosciutta Castelnovese (1973). These cured meats have been perfected by years of practice, but the production of the niche items remains limited. The cured meats do, though, make interesting use of spices, berries and herbs, with plenty of bay leaf, dandelion, fennel, rosemary and borage being used, especially in dishes from inland areas. The cuisine tends to use more of the aromas and flavors from the Mediterranean scrubland, focusing on simple dishes with good ingredients. This does not, though, limit the range of items, which runs from marjoram to potato cakes and from the classic focaccia to the ever present trennete with pesto.

Coppa

This is a type of cured pork made mainly at Santo Stéfano d'Àveto in the province of Genova. A pig's neck is cured with salt and pepper, cinnamon, nutmeg and cloves before being pushed into casings and then tied.

Mostardella

This is a type of salami made with the meat discarded during the making of the Sant'Olcese salami. Pork lard chopped into cubes is added to beef and then minced before being seasoned with salt, pepper and garlic. Saltpeter and ascorbic acid are then added in to make the salami last longer, before the mixture is pushed into cow gut casings and tied into small salamis. These little salamis are then dried for a week in a room heated by a wood-fired stove, where the temperature is about 30ºC. It is then seasoned for 15 more days at about 18 ºC. When cut, the color is bright red with sizeable pieces of lard.

Prosciutta

Originally from Castelnuovo Magra, in the province of La Spèzia, this ham is a recent "invention". It is made only with pork – a top quality leg of pork is needed – from animals reared in Italy that weigh over 200kg and are fed naturally. The leg is boned shortly after the animal is butchered (even the shin is removed) and then the nerves and fat are carefully removed. It is then opened to take out the loin and seasoned with salt and pepper.

The ham is then kept pressurized for about 10 days, before the excess salt is washed off. The meat is flavored with herbs and spices before being allowed to cure for 30 days. When this period is finished, the skin is rubbed with extra-virgin olive oil and left to season for 7 months in special rooms. When ready, it looks like speck but the taste is completely different. Indeed, the meat is quite dry and the taste is more reminiscent of cured game meat.

Prosciutto Cotto

This ham is made in limited quantities and only at Sassello, in the province of Savona. Pork legs from animals reared in Piedmont are used. The meat is placed in brine for a period of time that is determined by the weight. The legs are then boned and seasoned with salt, sugar, coriander, juniper berries, herbs, spices, Marsala wine and additives. The meat is placed in molds and boiled in special tanks. When done, it is moved to refrigeration cells to cool before being cleaned and vacuum packed, ready to be sold.

Salame Genovese

This salami is made with various types of lean meat and comes from Sant'Olcese, an inland town in the province of Genova. It is made using prime cuts of beef from Bruna Alpina and Piemontese cows (about 50%), top-quality pork from heavy pigs – generally, the pigs weigh 150-160kg – and a small amount of pancetta and

Products with the DOP and IGP labels

Protecting food production is the first step to safeguarding a heritage which is not only of economic significance, but also, and more importantly, of cultural importance. It is an act which confirms and aims to preserve the quality of a product. The DOP and IGP labels protect a product's environment, the human input and its quality. Products carrying the DOP (Protected Designation of Origin) label are products which, first, must comply with a strict set of production regulations, based on the local tradition, which specify what raw materials must be used and how they are processed. Secondly, they must be produced in a particular geographical area, although the "typical production area" may extend beyond the territory of a town and refer to a whole region. Products carrying the IGP (Protected Geographic Indication) label are protected in a similar way to DOP products (in terms of complying with production regulations and the particular area in which it may be produced) but the processing and packaging may be conducted in a wider area. The IGP label is the form of protection most often applied to fruit and vegetable products and their derivatives.

lard. The ingredients, once the fat and nerves have been removed, are minced, but not finely, and then salt, peppercorns, garlic powder and some local herbs and spices are added. Some saltpeter and ascorbic acid are also added to help preserve the product. The mixture is then pushed in cow-gut casings and tied to form medium-sized salamis. These are stored for 5 or 6 days in a ventilated room where they are smoked using alder and oak wood. After this, the

salamis are placed in a room where the humidity and temperature is controlled for 2 to 3 months. The Sant'Olcese salami has a rather unique, slightly smoky aroma and, when cut, it is bright red with fairly large pieces of fat.

Sanguinaccio

This sausage, eaten cold, is found across Liguria. The paste is made of pig's blood and fresh milk (in equal quantities). Pine nuts and sweetbreads (fried in onion) are then added in. All of the ingredients are mixed together thoroughly before adding salt and pepper. The paste is then pushed in pig-gut casing and tied into medium-sized salamis.

Testa in cassetta

Made only with pork cuts, it is produced across the whole of Liguria using the head, tongue and shoulders. These cuts are cooked in salted water for 3 to 4 hours before being allowed to cool. They are then chopped into small pieces using a knife.

This "minced" meat is seasoned with salt, pepper, cinnamon, cloves, nutmeg, pimento, mace, sugar and pistachios. Saltpeter is then added and everything is poured into molds – lined with nets made of veal – to be pressed into shape.

The cured meat is then placed in a cool room to settle before it is removed from the mold. It is best eaten soon afterwards.

The fire helps to dry the salami paste and give it its characteristic smoked taste.

GENOVA/GENOA

Salumeria Centanaro
Via S. Vincenzo 103/r, Tel. 010580841
A deli where the products are made next door. You can buy their testa in cassetta, various types of sausage and hams. The deli also sells oil, various sauces and cheese.

CASTIGLIONE CHIAVARESE
Macelleria Fratelli Perazzo
Via Canzio 60, Tel. 0185408025
Production and sale of testa in cassetta and various types of salami, cured meats and sausage.

here is the Ceriana sausage, although they also sell a range of other products.

LA SPÈZIA

CASTELNUOVO MAGRA
Antica Salumeria
Elena e Mirco
*Molicciara, Via Canale 52,
Tel. 0187673510
www.prosciuttacastelnovese.com*
The shop sells salamis and cured meats. The specialties include prosciutta castelnovese, salami-mostardella, testa in cassetta and much more.

Some specialties from Liguria.

SANT'OLCESE
Salumificio Cabella
*Via Sant'Olcese 38, Tel. 010709111
www.cabellasalumi.com*
The specialties include Sant'Olcese salami that has been dried in a wood-fired oven, mostardella, testa in cassetta and sanguinaccio.

SERRA RICCÒ
Salumificio Orero
*Orero, Via Torre Natale 29,
Tel. 010758025*
They make their own salami, mostardella and testa in cassetta.

IMPERIA

CERIANA
Macelleria Giacumin
Via Roma 24, Tel. 0184551042
Located in the old center, the specialty

SAVONA

PONTINVREA
Macelleria Pastorino
Via Giovo 16, Tel. 019705105
This shop is far more than a simple butchery as it rears and slaughters some of its own animals. It also makes some local cured meats, including various different salamis and sanguinaccio.

SASSELLO
Salumeria Macelleria Giacobbe
Piazza Rolla 7, Tel. 019724118
Located in the center of town, this butchery mainly sells local meat products as well as making various regional cured meats and salamis, such as testa in cassetta, ham, seasoned pork filet and a lard and herb pâté.

FOOD

CHEESE

Liguria is an arch, with the coast bending around the sea and the cliffs soaring above. In parts, these hills have been molded, one by one, into terraces by the stubborn perseverance of man. The cliffs rise sharply, but soon change, becoming part of the mountains. Here, the valleys are deep, woods dominate the landscape and the small, medieval hamlets – often perched on ledges – have a history of farming and not fishing. Yet, the sea always seems to be on the horizon. The distance is short, compact. This is a region that is open to the see and enclosed by the Alps and the Apennines. For the cuisine, this means it has made use of products from the sea, but also taken ideas from the interior. Pesto is a lovely union of this diversity: oil, basil and garlic hint at Mediterranean aromas, while the pecorino cheese suggests centuries of rearing animals, flocks and mountains. The most famous Ligurian cheese is from Santo Stéfano in the upper Àveto valley. The best known focaccia with cheese is from Recco: originally it was made with *prescinseua* cheese, but now crescenza has become more common. The torta pasqualina is made with milk curds, while the pansoti, ravioli and *cima* are made with ricotta or hard cheeses, bringing flavor to the filling.

Bruzzo della Valle Arroscia

A fermented ricotta made with sheep's milk. It is grayish-white and quite creamy. The taste can be more or less spicy, depending on the seasoning. It is fermented by adding grappa, vinegar, olive oil, pepper and chili pepper. In some zones, it is also salted. It is then kept in a cellar and stirred every day. It can be eaten after about a week.

Caprino di Malga

This fatty cheese can be fresh or seasoned. It is made with goats' milk and is cylindrical in shape with either no crust or a very fine one (darkish in color), depending on the ageing. The fresh version is white or pale yellow, while the aged one is darker, with touches of green. It is quite compact. Ageing takes 30-40 days. Seasonal product. In the Argentina valley, the *caprino di alpeggio* (using milk from goats grazing in the high-mountain pastures) is aged for a few months in a crotta (cave/cellar). This version can be grated and is sometimes used in pesto.

Formaggetta

It comes in a few varieties: Formaggetta di Bonassola and Formaggetta de Vàise. This cylindrical cheese is made with cows' milk. The diameter is about 15cm, and 8-10 cm thick. The outside is yellow, ranging from quite pale to more vibrant. The actual cheese is anything from milk white to deep yellow. It can be anything from soft to flaky, with no or very few holes in the cheese. The taste ranges from delicate to quite strong. In the Graveglia and Scrivia valleys, it is made by adding in some goats' milk, and in some place it can be salted (in Bonassola, it tends not to be salted). The cheese molds are rubbed with olive oil during the short ageing period. In the province of Savona, especially at Stella, you can find the Formaggetta Savonese or Formaggetta di Stella.

Formaggio di Santo Stéfano

Sometimes called San Stè, this is the best known cheese from the Genoa area, with the main production center being Santo Stéfano d'Àveto. It is made with low-fat cows' milk, generally from the Bruna, Cabannina and Meticcia breeds. It comes in rounds that weigh anything from 3 to 18kg. The crust is thin, flexible and smooth. The color ranges from pale yellow to brownish, depending on the ageing (at least 2 months). The taste is typical of a cows' milk cheese when fresh, becoming stronger with a hint of bitterness as it is aged. The locals love to eat this cheese after heating it on a stone slate.

Mozzarella or Mozzarella di Brugnato

This is a fresh, stringy cheese. It is round, milky white and must always be kept in water. It is made with pasteurized milk that has had some milk enzymes added. When ready, it is shaped in hot water to give it a rounded form.

Pecorino di Malga

This cheese can be eaten as is. It is semi-cooked and made with whole milk. The final form is rounded, with a diameter from

Pecorino cheese, seen here with the addition of chili pepper, is one of the major cheeses made in Liguria.

15-20cm. The cheese that is to be eaten fresh tends to come in slightly flat rounds and is normally aged from 20 to 60 days, meaning the crust is thin, smooth and clear, while the actual cheese is white, soft and compact (or with a few holes). The fresh version is either sweet or slightly bitter. The pecorino that is to be aged, from 2 to 12 months, tends to come in taller rounds, with a thicker, darker crust. The cheese is reasonably hard and the taste tends to be a little spicy. Pecorino plays a major role in Ligurian cuisine, both in pesto – as is well known – and as part of the filling for ravioli and savory pies.

Robiola della Valle Bormida

This sheep's milk cheese is mainly produced in the Bormida valley (Savona). It is a fresh cheese with a soft texture and weighs from 400 to 600g. It is made cold and can only be kept for a few days. It is dry salted and not aged.

GENOVA/GENOA

La Tavola del Doge
Piazza Matteotti 80, Tel. 010562880, latavoladeldoge@libero.it
This is the shop for the Cooperativa Agricola Tavola del Doge. On sale: goats' milk cheese from the Scrivia valley and the Savona hills, cheese from the Aveto valley and Varese Ligure, various formaggette from Savignone. There is also some extra-virgin olive oil, wines, liqueurs, honey, fresh pasta and pesto.

REZZOAGLIO
Caseificio Val d'Aveto
Rezzoaglio Inferiore 35, Tel. 0185870390
www.caseificiovaldaveto.com

Located in the Parco dell'Aveto, they make local cheese using untreated (and unpasteurized milk). You can buy San Stè – the local specialty – as well as *sarazzu*, ricotta, *prescinseua* and *morbidezza*.

IMPERIA

PIGNA
Trattoria la Posta
Via San Rocco 60, Tel. 0184241666
Located in the center, this deli sells a range of local formaggette (made with goats' and cows' milk) as well as local extra-virgin olive oil, olives in oil and brine, savory pies and focaccia bread. There is also a trattoria serving local dishes.

LA SPÈZIA

BRUGNATO
Caseificio Esposito
Via Regurone 13, Tel. 0187894103
www.caseificioesposito.com
This cheese store has been in business since 1956, using only Italian cows' milk. The products still have their traditional taste. In addition to the Mozzarella di Brugnato, you can buy yogurt and a range of cheese, including ricotta.

VARESE LIGURE
Cooperativa Casearia Val di Vara
Perazza, Tel. 0187842108
www.coopcasearia.it
They sell a wonderful range of organically produced cheeses, including Borgorotondo caciotta, Stagionato de Vaise Bio, Tomini Bio, Boscaiola, Divino Macerato nel Ciliegiolo and Stagionato di Varese Ligure allo Sciachetrà. They also have organically produced yoghurt and ricotta cheese.

SAVONA

STELLA
Codara Enrico
Cascina Pasti, Tel. 019706303
www.formaggettadistella.it
They make organic Formaggetta di Stella and have their own herd of goats.

FOOD

OIL

Liguria is a land of hills and mountains – often with steep slopes – that looks out across the Tyrrhenian Sea. The coast line is often dominated by cliffs, with narrow beaches. The climate is mild and temperate, being protected from the north by the hills and mountains, but enjoying a refreshing sea breeze. Space, though, is in short supply. As such, man has learnt to live with the mountains through patient work, creating terraces and small, protective dry walls that vary in size according to the dictates of the land. These little patches of land are where things are cultivated: vegetables, flowers, fruit, vines and, above all, olives, which bring a silvery luster to much of the region. Today, the surface area used for growing olives – although having been reduced somewhat in recent decades because of reforestation and fires – is about 14,000ha, which accounts for about 0.6% of the national production.

Fragmentation and quality

If one looks simply at the numbers, then the results might seem to be quite modest. However, if you take into account the rather unusual geography of this small region, then things seem more impressive. Indeed, the lie of the land not only tends to prohibit great swathes of cultivations, but also the use of mechanized cultivations methods. As such, fragmentation is a rule in these parts. The olive, though, does well despite being right along the northern boundary of the zone where it grows naturally. Olives are grown along the coastal strip, but also further inland, as far as the slopes allow. One advantage is the relative protection from the olive fruit fly.

The olives are generally collected – this is the best word – by hand, meaning that the annual oil production is less than 60,000 lb. As such, the fame Ligurian olive oil and especially extra-virgin olive oil have achieved both across the country and the world is definitely not tied to quantity but rather to the goodness of the product. Indeed, oil from this region is one of the most loved types, because of its gentle taste that tends to exalt the flavors of a dish rather than change or overpower them.

A heritage worth defending

In January 1997, the genuine, local nature of the extra-virgin olive oil led to Liguria receiving the Riviera Ligure DOP (Protected Denomination of Origin, sometimes called PDO) recognition from the European Union. According to this, for extra-virgin olive oil to be recognized as Riviera Ligure DOP it must be made using olives collected directly from the tree before 15 March

each year. No more than 7,000kg of olives can be collected from the specialized olive groves and no more than 25% of this total can be turned into oil. Of course, it must also have the special flavor and smell of Ligurian oil.

The DOP zone for the extra-virgin olive oil covers the whole of Liguria, although there are three, smaller areas that carry a specific geographic mention. The predominant olive in the region is the Taggiasca and this is the source of the specific taste and smell of Ligurian oil. This variety of olive is medium-large in size, producing a good number of olives per tree and a high oil yield.

Despite the widespread nature of this variety, each province has its own, lesser known (but autochthonous) varieties that give the oils their lovely nuances. The geo-

TCI HIGHLIGHTS

FOCACCIA AND FARINATA

Focaccia – a flat bread – is a symbol of Liguria, with its delightful olive oil taste. In Liguria, it can be eaten at any time of the day: with coffee for breakfast, with a glass of wine as a snack or an appetizer. The *focaccerie* – an early type of fast food stall – started in Genoa and can now be found across the world. The dough is made using soft wheat flour, water, olive oil, natural yeast, brewer's yeast and salt. It is then rolled out into a thin layer and placed on a baking tray. Fingers are used to mark it and then it is covered with oil, which tends to accumulate in the depressions. Finally, coarse salt is sprinkled on to it and then it is baked. This is focaccia in its simplest form. It can then be flavored with rosemary, oregano or sage; or olives can be added to the dough; or it can even be covered with a layer of onions. Cheese focaccia is something slightly special, closely associated to the Recco area. The base is a double layer of durum wheat dough; the filling is either fresh formaggetta or stracchino. It also includes

oil and it should be baked in a wood-fired oven. Farinata falls into the same category. It is made with chickpeas, water and salt and then cooked in large tin-coated copper pans. Once again, it can be garnished with herbs or vegetables: rosemary, borage, artichoke, mushroom and much more. One of the most interesting versions sees the addition of *gianchetti*, which are young anchovies, soaked in oil and lemon.

FOOD

graphic label Riviera dei Fiori relates to the province of Imperia, which is the most westerly in the region and the largest producer of olive oil. The extra-virgin olive oil DOP from this zone is made from Taggiasca olives. The province of Savona is covered by the geographic label Riviera del Ponente Savonese. The local extra-virgin olive oil is made from a minimum of 60% of Taggiasca olives, with the addition of various local varieties (Lizona, Morino, Arnasca etc.). As a whole, the Ponente or western section of Liguria has seen a slight reduction in olive growing in recent years, with some new cultivations, such as flowers, taking over. However, it still remains a strong olive-growing area and the products produced here have a special, clearly recognizable taste. The oil is refined, smooth and fluid, with delicate hints of wild herbs and nuances of almond or pine nut.

The products from the eastern section of Liguria, under the geographic label of Riviera di Levante, are more distinct in terms of flavor and color. Those oils are made from Lavagnina (sometimes called the "little Taggiasca", from the zone around Chiàvari), Razzola and Pignola olives. The province of La Spèzia, which also takes in parts of the historical areas of Lunigiana and Versilia, has far fewer olive groves and the cultivars tend to be similar to those found in Tuscany.

In Liguria, there is also a very small amount of Biancardo oil, which is made from over-ripe olives harvested in April.

Techniques that mix the past and the future

The delicacy and the mildness of the oils is not only due to the varieties of olives grown, but also to the methods and times of the harvest and then how the olives are processed. Nowadays, Ligurian oil is more aromatic than before because the new shapes of many olive groves – less tightly clustered and not as steep – allows the use of more modern machines. In recent years, the granite millstones and presses have started to give way to technology and have become more common as memorabilia in museums. Finally, it needs to be mentioned that the fame of Ligurian oil is also linked to the oil refining and selecting industry in the region as well as the bottling industry, which is mainly centered in Oneglia di Imperia. For centuries, these parts of Liguria have produced and bottled considerable quantities of oil both for the local and export markets.

Food and oil

Oil is a fundamental part of regional cuisine, being used in everything from starters to main courses and from fish to meat dishes. For example, there is the famous Ligurian fish, cooked in the oven with olives and potatoes, or the Ligurian rabbit, which is flavored with oil and olives. Yet, the emblem of the region is pesto. Liguria is extremely proud of this product and it comes in thousands of variations with subtle changes. Of course, the essence remains local basil, which is rich in aroma, mixed with oil, a touch of garlic, pine nuts and pecorino cheese. Ligurian oil is also ideal for frying fish, for dressing salads and for making sauces for a range of dishes. It is also essential with the popular local focaccia that is soft, flavorsome and aromatic, leaving you with an unforgettable taste of simplicity.

GENOVA/GENOA

SESTRI LEVANTE
Frantoio Bio
Via della Chiusa 70, Tel. 0185481605
www.frantoio-bio.it
In business since 1867, they make various types of extra-virgin olive oil using Lavagnina and Razzola olives. They also produce olives in brine and in oil.

IMPERIA

Benza Frantoiano
Via Dolcedo 180, Tel. 0183280132
www.oliobenza.it
This agritourism with an oil press is in the lovely Prino valley, near Imperia. They produce cold-pressed extra-virgin olive oil DOP using only Taggiasca olives that they grow. You can also buy Taggiasca olives preserved in brine and olive pâté.

Frantoio di Sant'Agata d'Oneglia di Mela
in Oneglia, an der Kreuzung
Via S. Agata Strada dei Francesi, Tel. 0183293472
www.frantoiosantagata.com
They make five types of extra-virgin olive oil, including one DOP with Taggiasca olives. They also produce a range of vegetables preserved in oil and some Ligurian sauces.

BADALUCCO
Olio Roi di Boeri Franco
Via Argentina 1, Tel. 0184408004
www.olioroi.com
In business for over a century, they produce cold-pressed extra-virgin olive oil from Taggiasca olives. Their other specialties are Taggiasca olives in brine and pitted olives in oil. They have a range of flavored oils, vegetables preserved in oil and some Ligurian sauces.

 ## TCI HIGHLIGHTS

THE CARLI BROTHERS' OIL MUSEUM

The olive museum is located in the heart of the western side of the Ligurian Riviera, which is one of the main oil producing zones of the modern age. The museum is part of the Carli oil production plant and it allows the visitor to learn more about the processes and dynamics that are the origin of many aspects of the contemporary Ligurian landscape. The museum was born of the Carli families passion for olives and olive oil and from some of the material that the family itself had collected over the course of a century. After many years of research and study, the museum was opened in 1992 in an art nouveau building that was the company's first headquarters. In 2002, the museum was extended to illustrate more clearly the importance of olives in various Mediterranean countries. It also has a

CAMPOROSSO

Azienda Agrituristica Il Bausco

Brunetti, Tel. 0184206013
www.ilbausco.com
This organic farm produces extra-virgin olive oil DOP using Taggiasca olives (first pressed cold) and Rossese di Dolceàcqua DOC wine. They also sell a range of other organically grown fruit and vegetables.

CHIUSAVECCHIA

Anfosso

Via IV Novembre 96/bis,
Tel. 018352418
www.olioanfosso.it
In business since 1955, this farm produces cold-pressed extra-virgin olive oil from Taggiasca (DOP) and Tumai olives. They also make a range of pesto and other sauces.

LA SPÈZIA

LÈVANTO

Coop. Agricoltori Vallata di Lèvanto

Le Ghiare, Via S. Matteo 20,
Tel. 0187800867
www.levanto.com/cooperativa
The shop of this cooperative sells cold-pressed extra-virgin olive oil DOP from Razzola olives, various items preserved in oil, olives in brine, wine, honey and jam.

SAVONA

Azienda Olivicola Canaiella

Via Canaiella 4, Tel. 019860190
www.canaiella.it
This farm, with Aiab organic certification, sits about 135m above sea level on a natural terrace surrounded by woods of lush, wild vegetation. They produce cold-pressed extra-virgin olive oil from Taggiasca olives as well as olive pate and pesto.

ALBENGA

Antico Frantoio Sommariva

Via Mameli 7, Tel. 0182559222
www.oliosommariva.it
For over 100 years, this oil press, located within the Medieval walls of the town, has been making Nuovo Mosto extra-virgin olive oil by cold pressing organic olives. It also has other typical Ligurian specialties: pesto, walnut sauce, artichokes in oil and Taggiasca olives in brine.

LOANO

Oleificio Polla Nicolò

Via Ghilini 46, Tel. 019668027
www.oliopolla.it
For over a century, they have been making cold-pressed extra-virgin olive oil from Taggiasca olives. Tradition remains very important here, especially when it comes to drawing out the flavor in the olives. Also sell olives in brine.

FOOD

library, which can be visited on request. The building opposite the museum now houses a conference center, various places to get something to eat and a souvenir shop, obviously selling items linked to olives and producing olive oil. During the olive harvest, you can also see how the fruit is processed using the modern machinery owned by the Carli brothers. The museum itself has a range of objects, including archaeological finds, books, texts, old machinery and equipment used in making oil. The oldest items are 4,500 years old and come from various places. All of this material tells the story of the tree that is the symbol of Mediterranean culture as well as examining the botanical, technological and commercial elements of olives and olive oil as their symbolism and uses. The garden, with its numerous age-old trees, has reconstructions of some ancient presses and mills from various countries across the Mediterranean: perhaps the most notable ones are an ancient lever press, various Ligurian ones and some Spanish ones. There are also some old jars and ceramic containers that, for thousands of years, were used to store the oil. These come from Italy, Turkey, Greece, Spain and Portugal.

The museum is in Imperia, at Via Garessio 13, Tel. 0183295762,
ww.museodellolivo.com

WINE

The growing of vines in Liguria is caught between two opposites: on the one side, the Mediterranean climate is particularly favorable to agriculture and on the other, the land is uneven and cultivable land is jealously guarded. This region consists of an "arch" of mountains that runs near the coast, often forming steep slopes and cliffs. Yet, on the other side, the wonderful sunlight pushes winemakers to grow vines and thus spend countless hours maintaining the terraced slopes that dominate so much of the coast. These restrictions have, though, meant the amount of wine produced in the region is and always has been limited, with small, specialized vineyards tending to be the norm. In recent years, the creation of some new DOC zones has led to a certain upturn in production, but it remains relatively rare to find Ligurian wines beyond the regional boundaries.

Numerous type of grapes, two great wines

One of the key characteristics of winemaking in Liguria is the high quality of the vines. Not long ago, the region had as many as 85 different types of wine, which is quite amazing considering the size of Liguria. Furthermore, the majority where whites, made from a mix of grapes (around 100 types of grapes are grown). This is a fairly common tendency for regions that face onto the sea, since the amount of sea traffic – and consequently of inland traffic – tended to encourage growing varieties from far-off and not-so-far-off lands. For example, it seems that Vermentino arrived here from Spain, after passing via Corsica. The Dolcetto came across the Apennine passes from Piedmont. Tuscany accounted for Canaiolo, Ciliegiolo Nero, Trebbiano Toscano and Vernaccia del Chianti. Many other grapes have been in the area for centuries, although little is known of their paths - or sea routes - here. This is the case for Rossese, which is the basis for Dolceàcqua DOC as well as for Bosco and Albarola, which are used to make various wines from Cinque Terre. The creation of DOC areas has greatly reduced the number of grapes grown, resulting in a higher, more homogenous quality of grapes. Of course, such development also leads to fears about what else might soon be lost from this long winemaking heritage.

A winemaking heritage with 7 DOC wines

Winemaking in Liguria is dominated by what could be termed two "historic" DOC areas, namely Cinque Terre and Rossese di Dolceàcqua (interestingly, located at opposite ends of the region) and five more recent additions, namely Collina di Lèvanto, Colli di Luni, Golfo del Tigullio, Riviera Ligure di Ponente and Valpolcevera. Some others have Typical Geographic Indication (normally abbreviated using the Italian intials, IGT), such as Golfo dei Poeti, Spezzino and Colline Savonesi. Yet, despite this recent reorganization of Ligurian wine, the tendency is still to see wine from this region as being tied to just a few products that have achieved renown across the country because of the fame they once enjoyed. For starters, Sciacchetrà is a sweet wine that is inseparably tied to the panoramic landscape of Cinque Terre. The name actually comes from the fusion of two local words: 'sciac', meaning to press, and 'trà', to keep (away, store), a reference to the long ageing of the product. The grapes – which have been turned into raisins – are pressed and then removed from the vat after only 24 hours. The most is placed in barrels immediately, after which it is moved from one vat to another about 3 times before eventually being bottled in April. This elaborate process keeps the level of sugar high and gives the wine the desired, smooth taste. Next on the list of the famed Ligurian wines is the Rossese di Dolceàcqua, the only truly notable red from the region. This wine is also tied to a specific part of the region inland from Ventimìglia in a zone of ancient beauty and alive with tradition.

Cinque Terre and Cinque Terre Sciacchetrà DOC

The zone for this wine includes the municipalities of Monterosso, Vernazza and Riomaggiore along with the villages of Biassa and Tramonti di Campiglia in the La Spèzia municipality. The Cinque Terre white is a pale yellow color, with a strong nose. It goes best with fish and other dishes cooked in tinfoil. The Passito Sciacchetrà is a particular favorite, which is made with the same grapes as the normal version, but they are allowed to become raisins and the wine is only made after 1 November of the harvest year. It has a strong nose, with a clear sense of honey. It is best with desserts, at the end of meals or possibly as an after dinner drink.

Colli di Luni DOC

The zone for this wine is on the border between Liguria and Tuscany along the Magra valley. It comes in various forms: Bianco (white), pale yellow with a dry, smooth taste; and Vermentino, with a delicate, winy nose. There is also the Rosso (red), which is ruby red with a dry, smooth taste. It goes with various different dishes.

Colline di Lèvanto DOC

This zone is in the province of La Spèzia, in the municipalities of Lèvanto, Bonassola, Framura and Deiva Marina.

The recognised DOC area covers a Bianco that is pale yellow with a delicate, persistent nose with slightly fruity hints and a smooth, dry taste. It also includes the Rosso. It is ruby red, with a delicate, smooth and medium-bodied taste. Finally, the DOC also includes a Novello (new or nouveau) version.

Golfo del Tigullio DOC

This zone covers the hills inland of Genoa, including 35 municipalities (some municipalities are only partly covered) in addition to the regional capital. The DOC label covers: Bianco (also in a sparkling or Frizzante version), with a delicate nose and a dry, full-bodied taste that goes well with fish dishes and starters; the yellowy Bianco Passito, which is best at the end of a meal and is aged from somewhere between 1 and 5 or 6 years; Bianchetta Genovese (also in a Frizzante version), which has a dry, full-bodied taste and goes well with a starter or most fish dishes; the Moscato and Moscato Passito are sweet and smooth, going best with desserts or enjoyed alone, perhaps after a meal; the pale yellow Vermentino has hints of green and also comes in a Frizzante version; the Spumante, which has a refined nose and a dry, fresh taste that makes it ideal with summer meals and desserts;

FOOD

TCI HIGHLIGHTS

WINE CATEGORIES

Three labels define Italian wines according to quality. The top label is DOCG (Guaranteed and Controlled of Denomination of Origin); there are around 20 DOCG wines in Italy. DOC (Controlled of Denomination of Origin) indicates conformity to regulations for a given area of origin, and production and maturation procedures. IGT (Typical Geographic Indication) guarantees vine cultivation according to certain regulations. VDT is for table wine with an alcohol content of at least 10%.

Rosato (also Frizzante), which is aged for 2 years and goes well with various dishes; the ruby-red Rosso that is dry and full bodied with some tannins (also produced in Frizzante and Novello versions); and finally, the Ciliegiolo, with a lasting, fruity nose and a color that varies from cherry to ruby red. The latter also comes in Frizzante and Novello and can be drunk with various dishes.

Riviera Ligure di Ponente DOC

The zone covered by this DOC is quite large, mainly being concentrated in the wine-growing areas of the provinces of Imperia and Savona in the western section of Liguria. The following wines are covered by the DOC recognition: Ormeasco (Riviera dei Fiori sub-zone), a ruby red wine with a dry, pleasant but slightly bitter taste that is largely the result of the recommended 3 years of ageing; the Superiore version, which must be aged for 1 year (and can be aged for up to 4) and goes well with red meat and a range of game dishes; Rossese (Riviera dei Fiori, Albenga and Finale sub-zones), a clear, ruby red with a delicate, winy nose that is normally aged for 3 years and goes well with various dishes; the coral-pink Ormeasco *Sciac-trà*, with a pleasant, dry taste; Pigato (Riviera dei Fiori, Albenga and Finale sub-zones), a dry, slightly bitter, almondy wine that tends to be pale yellow and is best served with fish dishes; and the Vermentino (Riviera dei Fiori, Albenga and Finale sub-zones), which has a fresh, dry taste and a pale yellow color. The latter is best aged for up to 2 years and goes well with a variety of fish dishes.

Rossese di Dolceàcqua or Dolceàcqua DOC

This DOC zone covers the best area for the Rossese grape, which includes the Dolceàcqua municipality (in the province of Imperia) and various other neighboring centers in the Nervia valley. This is a unique type of wine that is ruby red or pomegranate (when aged) in color. The nose is winy and intense but delicate and the taste is smooth, aromatic and warm. It is normally aged for 4 to 5 years (for the Superiore version, it must be aged for at least a year and can be aged for 5/6 years or even more). It goes well with red meat, game dishes and some types of aged cheese.

Valpolcevera DOC

This is produced in the area inland of Genoa, in the Sant'Olcese, Serra Riccò, Mignanego, Campomorone, Ceranesi and Genoa municipalities. It comes in various types, all of which are covered by the DOC recognition. The Bianco is pale yellow with a delicate, persistent nose. It goes well with starters and fish, and comes in Frizzante and Spumante versions. The Rosso is a dry, medium-bodied wine with a pleasant nose with winy hints. It goes well with vegetable soups and light meals. It also comes in Frizzante and Novello versions. Rosato (also availabe in a Frizzante version) has a fresh, dry and smooth taste, making it better with light meals than heavy feasts. The color ranges from reddish to ruby red to clear. The Bianchetta Genovese is pale yellow

Dolceàcqua, the bridge over the Nervia.

in color, with a nose that can be intense although it is not always so. It goes well with starters and fish dishes (also available in Frizzante and Spumante versions). The pale yellow Vermentino has hints of green and the taste is dry and smooth. The Coronata is a white wine with an easily identifiable, delicate nose. Both the Coronata and Vermentino go well with fish dishes and a range of starters. Finally, the last version covered by this DOC is the Passito. It is ideal with desserts as it has a sweet, warm flavor that is quite persistent and full-bodied.

GENOVA/GENOA

CHIÀVARI
Bisson
Corso Gianelli 28, Tel. 0185314462
www.terredetrinci.com
- ● D.O.C. Golfo del Tigullio Rosso Il Musaico
- ● D.O.C. Golfo del Tigullio Rosso Ciliegiolo
- ● I.G.T. Granaccia
- ● I.G.T. Musaico 2005 Rosso
- ○ D.O.C. Golfo del Tigullio Bianchetta Genovese U Pastine
- ○ D.O.C. Golfo del Tigullio Vermentino Vigna Erta
- ◐ D.O.C. Cinque Terre Sciacchetrà
- ◐ D.O.C. Golfo del Tigullio Passito Acinirari

IMPERIA

Tenuta Colle dei Bardellini
Bardellini, Via Fontanarosso 12,
Tel. 0183291370
www.colledeibardellini.it
- ● D.O.C. Riviera Ligure di Ponente Rossese
- ○ D.O.C. Riviera Ligure di Ponente Pigato Vigna La Torretta
- ○ D.O.C. Riviera Ligure di Ponente Vermentino Vigna U Munte

CHIUSANICO
La Rocca di San Nicolao
Gazzelli, Via Dante 10,
Tel. 018352850
- ○ D.O.C. Riviera Ligure di Ponente Pigato
- ○ D.O.C. Riviera Ligure di Ponente Pigato Riviera dei Fiori Vigna dei Proxi
- ○ D.O.C. Riviera Ligure di Ponente Vermentino Riviera dei Fiori Vigna dei Proxi
- ○ D.O.C. Riviera Ligure di Ponente Vermentino Riviera dei Fiori Vigna dei Proxi Barrique

LA SPÈZIA

DOLCEÀCQUA
Terre Bianche
Arcana, Tel. 018431426
- ● D.O.C. Rossese di Dolceàcqua
- ● V.D.T. Arcana Rosso
- ○ D.O.C. Riviera Ligure di Ponente Pigato
- ○ D.O.C. Riviera Ligure di Ponente Vermentino
- ○ V.D.T. Arcana Bianco

ORTONOVO
Lunae Bosoni
Luni, Via Bozzi 63, Tel. 0187669222
www.cantinelunae.com
- ● D.O.C. Colli di Luni Rosso Niccolò V
- ○ D.O.C. Colli di Luni Bianco Onda Luna
- ○ D.O.C. Colli di Luni Vermentino Cavagino
- ○ D.O.C. Colli di Luni Vermentino Etichetta Grigia
- ○ D.O.C. Colli di Luni Vermentino Etichetta Nera

SAVONA

ALBENGA
Cascina Feipu dei Massaretti
Bastia, Tel. 018220131
- ● V.D.T. Riviera Ligure di Ponente Rossese di Albenga
- ● V.D.T. Russu du Feipu
- ● I.G.T. Granaccia
- ○ D.O.C. Riviera Ligure di Ponente Pigato Cascina Feipu

Amaretto di Sassello, named after the well-known amaretto biscuits, is definitely the best known regional liqueur. It is not, though, as some people think, the only regional liqueur; indeed, there are plenty of other ones, many of which are still made using age-old recipes. The production of beer only originated in the previous century. However, this relative lack of tradition does not seem to have hampered this industry. Much of the beer is quite unusual and so well worth trying.

Amaretto di Sassello

This liqueur originated in Sassello, a small place in the Ligurian section of the Apennines in the province of Savona that is famous for its amaretto biscuits. The drink is made by mixing, whilst cold, water, alcohol, various herbs and caramel. All this is done in a specific blender and using filters. The result is a sweet liqueur that is caramel in color with an alcohol percentage of 25%. The aroma is strong and the taste has clear traces of caramel. It is bottled in special glass bottles and then labeled with traditional labels. There is a variant, called Amaro di Sassello, which has a higher alcohol percentage (30%). The history of this drink dates back to 1850 when, according to the tradition, a local family invented the drink for themselves. Amaretto di Sassello is still produced using the original recipe and the traditional artisan methods. It is a dessert liqueur, but it can also go well with fruit salads or coffee.

Birra di Savignone

This beer is made in Busalla and Savignone (Genova). In 1878, two Swiss entrepreneurs opened a brewery. Today, the factory makes a range of beers, including more traditional larger and ale as well as some unusual beer with honey and, in season, chestnuts (collected by hand from the mountains around Genoa, then dried and crushed using stone – all this gives the beer a special aroma). The beer from here tends to be quite low in alcohol, focusing more on being a refreshing, energizing drink.

Distillato di Prugna

This prune schnapps (or grappa) is made by crushing and then fermenting the fruit. After the harvest, the fruit is left in special, humidity-controlled rooms in barrels for 2 months. The mixture is then distilled using copper alambic stills and the foreshots and feints are separated until the liquid reaches an alcohol percentage of 45%. Once the liquid has been aged, it is bottled in glass bottles. The majority of this grappa is produced in Varese Ligure.

Sciroppo di Rose

Production zone: Genoa, Scrivia valley and Stura valley. Literally meaning rose syrup, this drink is made with rose petals and has an intense color and smell. By adding water, it becomes an excellent, thirst-quenching drink for the summer or, in winter, by combing the syrup with some warm water, it becomes an effective cough remedy. It seems that there is no single, precise recipe for making this syrup as every producer has its own specific method. In general, the rose petals are collected in late May or early June, and then soaked in water before being boiled and allowed to infuse for about 24 hours. After this, the leaves are filtered and pressed. Sugar is added and then the mixture is boiled, but the temperature must be kept as low as possible to ensure the syrup does not cook. In the Scrivia valley variant, a touch of lemon is also added. The liquid is then bottled while still warm to help its preservation.

Vin de Meie (or peie)

This drink can also be called a cider. *Vin de meie de Monteuggio* or *aegua de meie* is produced in the upper Scrivia valley in the province of Genoa. This apple cider has a deep color and a delicate, yet persistent smell. The taste is pleasantly sweet and fresh, making it ideal with desserts and cakes, such as canestrelli, a type of biscuit shaped like a donut and made with short pastry.

CAKES

Italy has a wide range of cakes, sweet pastries and desserts, and Liguria – with the regional capital Genoa at its heart – forms an important and unique part of this. No other section of the peninsula has so much cultural history and such a steep coastline that has been cut into terraces where fruit trees and vines grow at the lower levels, followed by olive groves and then chestnuts slightly higher up before even these give way to pines. This history and landscape have ensured a mingling of traditions and flavors, many of which came from across the seas – especially the plentiful use of spices that has clear connections to more eastern and north African cuisines – and from across the Apennines, especially from Piedmont and Emilia, the source of many cakes. Against this general background, two rather unusual elements deserve mention. First, there is the tradition of *confetteria* or confectionary, which is linked to the abundance of sugar of Arabian provenance. This sugar supply is also a reason for the many syrups and candied fruits, including the rare sour orange. Secondly, there is an age-old passion for chocolate, which arrived in Piedmont with the Spanish court but then made its way across the mountains to Genoa and the whole of the Riviera. In recent times, the trappings of tourism have added to this: pastry houses, cabaret bars, grand hotels and cruises all brought a desire for sweet things. Of course, such a tradition would be amiss without some wine that evokes centuries of sun-washed sweetness, namely the mythic Sciacchetrà delle Cinque Terre.

Amaretti di Sassello

Sassello is a delightful little town inland from Savona. The town is closely associated with the amaretto, or almond biscuit; however, this biscuit does not merely represent part of the local cuisine, but also local entrepreneurialism. In 1860, a housewife named Gertrude Damia decided to take her passion for the baking and turn it into a business. The central element of her business was this small, round biscuit made with crushed sweet and bitter almonds, sugar, egg white and a touch of vanilla. The biscuits were wrapped in elegant, thin paper with frayed ends and had a delicate smell, combining a consistent texture with lightness. Indeed, the idea was as effective as it was simple and in no time at all, the oven where the biscuits were made became an attraction. The bakery was even drawn on local postcards, with the caption "Piazza degli Amaretti Virginia". For many Italians, the tin boxes with careful illustrations are part of the collective memory.

Amaretti di Sassello biscuits are unmistakable, especially the almondy aroma.

Baci di Alàssio

These soft biscuits have two halves of almond biscuit (simple or with chocolate) with a soft cocoa cream in the middle. In Albenga, they are called *baxin*. Variants of this biscuit are found across the region.

Biscotti del Lagaccio or Biscotto della salute di Sarzana

Made across the region. This dry biscuit is ideal for breakfast. It is made with soft wheat flour, sugar and, in some versions, sweet fennel. These large

Baci di Alàssio.

biscuits are like long pieces of bread with small cuts on the surface.
They are baked in an oven to dry them out and then cut along the incisions before being baked some more.
The lightness, simplicity and durability of these biscuits have earned them the nickname "health biscuits".

Biscotti di Genova

These biscuits are made with soft wheat flour, castor sugar, peeled almonds, eggs, lemon rind and butter.
After being baked in the oven, the biscuits are shaped using a knife and then baked some more to turn them into crispy biscuits.

Buccellato or Ciambelon

It is produced in the Garzano area and the Magra valley. This donut-shaped cake is about 25cm wide and somewhere between 2-3cm thick. It is slightly golden in color, with a crispy exterior and a soft interior, thanks to various phases of rising and mixing. It is made with flour, eggs, sugar, milk, butter, yeast, lemon essence and orange blossom. It is then shaped like a donut and coated with egg yolk and some sugar. Next, it is allowed to stand before, finally, being baked.

Buccellato spezzino is sometimes called ciambelon.

Canestrelli

Made across the region, these short pastry biscuits are golden and shaped like little donuts. They are quite sweet with a soft, crumbly interior.
The dough consists of flour, sugar, butter and bicarbonate. The biscuits are coated with milk and sugar before being baked for 10 minutes at 150°C/302°F.

Canestrelli di Torriglia.

Canestrelli di Torriglia

These little donut-shaped biscuits are made with short pastry that is baked. The dough contains fine flour, butter, sugar and eggs.

Castagnaccio

Produced across the region, the name indicates a link to chestnuts since *castagna* is chestnut in Italian. In addition to chestnut flour, it is made with pine nuts, raisins, fennel seeds, olive oil and some salt. The result is an aroma that is unmistakable. The first step is to make a mixture of water, chestnut flour and salt, which is placed on a baking tray that has been greased with some oil. Soften the raisins in warm water, then strain the water and sprinkle the raisins on the mixture along with the pine nuts and fennel seeds. Cover with some more oil and then bake in an oven at 190°C/374°F until cracks start to appear on the surface. It can be eaten hot or cold.

Chinotto Candito di Savona

The chinotto is a small, sour orange that is inedible in its natural state. It comes from a tree of Chinese origin and it is mainly grown in western Liguria. Today, it is only found in the cuisine of Savona and only on an artisan level. After the fruit has been candied in sugar, it is bottled in slightly alcoholic syrup. This is not a true dessert, so to speak, but was traditionally offered to guests.

Marzapani Quaresimali

This age-old recipe is derived from the Torta Genovese that, in the 14th century, the Sediario family of Genoa would send to the courts in Ferrara and Mantua. The modern version consists of small almond pastries coated in icing flavored with chocolate, vanilla, mint or the like. They are baked for a short time in the oven and then decorated with colored, coated almonds.

Pandolce Genovese or Pan-a-duse

According to the legend, it was the Doge Andrea Doria in the 16th century who organized a competition between the master pastry chefs in the city to create a cake that was a fitting symbol of Genoa's wealth and true to the city's marine history. The cake also needed to be nutritious and able to keep for a long time so that it could be taken aboard the ships on their long journeys. That was the origin of the pandolce (literally, sweet bread), which is a sort of focaccia made with a risen dough of eggs, butter and honey. This bread is filled with raisins, pine nuts, pistachios and candied fruit. Fennel seeds, vanilla, orange blossom water and a sweet wine (perhaps Marsala) are also used to added flavor. The legend cannot be verified, but pandolce has definitely become the Christmas cake for Liguria. Eating the cake – at New Year – is also filled with symbolism: the youngest member of the family has to place an olive or bay twig on top, as a sign of devotion; the oldest member has to cut the cake in such a way as to ensure there is an extra slice for the first needy person who comes to the door. The cake can stay fresh for up to a month. Then it dries out and can be kept for ages, as it only needs to be popped in the oven to "resuscitate" it. These days, it can be

Pandolce genovese has a long tradition.

found in pastry houses throughout the year. The traditional form – tall and well risen – is often found side-by-side with the flatter, more compact modern one.

Spungata di Sarzana

This round, fairly flat cake is quite spongy in the upper part. It is cream colored with clear icing. It is made with puff pastry filled with apples and pears chopped in pieces (or as jam), pine nuts, almonds, spices and natural flavorings. It is made in a wooden bowl: a layer of pastry is placed on the bottom

A typical spungata.

and then covered with the filling before a second layer of pastry is added. The edges are carefully closed and then the top is covered with icing made of icing sugar and egg white. The top is then perforated to help it bake (180/200°C-356/392°F).

Torcetto

The biscuits are from the Bormida valley and are normally associated with the town of Mallare. They are fried, sweet biscuits flavored with liqueur. The ingredients are flour, sugar, butter, rum, egg, yeast, grated lemon rind and olive oil. The eggs are beaten with the sugar, then the liqueur, lemon rind and softened butter are added in. The flour is sieved together with the yeast powder and then the remaining ingredients are added in. This is all mixed together carefully to get a smooth, relatively uniform dough. This is then shaped into finger-sized pieces, which are bent into oval shaped rings. These are then fried in hot oil.

GENOVA/GENOA

Panarello
Via XX Settembre 154/r,
Tel. 010562238
Corso Buenos Aires 43/r,
Tel. 010591638
Via Caprera 4F/r, Tel. 010312414
Via Galata 67/r, Tel. 010561037
www.panarello.com
This shop is an icon for cakes and desserts in Genoa. They make traditional and modern pandolce, Biscotti di Lagaccio and various other local specialties.

CAMOGLI
Budicin
Ruta, Via Aurelia 186, Tel. 0185770523
A very traditional pastry house where you can buy traditional and modern pandolce, canestrelli, baci di dama and some other interesting cakes and desserts.

CHIÀVARI
Gran Caffè Defilla
Corso Garibaldi 4, Tel. 0185309829
In business for over 100 years, this is a good place to try some local specialties, including sorrisi di Chiàvari al maraschino, pandolce and many others.

IMPERIA

Pasticceria Angelo
Via Nazionale 8, Tel. 0183291814
This artisan pastry house is a good place to try baci di Imperia, torta sacripantina, pane del pescatore and, at Christmas, pandolce.

SANREMO
La Veneziana
Corso Cavallotti 227, Tel. 0184502050
They have been making baci di Sanremo, pane del pescatore, amaretti and treccia della nonna for over 40 years.

LA SPÈZIA

Stampetta
Corso Cavour 245 and 375,
Tel. 0187718029
They produce a range of fresh and dry pastries, including pandolce. If those are not enough to tempt one, then they also have an enticing range of chocolates.

SARZANA
Gemmi
Via Mazzini 21/23, Tel. 0187620165
gemmi2004@libero.it
This traditional pastry house in the old center produces a range of homemade cakes and biscuits, including amaretti, buccellato and focaccia di Sarzana.

SAVONA

Amaretti Astengo
Via Montenotte 16/r,
Tel. 019820570
This pastry house has been in business since way back in 1878. It makes amaretti, pandolce, torta sacripantina and various chocolate cakes and biscuits.

ALÀSSIO
Balzola
Piazza Matteotti 26, Tel. 0182640209
This old pastry house, founded over a century ago, produces a range of artisans cakes and desserts, including baci di Alàssio and a number of different types of chocolate.

ALBENGA
Grana
Via Palestro 7, Tel. 018250875
In the old center, they sell a wide range of local cakes, biscuits and pralines, including baci di Albenga, pane del pescatore, gobeletti and a special biscuit bread with chocolate and almonds.

SASSELLO
Amaretti Giacobbe
Pian Ferioso 62, Tel. 019724860
www.vislink.it/amarettigiacobbe/
In business for over 50 years, the company was founded at a time when many artisans where becoming industrial, but this company has always strived to keep its artisan roots. It sells the traditional amaretto di Sassello as well as some rather interesting variants of this classic (coconut, apricot, citrus fruit, cocoa, coffee, hazelnut and rum).

Food and Wine Festivals

MAY

⤷ Second Sunday in May
SAGRA DEL CANESTRELLO
Torriglia (Genova)

Town hall, Tel. 010944038
The festival is a relatively new addition to the calendar, but it is growing in popularity every year. Canestrelli, biscuits with six points, have become an integral part of this area and during the event, vast quantities of these biscuits are given out for free in the streets of the town.

⤷ Second Sunday in May
SAGRA DEL PESCE
Camogli (Genova)

Town hall, Tel. 0185572901
camogli.cultura@libero.it
The festival, celebrated since 1952, is linked to the anniversary of St Fortune, patron saint of fishermen. The town has an enormous frying pan (4m wide) that hangs on the side of a house for the rest of the year. On the Sunday morning, the pan is blessed, filled with oil and heated on a large fire. Once warm, fish are fried and then given out for free for a couple

of hours. During the afternoon, a massive amount of frying is done, with 2 tons of fresh passing through the pan!

⤷ Fourth Sunday in May
SAGRA DELLA FOCACCIA
Recco (Genova)

IAT Tel. 0185722440
The famous focaccia di Recco is at the center of this festival, which is the pride of this sea-side town. Two stalls are set up, one along the seaside promenade and the other on the main square, where two types of focaccia are given away: in the morning, you can get the one with onions as well as the traditional one with cheese, while in the afternoon only the traditional one is given away.

JULY

⤷ Second last weekend in July
SAGRA DEL BAGNUN
Sestri Levante (Genova)

Associazione del Bagnun
Tel. 01854781
www.bagnun.it
info@comune.sestri-levante.it
One of the most deeply-rooted traditions in Riva Trigoso, a seaside district of Sestri Levante in eastern Liguria, is the Sagra del Bagnun. This wonderful festival has been held on the third weekend of July for over 40 years. At the festival, thousands of dishes of Bagnun – a tasty, typically seaside dish made with anchovies – are given away to participants. Over the years, this event has become a highlight for tourists and locals alike. Every thing kicks off with the Bagnun being given out and then continues with dancing to music performed by an orchestra and a fireworks display over the sea.

⤷ Third weekend in July
FESTA DEL MARE - MUSCOLATA
Loano (Savona)

Town hall, Tel. 019676007
www.forchettina.it/
sagre_feste_liguria
info@comune.rapallo.ge.it
The Festa del Mare: Muscolata d'Estate is held at the seafront at the Casetta dei Lavoratori del Mare. Seafood is the key, especially mussels. Over 12 quintals of mussels end up in the massive frying pan (2m wide) and are cooked using a traditional local recipe that uses fresh regional tomatoes, garlic, parsley, white wine and extra-virgin olive oil. The event is organized by the Comitato Sagra del Crostolo with backing from the municipal office for culture and tourism.

AUGUST

⤷ First Saturday in August
SAGRA DU PIGNURIN
Ospedaletti (Imperia)

Town hall, Tel. 018468221
www.comune.ospedaletti.im.it
During this festival, 10 quintals of pignurin, a small fish that is common along the Riviera di Ponente, is cooked in enormous pans and then given out with bread and some local white wine. There are also various dishes available with prawns, swordfish, potatoes chips and meat. The event, which dates from 1970, recalls the time when the fishermen would meet at the shore to celebrate the arrival of summer and the return of the fishing season.

⤷ 14 August
TORTA DEI FIESCHI
Lavagna (Genova)

Town hall, Tel. 0185367284
www.comune.lavagna.ge.it
Every year, Lavagna comes alive with colors, lights, outfits and old music in the traditional pageant known as the Torta dei Fieschi. It involves a parade with people in medieval outfits that winds its way through the old streets of the town. The characters who parade are from the 6 traditional town districts. This is accompanied by giving out slices of an enormous cake. Every participant gets a ticket with an imaginary name on it and has to find the person who was given an identical ticket. Only those people who have found their "other" can get a slice of the cake.

SEPTEMBER

⤷ Fourth week in September
FESTA DEL FUNGO
Triora (Imperia)

www.comune.triora.im.it
Mushrooms are the heart of this festival. Porcini mushrooms, cooked in a range of different ways, abound.

⤷ Second last weekend in September
FESTA DEL TARTUFO
Millèsimo (Savona)

Comunità Montana Val Bormida, Tel. 019564344
Local restaurants and special stalls offer various delights based on truffles. Piazza Italia is the center for various events and shows.

FOOD

The patient and industrious people of Liguria are proud of their land, as can be seen from the wonderful array of handmade objects that they have been producing for centuries. The limits on local raw materials meant that quality was always prized over quantity. A good example of this is the glass-making of Altare. Albisola is the home of ceramics, while Campo Ligure is famed for its artisan filigree production. The Tigullio Gulf and the Fontanabuona valley are both known for their fabrics: velvet, damask, brocatel and various types of lace, including pillow lace. Flint is another important local material, being used for roofs as well as for decorating church facades, cooking over fires, make school blackboards and as the base for pool and snooker tables. Chiàvari is synonymous with wood-working, especially in the form of the Chiavarine chairs. The earliest chairs were designed and created, in the early 19th century, by Gaetano Descalzi,

🔵	**CERAMICS**
🔵	**SLATE**
🔵	**FABRICS AND EMBROIDERY**
🔵	**WOOD**
🔵	**GOLDSMITHERY**
🔵	**GLASS**
🔵	**FASHION**

known as "Campanino". His nickname is still used for his original chair, which became the basis for the far more famous Chiavarina chair. Indeed, the latter achieved renown across the world with its simple, robust lines and lightness.

Shopping

Highlights

- For over 8 centuries, the Albisola ceramic industry has continued to thrive.
- In the late 19th century, Campo Ligure became one of the leading European filigree production centers.
- Wrought iron working was once a thriving local industry and is still practiced in the hinterland.
- From the great, international trade fairs to the small arts & crafts markets.

Inside

ARTS AND CRAFTS

Liguria might be a heavily industrialized area, but it is not hard to find evidence of older – but not always that old – crafts. The artisan world in Liguria is rich in valuable, interesting items that are the fruit of centuries of experience that has been handed down through the generations and refined by dedicated research. Furthermore, the people of Liguria are by nature and by history – one need only think of the centuries spent trading with peoples from far-off lands – driven towards forms of expression that are neither banal nor superficial. Ligurian crafts are undoubtedly filled with effort, but they are also linked to the land's cultural past and to the inner questioning that helps transform objects that are beautiful and functional into gateways to a world that is far more complex than it might initially seem. As such, at least for Liguria, one cannot judge the importance of crafts merely from the number of craftsmen or assistants. Indeed, no artisan trade can be considered extinct in these parts as long as even a single practitioner remains active.

Ceramics

The world famous Albisola ceramics have a recorded history in the Savona area dating from the 12th century AD. These ceramics are easily recognizable because of the use of blue decorations and figures – obtained using cobalt oxide – on a white or blue-gray background. The 13th century saw the introduction of tin-based glazes, leading to the advent of the early majolica, often called archaic majolica. In the 16th century, during the time of the Republic of Genoa, this craft enjoyed an unprecedented period of growth as both the quantity and the quality of production bounded forward, led by a series of famous artisan families from the Albisola area that brought international recognition to this ceramic production. This was also a great time of cultural exchange, favoring improvements in the degree of expression contained in the work. By the 17th century, the ceramic market was well established, allowing artisans to focus more on aesthetic and stylistic questions. In the first few decades of the century a form of Chinese decoration known as "naturalistic calligraphic" was introduced, but western stylistic elements – castles, landscapes and human figures - were soon combined with these more oriental ones. The second half of the same century saw this style of work being joined with another known as "tapestry style", in which mythological and historical figures were placed amid decorations of leaves, clouds and little birds. From here though, it was not until after the middle of the 18th century that any major new development took place. At that time, the traditional cobalt blue work of Albisola was transformed, with the addition of purple and pink manganese backgrounds (called Levantino) and light brown colors (Seirullo). In the 19th century, the growth of industry sparked a radical change for crafts in the Savona area: on the one hand, a new form a ceramic production – for the mass market – saw the use of black decorations; on the other hand, a section specialized in highly artistic work. In the 20th century, Albisola ceramics became part and parcel of avant-garde artistic movements, most notably

A part of one of the ceramic works along the seafront walk in Albisola.

TCI HIGHLIGHTS

CERAMICS: PAST AND PRESENT

As is clear from looking at this guidebook, much of the local ceramic art tradition is preserved in a variety of places: both the Genoa art gallery and the municipal museum of Finalborgo have specific sections dedicated to these ceramics; Villa Faraggiana and the G. Mazzotti museum in Albissola Marina; and the Manlio Trucco museum in Albisola Superiore. Yet, each of these places represents little more than a taster of the marvelous tradition that this area is so rightly proud of.

The ceramic tradition in the Savona area dates from the 12th century, with ceramic art

flourishing in Albissola from the 16th century onwards, partly because the deposits of clay and the white earth quarries ensured a plentiful supply of the necessary raw materials. The sizeable beach near the town was used to dry the recently created objects before they were packed on boats and dispatched to faraway destinations. The most famous – and most widely appreciated – form of decoration for Albissola ceramics is the monochrome light blue, which became fairly widespread from the early 17th century onwards. The most luxurious and sought after ornamental style is the historiated one, sometimes known as baroque, that arose in the 17th century along with the equivalent painting movement in Genoa. Here, the backgrounds tend to be of castles set high in the mountains, with biblical or mythological characters in the foreground.

Both ceramic production and the related cultural initiatives are still very much alive in the Savona area. Yet, perhaps the one place that really does justice to this illustrious tradition is the seafront walk in Albissola Marina that has a delightful mosaic floor that was created in 1963 by internationally renowned painters and sculptors.

Futurism, and even today numerous artisans work using the kilns along this section of the Riviera. Albisola has a lovely seafront walk that has 20 ceramic panels – testifying to wonderful ceramic past – by a range of famous artists, including Capogrossi, Crippa, Luzzati, Fontana and other leading exponents of contemporary art.

Slate

The first inhabitants of the Tigullio Gulf were known as the *Tigulli*, which was derived from the Latin word *tegula*, meaning roof tile. The reason for this is simple enough: even before the age of Roman denomination, slate was quarried from the ring of mountains that runs behind this area (from Rapallo to Sestri Levante). Slate, a metamorphic shale-type rock formed by the gradual sedimentation of very fine lime, was mainly used to cover roofs. As the centuries past, it crept

out from being exclusively used in the building sector and started to find applications in the world of art and, more specifically, in the field of decorative sculpture. The results were extremely varied, with numerous different types of objects being created. For example, slate became common in Renaissance doorways, often with relief decoration, as well as being used as a support oil paintings, tempera work and even frescoes. The use of slate definitely predates Roman times, as can be seen from an Iron-Age necropolis in Chiàvari that has tombs made entirely with slabs of slate. However, it took until the 12th century (in Uscio and Recco) before slate quarrying took on notable dimensions. At that time, the slate-center of Liguria was Mt San Giacomo, behind Lavagna, but by the middle of the 19th century, the Fontanabuona valley was almost the only slate-quarrying destination. These days, the main use of this stone is "hidden" by the green cover of the pool table, where the inability of the material to lose its shape is an ideal property. In addition, since the 1970s, slate has become

An antique wooden wool winder with a foot pedal.

increasingly popular in the building sector once more, being used for interior decorations, tiling and in the restoration of old buildings. The reason for this rebirth is probably simple: slate is a sober and elegant stone with a color that can fit in just about any environment.

Damask

Damask production still thrives in Lorsica, a small hamlet east of Genoa that nestles halfway up the valley cut by the Tirello Stream, beneath Mt Ramaceto. Since about the 16th century, the artisans of Lorsica have been famed for their silk, brocade and lampas fabric. The fame of Lorsica damask is undoubtedly linked to two well-known designs: the crown one, used from the late 16th century onwards to paper the walls of noble mansions and to decorate the official summer clothes of *Doges*; and the one known as "of the palm" (late 18C on), which is filled with oriental hints and was commonly seen in most major European residences. The looms used these days in Lorsica are still similar to those used in the 16th century, with the untreated thread being dyed, wound onto bobbins and then used to make the warp yarn. In the next phases, eight threads at a time are passed through the loom, then one-by-one through the heddle and, finally, five at a time through the reed. To make a piece that is 130cm, you need to use an amazing 15,000 threads: such figures might seem excessive, but if you use less, it is likely that the fabric will lose the

characteristic raised effect (and indented on the reverse side). The results, though, are amazing, with wonderful interplays between gold and silver yarns forming patterns that stand out against the deep colors of the background. All in all, the fabric made today is worthy of the past, especially since it is made using the traditional method.

Lace, bobbin lace and knotted lace

In the late 15th century, Lyon became the primary silk producer, leaving Genoa in its wake. As a result, a new industry, Italian pillow lace, grew up in the void left by silk in Liguria. Although the origins of the lace industry lay very much in the economic need to convert the silk industry, the artisans of Liguria soon took this new industry to great heights, culminating in the 17th and 18th centuries, when Genoese lace could be found in all European markets. The industry thrived in the 19th century, but it slowly started to disappear and the last remaining lace makers are now found in the Rapallo, Santa Margherita Lìgure and Portofino area. The history of knotted lace (or macramé) is somewhat different, especially since the stitch used is of Arab origin and arrived in the Chiàvari zone in the early 17th century. Knotted lace was made exclusively by hand, with the highlight of the production being lace borders for linen towels. Indeed, these lace-bordered towels were, for centuries, the flagship of linen and hemp weaving in Tigullio. In the 19th

The damask production in the Ligurian region is a age-old tradition.

A section of a piece of lace in the Museo del Pizzo al Tombolo in Rapallo.

skilled artisans and the presence of labor made available by the declining local fabric industry. Within 20 years, Campo Ligure was one of the European filigree capitals. The industry continued to grow, achieving success across the world and reaching its peak in the 1940s. It did suffer somewhat in the general contraction of the artisan industry just after the turn of the century, but it remains one of the most thriving and lively crafts in Liguria, with an impressive number of businesses.

century, the mass migration towards Latin America led to a notable expansion in the production of this lace, but when this trend died down in the early 20th century, the industry faced a new crisis. Things finally headed back upwards in the 1960s, largely thanks to a new generation of lace makers who turned away from some of the traditional products and started to make new items, including shoe uppers, bags and items of clothing.

Filigree

Ligurian filigree artists, along with gold and silversmiths, are part of a long, rich tradition that dates from the Crusades. These campaigns led to a period of increased movement between the East and Europe, resulting not only in substantial trade but also in the exchange of techniques and the mixing of cultures. The next period of growth came later on, in the 17th and 18th centuries, when the Church went through a period of displaying its wealth, allowing artisans to break free of the shackles of financial constraints and give freer reign to their creativity. The development of the so-called "detailed filigree" industry was a later occurrence, dating from 1884 when the master silversmith Antonio Oliveri opened a filigree studio in his native Campo Ligure, a small town on the northern side of the Apennines. He was soon followed by other artisans and, not long afterwards, there were 33 similar studios. The result was a specialized, high quality form of craft that flourished both because of the various

Wood

Woodworking has inevitably been a part of this population's history as for thousands of years they have been a seafaring people and, naturally, it was important to develop techniques for the construction of boats. In addition, the physical nature of Liguria, with its prevalence of mountains and woods, ensured a plentiful supply of raw materials, which could also be exported and traded in foreign ports for more prized woods like ebony, mahogany and rosewood.

The development of the woodworking industry beyond the confines of ship-building is a more recent occurrence, taking place in the 19th century. At this time, the centuries-old experience of creating furnishings for sacred buildings combined with the woodworking skills, leading to increased wood inlaying. The results were mainly seen in the furniture field, but other areas were notable too, such as painting (frames) and gilding. In the same period in Chiàvari, Giuseppe Descalzi known as "Campanino" invented a chair based on a French model. It was known as the "Campanino" or "Chiavarina" and it marked the beginning of an age of great furniture making that lasted throughout the 19th century and was only thrown into crisis following the outstanding success achieved by the Viennese Thonet chairs across the whole of Europe. This crisis did not totally destroy the local artisan furniture industry – although it certainly left its mark – and many producers still

SHOPPING

145

exist. Some have survived by going down the industrial route, while others have held true to the more traditional techniques.

Iron

In Liguria, the architecture of the seaside towns and villages has been marked by a chronic lack of space, forcing the houses to be built almost on top of each other and the streets to be so narrow that, at times, it is scarcely possible for two pedestrians to walk side-by-side. Yet, this has not resulted in slapdash constructions, but rather careful building that is filled with detail, even in some of the more hidden spots. Amid this wealth of accessories, where a balance between function and decoration is constantly being sought, wrought iron and fretwork play a leading role. Both these skills have long traditions, although they are often only visible within the actual centers. By contrast, the areas where the geography allowed a little more space (Voltri, Masone, Sassello and all of the Polcevera valley), the artisan tradition of wrought iron working developed, especially from the 15th century onwards, into an industry

The unmistakeable Campanino chair.

closely linked to shipbuilding: making iron nails. Both these sectors went through crises in the 19th century, but while the nail-making industry largely died out (despite repeated attempts to get it going again), the tradition of wrought iron for decoration and in the building industry managed to survive, although greatly recluced. Indeed, it largely survives with individual artisans who make a living by creating gift objects, items commissioned by the building industry and restoring antique objects.

Glass

Altare is a village hidden in the mountains behind Savona. Its closed, taciturn nature seems almost to represent the people of Liguria. Substance is more important than form: there are many treasures, but they are never ostentatious and they are often tucked away. Arriving in this area, who could imagine that, for centuries, Murano has had a counterpart on the Tyrrhenian. Indeed, this center, with its centuries-old glass tradition, has nothing to envy – and much to compete with – from the more famous center on the Venetian lagoon.
According to tradition, in the 12th century

 TCI HIGHLIGHTS

THE LIGURIAN NATIVITY SCENE

The Neapolitan nativity scene (or *presepe*) is one of the most famous artisan traditions in Italy. Yet, part of this fame is due to the absence of genuine "competition" or, more accurately, of the disappearance over the centuries of similar forms of artisan expression that developed in other parts of the country. The most prestigious of these lost traditions was, without a doubt, the Ligurian nativity scene, which became popular, especially in Genoa, from the middle of the 16th century and reached its height about two centuries later. The original scenes had small, carved wooden statues that were copies of marble ones or depictions of the Nativity Scene or the Adoration of the Magi. These simple representations soon developed into more complex ones, drawing inspiration from the people and outfits of the age. Sometimes, the scene would be entirely made using wood, but other times, fabric and even precious elements

some French monks from the Bergeggi monastery near Savona who were officiating in Altare realized that these lands were rich in timber and raw materials for producing glass. As such, they built the first furnaces and called some glass-making families from Flanders and Normandy to come to the area. The secrets of glass-making – handed down jealously from father to son – brought riches and privileges (from the ruling authorities) to the local community. Success was so notable that within a few centuries it was seen as necessary, in 1495, to create the "University of the Art of Glass-making", which was actually a guild that protected the rights of master glass-makers and oversaw the system of privileges. The result was another boost to the local glass-making industry. The Consulate, which was the ruling body of the University, played a fundamental role in determining artisan production in the Altare area and thus had a notable impact on the local community.

The key distinction between Murano glass and that from Altare lies in the different process used: Altare developed a method that meant glass could be smelted at lower temperatures. This brought both advantages and disadvantages (the method used in Murano was less efficient, but it gave the artisan more time to manipulate the molten glass before it solidified, allowing more artistic work to be carried out), but overall both techniques reached about the same level, allowing each center to develop according to the needs of their reference markets and, of course, in line with the creative inspirations of the artisans. As such, Murano tended to favor colored glass, while the masters from Altare moved more towards see-through glass and industrial production (although they never lost the ability to make numerous shapes and colors). Glass-making is still the driving force of the local economy, although some new industries are growing. These days, you can still find various artisan workshops, often specializing in glass-blowing, cutting or decorating, that carry forward the torch of centuries of tradition and history in these parts.

GENOVA/GENOA

Ceramiche d'Arte
Via Gianelli Angelo 60, Tel. 0103725257
Ceramic Art

Il Ghirigoro
Via Rela 32/R, Tel. 010413246
Ceramic Art

Jac
Via E. Granello 1, Tel. and Fax 0103992181
Textile gift objects

La Filigrana Italiana
Via XX Settembre 2, Tel. 010585445
Filigree jewelry

like gold, silver, ivory and alabaster would be used. As it became more successful, the nativity scene became crowded with peasants, artisans, nobles and ordinary people, pages, beggars and animals. The techniques became more refined and some of the great artists of the age became involved.

It did not take long for depictions of the nativity scene to break out of the confines of the churches where they originated. For some of the more powerful families, they even became a way of competing or showing their superiority over other such families. The French Revolution and the decline of the powerful Genoese families, though, marked the end of this era. As the sun set on this period of competing noble and bourgeois families, the tradition returned to its natural routes – with the church. The tradition of building a nativity scene in the house did, though, live on among the lower classes, but simple economics meant they could not recreate the lavish scenes filled with innumerable accessories that characterized the 17th and 18th centuries. In these poorer scenes, the statues tended to be clay, often made in series using molds. In essence, the tradition of the Ligurian nativity scene carried on throughout the 19th century, but the age of masterpieces had drawn to a close. At present, industrial production has replaced artisan production, although one can never take away its place in the history of local art.

SHOPPING

CAMPO LIGURE

Arianna
Via Trento 68, Tel. 010921054
Textile gift objects
Effe-Erre
Via Vallecalda 5/7, Tel. 010921381
Production and sale of filigree
Eredi Bongera
Via Saracco 1, Tel. 010921067
Filigree jewelry and bric-a-brac
F.P.
Via Don Minzoni 47, Tel. 010920570
Production of precious objects
Giuseppe Oliveri
Via M. Olivero 13, Tel. 010921080
Precious fabrics
Pastorino Filigrana
Via Convento 13, Tel. 010920905
Production of precious objects

CHIÀVARI

Adriano Podestà
Via A. Gastaldi 17, Tel. 0185308208
Production of original
Chiàvari chairs
Levaggi A & F.lli
Via Parma 469, Tel. 0185383092
Production of Chiàvari and sailing chairs

CICAGNA

Consorzio Artigiano Ardesia - Le Pietre
Via Alberogrosso 10,
Tel. 018592394
Slate working for
interiors and
exteriors
A. Cuneo & C.
Via Molinazzo 21,
Tel. 0185929983
Urban and
interior
furnishings,
fireplaces, tables
and slate pool
tables

Pillows in damask fabric.

LORISCA

Figli di De Martini Giuseppe
Via Scaletta 78, Tel. 0185977302
Damask

SAMPIERDARENA

Beccuti
Via G. Buranello 155r,
Tel. 010466119
An old-style workshop has corks,
bizarre-shaped bottles,
vases and glass work.

ZOAGLI

Tessitura Gaggioli
Via dei Velluti 1, Tel. 0185259057
This company dates from 1932 and was
founded to combine artisan skill with
industrial production. You can watch old
artisan methods being practiced to
make silk, velvet and damask.

LA SPÈZIA

Miriam Consolari
Via Prione 116, Tel. 018729140
Embroidery

SARZANA

Isoppo & Parma
Via Pecorina 114, Tel. 0187621144
Furniture

SAVONA

ALBISOLA SUPERIORE

Ceramiche d'Arte
Francesco Guarino
Corso Mazzini 46, Tel. 0194004003
Traditional Albisola décor, natural
and landscape ceramics,
as well as sculptures and pictures.
Ceramiche Esa Mazzotti
Corso Matteotti 25,
Tel. 019481626
Artistic ceramics.
**Ceramiche e
Maioliche
Artistiche G.
Mazzotti 1903**
*Corso
Matteotti 29,*
Tel. 019489872
A traditional
company that has
made artistic
ceramic and
majolica objects since 1903.
La Nuova Fenice
Via Ferrari 1, Tel. 019481668
Production and sale of artistic ceramic
and majolica objects.
Pastorino Mario
Via L. Grosso 6/2, Tel. 0194004653
Artistic ceramics.
Studio Ernan Design
Corso Mazzini 77, Tel. 019489916
Single and series of artisan
ceramic pieces.

MARKETS

Creating and maintaining are the two faces of Ligurian craftsmanship, which seeks both to endure and to keep alive the evidence of the past. As such antiques and crafts markets – along with actually visiting the workshops where artisans often still use the traditional tools and methods – are an ideal way to discover the crafts, literally and figuratively. Perhaps the best of all such events is held in August: the Filigree Exhibition held in Campo Ligure. This is, though, by no means the only such event. Liguria also hosts a number of other trade fairs, some of which are international in scope while others are more national or local. In all, there are many opportunities to encounter the world of Ligurian crafts.

GENOVA/GENOA

Euroflora/International exhibition of flowers and ornamental plants

Next exhibition: 22 April to 1 May 2011
Every five years, the Genoa fairgrounds host Euroflora, a spectacular event. During the exhibition, the fairgrounds turn into a 150 000 m² garden with varieties from five continents. Every fair focuses on a special theme, with Euroflora 2006 choosing the theme of water. Since 1966, it has become the key promotional event for Italian flower growers. Each fair combines a message of love for the environment with a chance to spread knowledge among the public about the numerous ways of using plants and greenery.
Information: Tel. 0105391265,
www.euroflora06.it

One of the enchanting, colorful displays at Euroflora.

Fiera Primavera/Spring Fair

April
This is the Fiera di Genova's major trade fair. For ten days and ten nights, people can enter the fairgrounds for free and browse around, looking for purchases to make for the house, the garden and one's free time. Of course, there are also plenty of traditional edible items to choose from!
Information: Tel. 0105391265,
www.fiera.ge.it

Salone Nautico/Nautical Show

October
This is a must-attend event for all lovers of pleasure boating. The event now uses an impressive 300 thousand m², making it one of the world's leading such events.
Information: Tel. 0105391265,
www.fiera.ge.it

The Nautical Show is now a major international event.

BOGLIASCO
Mercato dell'antiquariato/ Antiques Fair

Last Sunday of the month
50 antiques dealers display their wide variety of wares on Piazza 26 Aprile, giving visitors a chance to admire old-time objects.
Information: Tel. 0103470429

CAMPO LIGURE
Mostra mercato della Filigrana/ Filigree Market

End August/Start September
The Salone del Consiglio Comunale is the setting for this historic event (begun in 1967). The best local filigree experts and producers show what they have to offer, next to stalls with jewelry and other precious objects. You can also visit the precious "La Galleria del Sole" ceramic plates.
Information: Tel. 010921003/920963

SARZANA

La soffitta nella strada/
Attic sale on the street

August from 5pm to midnight
This market owes its birth to the desire of local antiques dealers to have an opportunity to display a variety of wares. These days, the event attracts dealers from all over Italy and also from abroad. You can find a truly wide range of items, including period furniture, modern antiques, gift items, vintage objects, oriental antiques, carpets, rugs, paintings, lace works, table cloths, stamps and antique books.
Information: Tel. 01876141

The "attic sale on the street", an antiques market in Sarzana.

IMPERIA

DOLCEÀCQUA

Mercatino biologico, artigianato e antiquariato/Organic and antiques market

Last Sunday of the month
Piazza Padre G. Mauro is the setting, from 9 in the morning to sunset, for a series of stalls selling a wondrous range of items.
Information: www.dolceacqua.it

OSPEDALETTI

Arti e mestieri/Arts and crafts

First Sunday of the month from 10am; in July and August, also Tuesday 7pm to midnight.
As you walk along the chic Corso Regina Margherita you can see artisans and artists not only selling their wares, but also creating them. It is like an interactive workshop where the public can follow the journey from an idea, through the various stages of development, to the creation of a final product. This is, obviously, a good chance to admire creativity, but it is also a chance to learn more about the techniques involved in working wood, metal, glass, stone, ceramics, textiles, wax and other materials. In doing so, one invariable gains a renewed appreciation for the dexterity and ingenuity of the artisans.
Information:
www.comune.ospedaletti.im.it

LA SPÈZIA

Barcamercato Golfo dei Poeti
March and April
The small Assonautica harbor and the Morin promenade are used for an exhibition of new and old in the nautical world, from accessories to services linked to sailing. It is an excellent chance for private buyers and sellers, especially since boats can be tried there and then in the water. If you like sailing boats, catamarans, yachts and other such craft, then this is a wonderful event to go to.
Information: Tel. 0187728232

Cercantico in the La Spèzia Gulf
First Sunday of the month (except August)
This interesting and enjoyable antiques and collectors' market is held in the city streets. The name, roughly translated as, look for antique, really sums things up as the number of people who come to sell items ensures that even the most demanding, passionate and curious collector will find something.
Information: Tel. 0187728296

SAVONA

ALBISOLA SUPERIORE AND ALBISSOLA MARINA

Festival Internazionale della Maiolica/ Majolica International Festival
April/May
Ceramic objects from Liguria, trails and guided tours amid the shops, buildings, churches, newspaper kiosks and museums. This international festival brings the area to life.
Information: Tel. 019485785,
www.comune.albisola-superiore.sv.it

FASHION

Factory outlets are managed directly by the production houses themselves, thus ensuring the items available are not only original, but also high quality. In essence, they are ideal places to go shopping for quality items – and save money. At factory prices, you can buy items from the current season (in all sizes) as well as browse through what remains from previous collections, and end-of-line or second-choice items. If you are patient and prepared to spend some time looking, there are high-quality bargains to be found. Below is a list of some outlets that are definitely worth visiting.

GENOVA/GENOA

Diffusione tessile
Corso F.M. Perrone 19,
Tel. 0106591235
They have items left at the end
of the season from one of the main
female clothes groups in Italy.
The clothes range from garments for
girls to more classic numbers.
Wide range of sizes. Good selection of
leather bags and belts as well as shoes
and scarves. Underwear, costumes and
accessories for the seaside,
such as, towels, flip-flops and beach
bags. There is also an interesting
array of "leftover" fabrics. The minimum
saving is 50% (on the seasonal
sale price) with an additional
30% during sales.

Imago Tricot
Via Goito 26/5, Tel. 010814486,
www.imagotricot.com
Cashmere clothing for men and women
made by Imago Tricot.
The range includes classic, elegant
and sporty garments such as jerseys,
cardigans, knitwear, turtlenecks,
suits, skirts, dresses, scarves
and headwear. Collection and first
choice items available.
Factory prices throughout the year;
20% discount in January.

Spaccio Cream
Via Isonzo 16/rosso,
Tel. 0103739632
They make and sell gloves for women,
men and children in a range
of leathers (including from rams,
chamois, deer) with linings in merino
wool and cashmere.
The choice of items is vast, ranging
from casual to classic. You can also
order tailor-made items. Factory prices
throughout the year, but only first
choice items.

CASARZA LIGURE
Maglificio Elsa Massucco
Via De Gasperi 68,
Tel. 018546032
The company makes handcrafted pure
cashmere items under the Maglificio
Gallo brand. The outlet also has the
Robe di Kappa and Navigare labels.
There is a wide range of items for men,
women and children, including jerseys,
tops, dresses and tracksuits. Factory
prices throughout the year, with 30-40%
discounts on end-of-season items.

ZOAGLI
Cordani Velluti e Seterie
Via S. Pietro 21,
Tel. 0185259141,
www.seteriecordani.com
They make fabrics for clothing and
furniture. The material is high quality
and quite varied (flax, cotton, silk). It
can be used to make wedding dresses.
The range of articles includes scarves,
ties, neckerchiefs and tablecloths.
Factory prices throughout the year, with
special discounts for certain items.

IMPERIA

VENTIMÌGLIA
Mavil
Via Martiri della Libertà 11,
Tel. 0184357079
Females clothes by Mavil and Mode
as well as by Elena Mirò, Krizia,
Salvalaglio and Weichiss. The range
is impressive: formalwear, elegant,
casual, suits, dresses, trousers,
tops, blouses, jerseys, cardigans,
raincoats, jackets, coats, shoes, belts,
hats and neckerchiefs. The sizes range
from 42 right up to 62. Factory prices
are available throughout the year,
with discounts of 20 to 40% on end-of-
line items.

In summer, Liguria becomes a natural stage for open-air shows, concerts and festivals as well as many other enticing events. Autumn also has an interesting array of options that are ideal for an unusual weekend getaway, perhaps to overcome a post-summer malaise. The range of events held in Liguria helps to make this a thrilling region to visit, to discover the key moments of local history and to learn more about the regional traditions. Like in many other Italian regions, theater and culture – especially opera in this case – enjoyed an extraordinary period of growth in the 19th century with the rise of the middle classes. The Carlo Felice theater in Genoa opened in 1828, becoming a model, quite literally, for other theaters and concert halls constructed across the region. By the end of the 19th century, Liguria could boast over 100 theaters, with the vast majority focusing on opera. In the 20th century, as the novelty of opera wore off and the two world wars genuinely changed everything, theater and especially opera suffered.

Events

Today, concerts are alive once more, although tending to be clustered in the main centers. Folklore has also become important, playing a vital role in the many religious and non-religious festivals that evoke the rich past with their pageants, processions and parades.

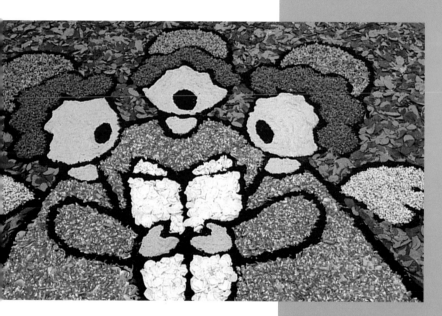

Highlights

- Genoa, with Amalfi, Pisa and Venice, was one of the Maritime Republics and now hosts, cyclically, the annual Maritime Republics Regatta, held at the end of a wonderful historical parade.
- In the early 1960s, Genoa experienced an extraordinary flourishing of musical talent, including Fabrizio De Andrè, Gino Paoli, Luigi Tenco and Bruno Lauzi.
- The Sanremo music festival, started in 1951, is the most famous song festival in Italy and is also fairly well-known abroad.

Inside

MUSIC

The main musical centers in Liguria are undoubtedly the main cities, although the geographical formation and the importance of tourism mean that there is a scattering of musical life right across the region. The main center is, of course, Genoa, especially because of the Fondazione Teatro Carlo Felice (Carlo Felice Theater Foundation). Savona, La Spèzia and Sanremo all play important roles. A range of musical associations are dotted across the rest of the region, especially in the tourist areas. Indeed, tourism is a driving force for music, particularly in combination with the extraordinarily beautiful landscape. Many towns and villages in Liguria have managed to find a wonderful harmony between music, history and landscape.

GENOVA/GENOA

Teatro Carlo Felice
Piazza De Ferrari,
Tel. 010589329/010591697
www.carlofelice.it
The theater was inaugurated on 7 April 1828 with Vincenzo Bellini's *Bianca e Fernando* watched by King Charles Felix (or Carlo Felice, hence the theater's name). It soon became a leading theater. It had been designed by Carlo Barabino, drawing on already established Italian models: La Scala in Milan (by Piermarini) and the Royal Theater in Turin (by Benedetto Alfieri). The structure had a large pronaos with a portico all around (both elements survived the wars and were kept for the new building) and was, like the rest of the furnishings, in Neoclassical style. Throughout the

A picture from 1905 of the Carlo Felice Theater and Piazza De Ferrari.

19th century, the theater was the social focal point for high society, thus becoming more a place to be seen than a cultural and musical dynamo. During World War II, the theater was heavily bombed, causing severe damage and resulting in other

TCI HIGHLIGHTS

THE GENOESE SCHOOL OF SINGER-SONGWRITERS

The term "Genoese school of singer-songwriters" generally refers to an exceptionally talented group of singer-songwriters from Genoa that arose and trained during the 1960s and, despite having notably different cultural and musical backgrounds, crossed paths in the Ligurian capital, which has long been a cultural crossroads. Artistic influences from beyond the Alps and the specific nature of that period in time (the contradictions of the economic boom, the unease with the dehumanization of certain values that capitalism was causing, the tension created by historical and political events, and the foreboding of difficult years to come) were the key factors in the poetry of the singer-songwriters from Genoa, who primarily sought anarchy and liberty. The leading lights of this movement are among the major names of Italian singing of that age: Fabrizio De André, Luigi Tenco, Umberto Bindi, Gino Paoli, Paolo Conte and Bruno Lauzi. Their songs spoke the same language as the youths as they dealt with themes like love, social contestation, war and looking after the less fortunate. The songs often used dialect. De André took the side, in is poetic songs, of losers, of those who had been disinherited and those who were excluded. These elements, along with the fact that his music was really very good, helped make him a

venues hosting the theater's playbill. The reconstruction was a long, arduous process that took decades, eventually being inaugurated on 20 October 1991 with Giuseppe Verdi's *Il Trovatore*. The new structure has the original pronaos and porticoes, and the general shape of the exterior mimics the original. The square tower is a new addition, but has already become an accepted part of the skyline. The interior is impressive, with the gallery, side balconies and main seating area capable of holding 2,100 people. It is designed on the concept of a pizza with windows and balconies overlooking it. The new theater is also technologically advanced, allowing major, complex shows to be staged. It has won various national and international awards.

Goa-Boa Festival
July
This festival, held in the old Cornigliano steel mill, is an international event dedicated to pop and rock music. In recent years, the event has grown, becoming famous even beyond the borders of Italy.
For further information:
Tel. 010593650/010592984,
www.goaboa.net

PORTOFINO
Liguria Jazz Summer
July and August
This thrilling festival involves the Portofino, Santa Margherita Lìgure, Recco and Camogli municipalities. These four municipalities overlooking two inlets (Paradiso and Tigullio) combine to produce one, major event that combines jazz with the tourist and cultural promotion of the area. The result is that the Monte di Portinfino area becomes awash with the festival, as the piazzas become packed for the various concerts. For further information: Tel. 010/585241, www.italianjazzinstitute.com

Portofino Classica International Music Festival
July-September
Every Saturday from early July until late September Portofino hosts various international artists as part of the Portofino Classica International Music Festival, which has now been running for seven years. The concerts are organized by the San Ambrogio Musical Association (A.MU.S.A.) and are held either in the S. Giorgio churchyard or the small theater.
For further information: Tel. 0185267732, www.comune.portofino.genova.it; www.amusa.it

SESTRI LEVANTE
Premio Hans Christian Andersen
May
The streets and squares of this town come alive with a series of shows, scenes and sounds.

favored singer of youth movements. In 1983, he released *Creuza de Mâ* entirely in dialect. Critics acclaimed it as his best album ever and it was awarded the best album of the 1980s. His last works showed that he had not lost his enormous creativity, even in his more mature years. Indeed, he remained a key figure on the Italian music scene. To make sure that his musical path did not end with him, since 2006, Genoa has been home to the Accademia Ligure della Canzone d'Autore.

This is a key academy not only for music students, but also for practicing musicians, especially since it aims to support new artists and help them to achieve recognition and grow professionally. The academy is located in the heart of Genoa's old center, near Porta Soprana. It holds courses in musical interpretation and writing music as well as hosting actual shows and concerts.

EVENTS

For further information:
Tel. 0185478344/0185457011,
www.andersenfestival.it

IMPERIA

CERVO
Festival di Cervo
July and August
The Festival di Musica da Camera di
Cervo (Cervo Chamber Musical Festival)
has been going for nearly forty-five
years and is emblematic of all the
musical initiatives that are organized
during the Ligurian summer. This small
medieval hamlet sits on a headland
overlooking the sea. It was discovered
almost by accident by Sandor Vegh – a
famous violinists and Hungarian
orchestra conductor who also founded
the Quartetto Vegh – when he replaced
a fellow violinist for a charity concert.
He was truly taken by the beauty of the
place, deciding to establish a chamber
music festival that would also be an
opportunity for major musicians from
the world scene to perform.
Since the outset, some of the world's
best known musicians have taken part,

A lovely setting for the Cervo Festival.

brining life to the natural stage formed
by the courtyard of the Baroque
Corallini church. In short, the Cervo
Festival has become a genuinely
international event.
For further information:
www.cervo.it

SANREMO
Festival Internazionale delle Bande
Late September/early October
Music bands from across Europe bring
music, color and folklore to the city
streets. There are two major finales, one

 ## TCI HIGHLIGHTS

SANREMO FESTIVAL
The Sanremo festival, also known as the Festival della Canzone Italiana (Festival of
the Italian Song), has been an annual appointment with Italian singing since 1951.
The festival was originally held in the Casinò di Sanremo, but it is now in the Ariston
Theater in Sanremo, sometime between late February and early March.

Over the years, the format has been tinkered with,
but in general, singers present new songs,
composed by Italians, that are then voted on
by the jury and the public. 1964 was the first year
when non-Italians were allowed, but they had to
sing in Italian.
Over the years, most famous Italian singers
have taken part and many famous international
guests have been involved as well.
The early festivals – from 1951 to 1954 – were only
broadcast on the radio, but it soon became a
television event. At present, it is shown live on
Italian TV and by Eurovision.

For further information: Ariston Theater, Corso
Matteotti 107, Tel. 0184507070,
www.sanremomanifestazioni.it

held in the Ariston Theater and the other on a stage erected on Piazza Colombo. For further information: Tel. 018459059, www.rivieradeifiori.org

LA SPÈZIA

Teatro Civico
Piazza Mentana 1, Tel. 0187733098,
This city theater (called the Teatro Civico) was designed in the 1830s by Franco Oliva and built on the site of an earlier theater. It was inaugurated in 1846. The playbill contained both opera and stage theater, however in the 20th century, both of these elements declined as the theater was used increasingly for cinema. The new Oliva city theater was seen as an important step in revitalizing local theater and music. It has a rectangular main hall with over a thousand seats – in the main seating area as well as in the balconies and galleries – and the new playbill is notably varied: theater, music and cinema. Many of the concerts are produced or backed by the Società dei Concerti (Concert Society), which has not only backed the theater and theatrical education, but also attempted to ensure that major international artists regularly perform here.

SARZANA
Festival Internazionale di Musiche & Suoni dal Mondo
July
This festival is one of the major Italian appointments for world music. This

The large audience area at the city theater in La Spèzia can hold a thousand spectators.

extensive festival began over 15 years ago, basing itself on the numerous music and cultural aspects of world music, jazz and, more generally, sounds from across the world. Every year, the festival attracts famous names from the tops of the various sectors. It is now backed by the Liguria Regional Government and, since 2004, it has also received support from the local government body entrusted with protecting historical and environmental heritage. It has also been chosen by the world famous Scuola Normale Superiore di Pisa as a cultural partner for "I Concerti della Normale" (Concerts of the Normal). There are also links to the main cultural events in Tuscany. In short, all of this support and recognition testifies to the excellent level of those involved and the originality of the project.
For further information: Tel. 0187716106 / 0187716172/0187620419

SAVONA

BORGIO VEREZZI
Festival Teatrale di Borgio Verezzi
July and August
The backdrop for this festival (the Borgio Verezzi Theater Festival) is the charming Piazza S. Agostino, a terrace overlooking the sea. The festival has both given the stage to well-known directors and actors, and revealed others who have gone on to achieve fame both in Italy and beyond.
For further information: Tel. 019610167, www.festivalverezzi.it

SPOTORNO
Spotorno Comics
August
The small square in front of the town library is the setting for this national gathering, backed by the municipality, for satire and humor. The highlight of the event – for the public and artists alike – is the "Notte delle Vignette" (Cartoon Night) when national and international artists draw "live". The "Oscar della Vignetta" National Competition has also become a part of the event. It is only open to high school students and gives them a wonderful chance to get to know some of the leading lights in the field.
For further information:
www.comune.spotorno.sv.it

FOLKLORE

The confraternities play a vital role in preserving and organizing traditional Ligurian festivals and fetes. These extraordinarily dynamic confraternities have often been around for centuries, allowing them to have accumulated a rich cultural history not only in terms of physical objects but also in the special ways they perform church music (different to Gregorian chanting) and ceremonies. Indeed, when many of these confraternities take part in processions, it is as much a show of strength as anything else, since enormous effort is needed to carry the heavy crucifixes that were often created by famed artists and are adorned with silver leaves, thorns and flowers. As these bearers make their ways through the streets at a measured pace, the silver decorations often tingle rhythmically, almost as if the bearers are dancing. The involvement of the confraternities brings a decidedly religious element to many Ligurian festivals. Interestingly, there are not an amazing number of festivals linked to the sea, sailing and fishing. There are a number of festivals linked to old European folkloristic practices, although in many cases the origins of these events are still waiting to be studied. This is the case for the bonfire for St John and the various tree and vegetation rituals connected to May Day and Pentecost.

GENOVA/GENOA

Processione di San Giovanni

24 June

The procession starts in the afternoon from the cathedral of S. Lorenzo, winds its way through the old center and heads to the old port, where the Archbishop blesses the city and the sea with the relics of St John the Baptist (conserved in a grand, gold and silver ark from the mid-15th cent.).

However, tradition holds that the festival is also blessed by a giant bonfires on the exposed river bed of the Bisagno Stream.

For further information:

Tel. 010576791,

www.apt.genova.it

Regata delle Repubbliche Marinare

May/July

There are four ancient maritime republics – Amalfi, Genoa, Pisa and Venice – and every year one of them hosts a regatta.

Each year, the event is preceded by a major historical parade in which each of the republics is represented by eighty costumed figures who act out important moments from the history of the republic.

This is followed by the regatta, where the boats are the same size and shape, but differ markedly in terms of color and the figurehead: Amalfi is blue with a winged horse; Genoa is white with a griffin; Pisa is purple with an eagle; and Venice is green with a lion. The teams are made

Some of the participants in the parade of the Ancient Maritime Republics at the Duomo in Genoa.

up of men born (or have resided for more than five years) in the city that they are rowing for.

The trophy is a medieval galley that is kept by the winner in its home city until the next regatta.

For further information:

Tel. 010576791, www.apt.genova.it

The spectacular fireworks competition involving the various districts of Rapallo at the end of the Feast of Madonna di Montallegro.

RAPALLO
Madonna di Montallegro
1-3 July
This feast lasts three days and the most salient moments are the procession with the silvery 18th-century Madonna, the parade of the confraternities and the grand fireworks display in which the various town districts battle for the best display.
For further information: Tel. 0185230346

IMPERIA

ARMA DI TAGGIA
Festa del Fùlgari
11-12 February
The feast celebrates a local 9th-century saint, Benedetto Revelli – elected by popular acclaim the Bishop of Albenga – and a legendary miracle he performed. Some Saracen pirates had come ashore during the night, intent on sacking the town. However, they took flight when they saw a mysterious display of lights in an arch and a fracas of explosions. According to the legend, each of the town districts built a massive bonfire that lit up the town and the youths set fire to gunpowder that had been poured in giant bamboo canes (the "fùlgari"), which burnt without exploding, forming an illuminated arch.
For further information:
Tel. 018443733,
www.taggia.it

BORGHETTO D'ARROSCIA
Le Milizie Celesti
Good Friday, every 5 years
The key feature of the Good Friday procession held in the small district of Gavenola (the last one was in 2005) is the series of five processional statues, called *casse*, depicting episodes from the passion of Christ. The polychrome wooden *casse* are wonderfully sculpted and are donated in the late 18th century by a nobleman of Dutch origin,

The elaborate and intriguing costumes of the Heavenly Hosts.

Francesco Maria Wannenes.
Probably the most unusual aspect
of the parade is the 24 children dressed
as angels, wearing precious velvet
outfits with silver embroidery and
appliqués in other colors.
These costumes were another gift
from Wannenes.
For further information: Tel. 018331061

CERIANA
Riti Pasquali
Holy Week
At the beginning of Holy Week,
the parish church becomes the setting
for a giant tomb scene with full-size
17th-century wooden statues, lavish
floral compositions, vases of cereal
crops (including grain) and enormous
candles, which are placed at the base
of Calvary. On the eve of Good Friday,
the four confraternities (Misericordia,
Santa Caterina, Visitazione and Santa
Marta) are called to the church
by the sound of enormous trumpets
made of rolled up chestnut bark.
Each confraternity then sings the
Miserere and other texts in its
traditional way, each of which is unusual
and differs from the normal Gregorian
way. The lay procession on Good Friday
has a truly penitential feel to it,
especially since only the singers
and children take part.
As a whole, the Easter rituals of Ceriana
are among the most complex and
emotional traditional religious rituals in
the whole of northern Italy.
For further information: Tel. 0184551017

DIANO MARINA
Infiorata
Corpus Domini
The roads where the Corpus Domini
procession passes are totally covered in
patterns made with flower petals. The
work is done by artists and volunteers
who work through the night prior to the
feast. The tradition has only recently
been taken up again.
For further information: Tel. 0183496956

DOLCEÀCQUA
L'Alloro di San Sebastiano
20 January
A laurel tree, cut from the nearby
woods, is adorned with hundreds
of large hosts in all different colors

The flower patterns in Diano Marina have become
a major event in recent years.

by the members of a confraternity.
The tree is then paraded through
the streets. The procession ends at the
church from where everything begins.
The tree is then planted and the faithful,
after placing an offering,
break off a branch, which is said to
represent the tree that St Sebastian
was tied to when he was martyred.
A similar ceremony is held in
Camporosso in the province of Imperia.
For further information: Tel. 0184206444

LA SPÈZIA

LÈVANTO
San Giacomo
24-25 July
On 24 July, a costume pageant recalls
the history of the town. The participants
climb up to the oratory of San Giacomo,
where they are solemnly received
by the prior of the confraternity.
The true feast, though, is on 25 July:
during the evening procession, a
number of confraternities parade
through the streets, wearing
characteristic outfits and carrying heavy
crucifixes adorned with silver filigree
flowers and leaves. The statue
of San Giacomo (St James) is carried
by men dressed in old sailor outfits.
A section of the procession continues
onto a series of boats, which then
head out a little way to sea with the

statue and reliquary of the saint, before returning to land so that the blessing with the reliquary of San Giacomo can take place.
A fireworks show then rounds everything off.
For further information:
Tel. 0187808125

VARESE LIGURE
Il Maggio
1 May

On 1 May every year, a group of people, preceded by a float adorned with broom, recite a chant that announces the arrival of May and spring.
The text they chant has been handed down orally from generation to generation, but it is very similar to a poem written by Giulio Cesare Croce (1550-1609), from Bologna, to be sung for the maidens at the beginning of May. The song ends with a request for donations and the promise to return the following year.
For further information:
Tel. 0187842094,
www.comune.vareseligure.sp.it

SAVONA

Processione del Venerdì Santo
Good Friday, but only in even years

This age-old procession starts from the cathedral at nine in the evening and then ends there as well, after heading through the streets in a roughly circular route. The procession begins with the rhythmic beating of drummers dressed for mourning and is led by a large processional cross bearing the

symbols of the passion of Christ. The evangelic story is recalled through the fifteen *casse* – splendid and heavy processional wooden statutes – that are carried by members of the confraternity. Originally, these bearers were hooded, but not any more. The rear of the procession is marked by the Arca della Santa Croce (Ark of the Holy Cross), decorated with a large silver crucifix. The Ark contains a reliquary of the True Cross.
For further information:
Tel. 01983101/019811818,
Freephone 800401525,
www.comune.savona.it

The flower patterns for Corpus Domini in the streets of Sassello.

The Good Friday procession in Savona; sculpture of Our Lady of Sorrows.

SASSELLO
Infiorata
Corpus Domini

At the first light, on the day of the feast, the inhabitants of Sassello cover the route of the procession with a carpet of leaves, flowers and petals, carefully arranged to form patterns or pictures of sacred symbols or religious scenes. In addition, the façades of the houses are covered with branches and tapestries, carpets, covers and altar covers are displayed from the balconies and windows.
For further information: Tel. 019724103

The wellness centers in Liguria are genuine 'temples' of wellbeing where the ceremonies and rituals focus on restoring the physical and psychological or mental balance of the body. These are authentic oases of relaxation that are much needed in an age of frenetic lifestyles, over working and generally having too much on our plates. Luxury is the key and any getaway is about indulging the self. This new sense of self awareness is now well accepted as wellness getaways are becoming increasingly popular. This probably relates to the new sense of health, linked to inner calm, physical form and aesthetic beauty. The old adage 'you are born beautiful' has given way to 'you become beautiful'. The connection between health and beauty is ever more important, making looking after one's body not narcissism but part of physical and psychological wellbeing.

As you enter one of these wellness centers, the rest of the world seems magically left behind as you are welcomed by relaxing infusions, candles, soft-lighting

Wellness

and relaxing music. This other worldliness continues as you move between the pool, beauty treatments, mud baths and massages. To top things off, many wellness centers are located in the leafy parts of the hinterland, making it easy to enjoy a calm, relaxing vacation.

Highlights

- Bordighera, located just before the French border, has two excellent centers with health trails and relaxing getaways.
- Pigna, in one of the most lovely valleys along the Riviera dei Fiori, has a major spa complex with thermal pools and small waterfalls.
- Portofino has a wellness center in an old monastery with a stunning view of the charming bay below.
- Uscio is home to a colonial style center set in a large park.

Inside

Grand Hotel Diana
Via Garibaldi 110,
Tel. 018262701
www.hoteldianaalassio.it
Open all year

The garden has some age-old pines, and there is also conference room and a bar. The two restaurants, including one with an outdoor area by the sea, serve typical seafood cuisine

The view from the restaurant at the Grand Hotel Diana.

Located on the seafront, this spa is completely air conditioned and has a parking lot with a "car ready" service. It is also near the old center and the harbor. The spacious, elegant rooms have balconies and small sitting areas. There is a reserved section on the beach for guests with sun beds and umbrellas.

accompanied by music. Barbecues are also held. Vegetarian and dietetic menus. The wellness center uses the elements of the sea, such as the salt and the seaweed, along with the goodness of the sea water. Indeed, sea treatments are the specialty. Gym, spa bath, sauna, solarium and indoor pool.

The garden of the Grand Hotel del Mare.

Grand Hotel del Mare
Capo Migliarese,
Via Portico della Punta 34,
Tel. 0184262201
www.grandhoteldelmare.it
Open all year
This elegant hotel is located in the final section of Liguria before the French border. It is right on the sea and surrounded by a splendid terrace garden. The private beach is only a short walk away. Elegance and discretion are the keys to hospitality here, where guests are carefully

looked after throughout their stay. There are plenty of common areas where you can read and relax. The rooms are furnished with attention to detail and contain all modern comforts as well as balconies overlooking the sea. The range of rooms is also good, running from more classic rooms to suites for those who really wish to indulge themselves. The restaurant tends to focus on Ligurian cuisine, although other Italian recipes and many international ones are often on the menu. There is also a beauty center that offers numerous "combination treatments" for the week or weekend. Guests can also enjoy all of the main beauty treatments and the various wellbeing routes, all of which helps to make this a truly relaxing place. There is also a sauna, solarium and heated salt-water pool in a splendid corner of the porch garden. The range of treatments is designed to help both physical and mental health, especially by rejuvenating the body and dealing with the stress of daily life.

Parigi

Lungomare Argentina 16/18,
Tel. 0184261405
www.hotelparigi.com
Open all year – disabled facilities
Famous since the early 20th century, this hotel is located right on the sea by the famous promenade in Bordighera. The hotel is run by the Sattanino family and combines a refined, elegant atmosphere with professional service. It has a range of rooms, including a suite, where the furnishings and comforts have been carefully selected. The lovely restaurant serves both regional and national dishes, and has an excellent wine list that combines well with the menu. The fifth floor of the building is where you will find the new wellness center that is light and welcoming. Guests can make use of the sauna, Turkish bath, spa bath and *thalassorelax* pool with heated seawater (37°C/98.6°F). There is also a terrace – used for sun therapy – with a splendid view of the sea. In summer, guests can use, for free, the reserved section of beach below the hotel. The center also offers personalized programs that include a diet controlled by a nutrition specialist. These programs are designed to match individual needs. A key aim of the center is to help guests genuinely relax, both physicaly and mentally.

The splendid view of the sea from the Parigi.

PIGNA

Grand Hotel Antiche Terme

Regione Lago Pigo,
Tel. 0184240010
www.termedipigna.it
Open from April to October and around Christmas
The spa complex is located in one of the most beautiful little valleys in western Liguria, between the Riviera dei Fiori and the Cote d'Azure. The complex contains the spa, a hotel and the wellness center. The furnishings are elegant and refined, with marble and wood creating a lovely atmosphere. There are plenty of large windows to help you take in the lovely surrounds. The rooms are designed around the concept of light elegance, avoiding minimalism or over elaboration. There are two restaurants,

San Michele and Bistrot del Lago, although the latter is only open in summer. The cuisine is a meeting of traditional regional cuisine and special dietary needs. Guests also have access to the business center, disco area and cinema hall.

Wellness center. The spa and wellness center are set across two floors below the hotel. The large windows help to make the place more relaxing, especially since you can see the Nervia Stream and the lovely old center of Pigna. The water, rich in sulfur, wells up from the ground at $30.8°C/87.44°F$ from the Madonna Assunta spring. The center is open both to hotel guests and non-guests. There are four heated pools, including two open-air ones that are linked by a small waterfall. Finally, clients can use the outdoor pool with spa, two gyms, Turkish bath, solarium and health route. All treatments are preceded by a visit to the onsite doctor. The products from the Terme di Pigna line are used.

The two pools at the Grand Hotel Antiche Terme.

PORTOFINO

Splendido
Viale Baratta 16,
Tel. 0185267801
www.hotelsplendido.com
Open mid-March to mid-November
This former monastery is situated on a headland, ensuring a charming and panoramic view of the surrounding bay. Guests can choose between rooms or suites which are furnished with taste and equipped with air conditioning, television with video machine and DVD, telephone, mini-bar, safe and hair dryer. The hotel also has a garage parking service, external parking, a private motorboat for outings and waterskiing, private garden, reading room, bar, babysitting service, daily laundry and dry-cleaning service, shuttle to the center of Portofino and tennis court. Nearby, you can also make use of an excellent golf course and riding center, which is ideal for those lovers of more active outdoor pursuits. There are two restaurants, including one with a terrace, that serve traditional Ligurian dishes, although guests personal dietary requests can easily be taken care of. The wellness center specializes in beauty and rejuvenation treatments, with various courses, including yoga. The setting is personal and reserved with attention to detail. Guests can use the heated outdoor seawater pool, sauna, Turkish bath and gym.

RAPALLO

Excelsior Palace Hotel
*Via San Michele
di Pagana 8,
Tel. 0185230666
www.excelsiorpalace.thi.it
Open all year*
This hotel has been famous since the early 20th century because it was home to Italy's first casino. It sits in the heart of the Tigullio Gulf, facing the marvelous and famous Portofino bay. The hotel has played host to a number of illustrious guests over the years and it was completely refurbished in 1995.
The Lord Byron restaurant has large windows overlooking the sea and serves both regional and Mediterranean cuisine.

A view of the Tigullio Gulf from the Excelsior Palace Hotel.

The Eden Roc restaurant, located right on the beach, is only open during the hot summer months.
There are also two bars, a conference center and a private beach club that has various well-equipped changing cabins.
Wellness center. A part of the Kursaal, the elegant early 20th-century villa linked to the hotel, is used for the Health & Fitness Club. It has a heated indoor pool, spa, Turkish bath, sauna and gym with a sea view. Qualified staff are on hand for both traditional treatments and more sophisticated programs.
The outside pool is often used for aqua-gym courses.

USCIO

Colonia della Salute Arnaldi
*Via C. Arnaldi 6, Tel. 0185919406
www.coloniaarnaldi.com
Open from April to October*
This complex was founded in 1906 by the chemist Carlo Araldi and it is located in a charming position, between Genoa and Portofino in a grand park. Guests can choose between colonial pavilions and buildings fitted with a range of comforts. The complex also has a private garden, bar, reading room, concert hall, gym, sauna, Turkish bath, health trail, tennis court, playground and indoor pool. The restaurant serves Italian cuisine, with a focus on eating well. Personal dietary needs can be catered for.

The wellness center is a cutting-edge complex specializing in preventative medicine and cures based on medicinal plants. The exact nature of the treatments required is determined by personal needs and takes into account one's diet. The aim is to reach one's ideal weight and optimum state of mental and physical wellbeing. The beauty treatments are done in collaboration with doctors and specialists and are aimed at removing some of the most common cosmetic flaws. The center also does a skin check-up using special equipment, has a skin clinic and offers mesotherapy, which is a form of non-surgical cosmetic medicine.

WELLNESS

THE A-Z OF WHAT YOU NEED TO KNOW

GETTING TO

By plane to Liguria

GENOA, Sestri Ponente - Cristoforo Colombo Airport Tel. 01060151, www.aeroportodigenova.it or www.airport.genova.it

For national and international arrivals, tickets and parking, Tel. 0106015273, for flight info, Tel. 0106015410, for lost luggage, Tel. 0106015407.

The airport lies a mere 6km from the center of Genoa and can be reached from the Genoa-Airport exit on the A10 highway. Public transport also links the airport to the center of Genoa: 100 AMT Volabus. Buses leave every 30 minutes from Piazza Verdi (in front of the Brignole train station) and run from 5.30am to 11.45pm. More information about how to get to the airport is available at the ticket office and AMT kiosks, on 800085311 or at www.amt.genova.it

There is also the option of a taxi, which can be booked by calling Radiotaxi on 0105966 or going to www.solotaxi.it

VILLANOVA D'ALBENGA
Villanova d'Albenga International Airport Viale Generale Disegna, Tel. 0182582033,

www.rivierairport.it
About 40km from Savona. An increasing number of private flights now arrive at this airport. It is open every day from 7am to 10pm.

By car

There are three main highways: A10 for the Ponente Riviera (provinces of La Spèzia and Genova), for people arriving from France; A12, for the Levante Riviera (provinces of Savona and Imperia) and connecting Liguria to Tuscany; and the A7 Milan-Genoa, which connects Genoa to the rest of northern Italy. The A6 Turin-Savona highway from Piedmont, the A15 La Spèzia-Parma highway and the A26 Alessandria-Genoa highway are other useful routes. The coastal area is served by the SS1 Aurelia road, which follows an old Roman route that started in Rome and crossed Liguria.

By train

The train network largely covers the coast, but a good bus network (linked to the train network) covers the hinterland. For more information on time-tables and stations: Ferrovie

dello Stato Trenitalia, Trenitalia info line 892021 or www.trenitalia.it. Services for Disabled Passengers – with the Disabled Assistance Center – provides assistance for people in 225 stations around the country; more info on 199303060 or www.regione.liguria.it and www.spaziliberi.it

By bus

The bus network connecting Liguria to other regions is good, especially since many companies provide connections (sometimes to other companies) that make it possible to reach Liguria from anywhere in the country.

IBUS: fixed lines 800148148 or cellular phones 899032042; www.ibus.it is the long-distance coach leader, bringing together 6 major Italian companies. The online site is clear and provides a booking option.

By boat

Sea connections have always been important for this region, especially since this has long been one of the Mediterranean's trading hubs.

TRANSPORT

How to get

Liguria is a 'long' region (about 270km) and getting around in a car in the main cities and along the coast in summer can be very taxing. Nonetheless, it is still the best way to explore the hinterland, where the traffic is less and parking is easier. The best ways to go from place to place in Genoa are the stretches of city trains, public transport and the motorbike. To head along the coast, the train is by far the best option.

CAR AND MOTORBIKE:
At http://car-rental.traveleurope.it, you can get real time quotes to find the best car hire deals.
AVIS Booking center 199100133, www.avisnoleggio.it
GENOA: Via dell'Aviazione, Tel. 0106515101
LA SPÈZIA: Autonoleggio

Rent-a-car, Via Rosselli Fratelli 76, Tel. 0187770270
SAVONA: Corso V. Veneto 246/R, Tel. 019811311, 019810873
HERTZ Booking center 199112211, www.hertz.it
GENOA: Cristoforo Colombo Airport, Tel. 0106512422
CHIÀVARI: Piazza Generale Negri Di Sanfront, Piazza Generale Negri Di Sanfront 32, Tel. 0185309424
LA SPÈZIA: Via della Pianta 6/8, Tel. 0187512140
SAVONA: Via Vittorio Veneto 98, Tel. 019815316
SANREMO: c/o Autorimessa Italia, Via XX Settembre 17, Tel. 0184500470

– Train

TRENITALIA: info line 892021, www.trenitalia.it
Genoa Regional Headquarters, Via Andrea Doria 5, Tel. 0102742687

– Bus

At www.orariotrasporti.regione.liguria.it you can get reliable information about timetables, routes, connections and journey times.

ACTS (Azienda Consortile Trasporti Savonese), Tel. 01922011, www.acts.it
ACTA SPA La Spèzia, Tel. 800322322, www.atclaspezia.it
AMT (Azienda Mobilità e Trasporti SPA), Tel. 800085311, www.amt.genova.it
ATP (Azienda Trasporti Provinciali), Tel. 800014808, www.ali-autolineeliguri.it
RT (Riviera Trasporti SPA), Tel. 800034771, www.rivieratrasporti.it
SAR (Autolinee Riviera SPA), Via Benessea 12, Cisano sul Neva (SV) Tel. 018221544, www.sar-bus.com

GENOA PORT: Genoa Port Authority, Palazzo S. Giorgio, Via della Mercanzia 2, Tel. 0102411, www.porto.genova.it and www.stazionimarittimegenova.com The port has a surface area of 7 million m² and offers connections to just about everywhere in the world as it is served by many major international companies.

LA SPÈZIA PORT: La Spèzia Port Authority, Via Molo 1, Tel. 0187546320, www.porto. la-spezia.it; for tourist information, Viale Mazzini 45, Tel. 0187770900; www.apttigullio.liguria.it

SAVONA PORT: Savona Port Authority, Via Gramsci 14, Tel. 01985541, www.porto.sv.it

IMPERIA PORT: Imperia Port Master and Maritime Authority, Via Scarincio 17, Tel. 0183666333 (Mon, Wed and Fri 9am-noon, Tue and Thurs 9am-noon and 3-4pm).
For information on the smaller ports and yacht ports: www.barcavela.it, www.golfoparadiso.it, www.navigazionegolfodeipoeti.it, www.battellirigenova.it, www.traghettiportofino.it

CLIMATE

The temperature in Liguria is relatively constant, with the winter being especially mild and the summer months enjoying plenty of sun. In recent years, the main cities have started to be afflicted by a few weeks of stuffy summer weather.

– Bicycle

You need some form of photo identification to hire a bicycle. It costs anything upwards of 10 Euros per day.

BORDIGHERA: Barale Giorgio, Corso V. Emanuele 479, Tel. 0184252616

CAVI DI LAVAGNA: Sporting Club Astoria, Traversa di via Aurelia 1475, Tel. 0185390189

RAPALLO: Chicco, Via Mameli 55, Tel. 018567194 (also mopeds)

SANREMO: Mussello Cicli, Via Volta 34, Tel. 0184502121, www.ciclimussello.it

SANTA MARGHERITA LÌGURE: Ciclomania, Via privata L. Bozzo 22, Tel. 0185283530 (also racing bikes and mopeds)

SESTRI LEVANTE: Cicli Enrico, Via Nazionale 415, Tel. 018544725 (also mopeds)

INFORMATION

www.regione.liguria.it, www.orariotrasporti. regione.liguria.it, www.provincia.genova.it, www.provincia.savona.it, www.provincia.sp.it, www.provincia.imperia.it, www.turismoinliguria.it, www.stradeanas.it. Web without barriers for disabled people: www.disabili.com, www.terredimare.it
For further information about the region, contact the regional tourism board:

AZIENDA REGIONALE DI PROMOZIONE TURISTICA
Palazzo Ducale, Piazza Matteotti 9, Genova, Tel. 0105308201
www.turismo.liguriainrete.it
For boat trips and outings:

CONSORZIO LIGURIA VIAMARE
Tel. 010265712/010256775
www.liguriaviamare.it

Inside

Tourist information
Hotels and restaurants
At night
Museums and Monuments

EMERGENCY NUMBERS

112	Military Police (Carabinieri)
113	State Police (Polizia)
115	Fire Department
117	Financial Police
118	Medical Emergencies
1515	Fire-watch
1518	Road Information
803116	Road Assistance

ALÀSSIO

ℹ️ **IAT Punto Informativo Riviera di Ponente**
Via Mazzini 68,
Tel. 0182647027

Hotels

Aida ★★★
Via F. Gioia 25, Tel. 0182644085
www.hotelaida.it
42 Rooms
Credit cards: American Express, Diners Club, Visa, Mastercard, Bancomat, JCB
The ideal hotel for sports enthusiasts and younger visitors, who will love the baby-club. Large, airy rooms and delicious cuisine with local specialties.

Al Saraceno ★★★★
Corso Europa 64,
Tel. 0182643957
www.alsaracenogroup.com
47 Rooms
Credit cards: American Express, Diners Club, Visa, Mastercard, Bancomat
Quiet elegance is the keynote for this comfortable hotel. All the rooms are stylishly furnished and have their own balconies.
The hotel restaurant serves both classic cuisine and typical local specialties.

Badano sul Mare ★★ ★
Via Gramsci 36,
Tel. 0182640964
www.badano.com
18 Rooms
Credit cards: Visa, Mastercard, Bancomat
A comfortable hotel on the seafront; the restaurant is reserved exclusively for guests and has picture windows overlooking the bay. Rooms with balconies.

Dei Fiori ★★★
Viale Marconi 78,
Tel. 0182640519
www.hoteldeifiori-alassio.it
35 Rooms
Credit cards: American Express, Diners Club, Visa, Mastercard
Centrally positioned, this well-run, comfortable hotel has floral decorations dating back to the 1920s. The restaurant serves classic cuisine and typical local specialties.

Diana Grand Hotel ★★★★ ⑁
Via Garibaldi 110,
Tel. 0182642701
www.hoteldianaalassio.it
57 Rooms
Credit cards: American Express, Visa, Mastercard, Bancomat
With a premium position on the seafront, the Diana has large, elegant rooms with balconies. Guests can relax in the pleasant surroundings of the terrace garden and enjoy a swim in the hotel pool, complete with whirlpool and wellness center. Dine in the classic "Sun Terrace" restaurant or at the more informal "La Marina".

Savoia ★★★ ⑁
Via Milano 14, Tel. 0182640277
www.hotelsavoia.it
35 Rooms
Credit cards: American Express, Diners Club, Visa, Mastercard
Seafront position, modern hotel with comfortable rooms and a barrel-vaulted, brick-faced lounge. Terrace with solarium. The "Profumo di Timo" restaurant serves local, Ligurian cuisine.

Restaurants

Baiadelsole ⑬⑬⑬
Corso Marconi 32,
Tel. 0182641814
mirella.porro@tin.it
Closed Mondays and Tuesday in winter, Monday in summer
Credit cards: Visa, Mastercard
Pleasing décor for the Baiadelsole, run by Angelo and Mirella, both passionate about hospitality. Angelo looks after the guests and Mirella holds sway in the kitchen. Must try specialties include grilled squid with lime rind and cinnamon pudding with pears in red wine.

Palma ⑬⑬⑬⑬
Via Cavour 11,
Tel. 0182640314
Closed Wednesdays
Credit cards: American Express, Diners Club, Visa, Mastercard, Bancomat
One of Liguria's top regional restaurants in an elegant, aristocratic setting. A deliberately limited choice of carefully thought-out dishes range from traditional fare to more creative items.

ALBENGA

ℹ️ **IAT Punto Informativo Riviera di Ponente**
Via Mazzini 68,
Tel. 0182558444

Hotels

Ca' di Berta ★★★ ⑁
Salea, Via Case di Berta,
Tel. 0182559930
www.hotelcadiberta.it
10 Rooms
Credit cards: American Express, Diners Club, Visa, Mastercard
This comfortable, romantic hotel boasts Roman origins. A sunny, airy, building in stone set in its own park nestling amidst olive groves and vineyards.

La Gallinara ★★★
Via Piave 66, Tel. 018253086
www.hotellagallinara.it
25 Rooms
Credit cards: American Express, Diners Club, Visa, Mastercard
Set on the outskirts of the town, this nautical style hotel has been completely renovated. The rooms have all mod cons and breath-taking 180° views over the sea and the coast. Guests can enjoy a sweet breakfast buffet on the hotel's panoramic terrace.

Rural Lodgings

Il Colletto ★
Campochiesa, Via Cavour 34,
Tel. 018221858
www.agriturismoilcolletto.it
Closed mid January-February
Credit cards: American Express, Diners Club, Visa, Mastercard, Bancomat
The property is divided into three parts: the first part contains the guest apartments surrounded by a garden with a swimming pool and gazebo, the second the stables and picnic area and the third the farm and farmhouse. Gardening courses available.

Restaurants

Babette ⑬⑬
Viale Pontelungo 26,
Tel. 0182544556
www.ristorantebabette.com
Closed Mondays and Tuesday midday
Credit cards: Visa, Mastercard, Bancomat
Babette's is just a stone's throw from Albenga's famous 'towers', with an intimate atmosphere and a small al fresco dining area for the summer. The two chefs are well-known for their creativity and take great care over the choice of ingredients. Extensive wine list.

Il Pernambucco ⑬⑬
Viale Italia 35, Tel. 018253458
massimoalessandri@libero.it
Closed Wednesdays (in winter)
Credit cards: American Express, Diners Club, Visa, Mastercard, Bancomat
This pleasant, modern restaurant is set in a large park and specializes in traditional local dishes, using fresh local ingredients such as "violetto" asparagus and artichokes. Coeliac menu available.

Osteria dei Leoni ⑬⑬
Vico Avarenna 1, Tel. 018251937
www.osteriadeileoni.it
Closed Tuesdays
Credit cards: American Express, Visa, Mastercard
The "Osteria dei Leoni", in its charming 14th-century palazzo, is run by Roberto, passionate

★★⨽ ★★★ ⋅★⋅ ★★★ ★★ ★ Hotels   ⑬⑬⑬⑬⑬ ⑬⑬⑬⑬ ⑬⑬⑬ ⑬⑬ ⑬ Restaurants   ⑁ Disabled   ★ Special TCI Rates

about hospitality. Locally caught fresh fish dominate the menu with dishes like braised tuna with mozzarella and oregano; lemon pie or meringue in green tea sauce are just two of the desserts.

Museums

Civico Museo Ingauno
Via N. Lamboglia 1,
Tel. 018251215
www.iisl.it
15 June-15 September: Tuesdays-Sundays 9.30-12.30, 15.30-19.30. 16 September-14 June: Tuesdays-Sundays 10-12.30, 14.30-18

Museo Diocesano d'Arte Sacra
Via Episcopio 5, Tel. 018250288
www.diocesialbengaimperia.it
Tuesdays-Sundays 10-12, 16-18

Museo Navale Romano
Piazza S. Michele 12,
Tel. 018251215, www.iisl.it
15 June-15 September:
Tuesdays-Sundays 9.30-12.30,
15.30-19.30. 16 September-
14 June: Tuesdays-Sundays
10-12.30, 14.30-18

ALBISOLA SUPERIORE

> ℹ️ *IAT Punto Informativo Riviera di Ponente*
> Passeggiata E. Montale 21,
> Tel. 0194002008

Museums

Museo Manlio Trucco
Corso Ferrari 193, Tel. 019482741
www.comune.albisola-superiore.sv.it
Temporarily closed

ALBISSOLA MARINA

> ℹ️ *IAT* Passeggiata E.
> Montale 21, Tel. 0194002008

Museums

Villa Faraggiana and Fabbrica-Casa-Museo G. Mazzotti
Viale Matteotti 29,
Tel. and Fax 019489872,
www.gmazzotti1903.it
Weekdays: 8.30-12.30, 14.30-19.30. Holidays: 9.30-12.30, 15.30-19.30

ANDORA

> ℹ️ *Comune*
> Via Aurelia 41, Tel. 0182681004

Hotels

Garden ***
Via Aurelia 60, Tel. 018288678
www.hotelgardenandora.com
16 Rooms
Credit cards: American Express,

Diners Club, Visa, Mastercard
Right on the seafront, a quiet, family-run hotel with home cooking. The dining room overlooks the garden and evening entertainment is provided.

Moresco ***
Via Aurelia 96, Tel. 018289141
www.hotelmoresco.com
35 Rooms
Credit cards: American Express, Diners Club, Visa, Bancomat
In an impressive position on the Levante seafront promenade, this modern four-story hotel has access to the beach. A pleasantly-decorated hotel with functional bedrooms. Sweet and savory breakfast buffet.

Restaurants

Casa del Priore 🍴🍴🍴
Via Castello 34, Tel. 018287330
Closed Mondays in winter
Credit cards: American Express, Diners Club, Visa, Mastercard, JCB
A cozy, romantic restaurant in the heart of the medieval downtown. Fish specialties such as spinato selvaggio alla ligure and lobster soup. Brasserie serving first courses and grilled fish and meat in the outdoor summer dining area.

Pan de Cà 🍴🍴
Strada per Conna 13,
Tel. 018280290
Closed Tuesdays (except mid June-mid September)
Credit cards: American Express, Visa, Mastercard
This cozy restaurant nestles amidst the green of the olive groves along the ancient Roman road to Conna. Traditional home cooking (make sure you try the capon and the ravioli or the homemade pasta tagliolini) at a fixed price.

APRICALE

> ℹ️ *Ente Turistico Pro Loco*
> Via Roma 1,
> Tel. 0184208641

Hotels

Apricus
Via IV Novembre 5,
Tel. 0184209020
www.apricuslocanda.com
5 Rooms
Credit cards: American Express, Diners Club, Visa, Mastercard, Bancomat
Lovely "locanda" in the historical downtown. A sunny place to stay with a romantic atmosphere. The rooms are simply, but tastefully, furnished with an eye to detail. Sweet and savory breakfast buffet.

Restaurants

Apricale da Delio 🍴🍴
Piazza Vittorio Veneto 9,
Tel. 0184208008
www.ristoranteapricale.it
Closed Mondays and Tuesdays (except in summer)
Credit cards: American Express, Diners Club, Visa, Mastercard, Bancomat, JCB
In the historic downtown, with an open air dining area and a garden overlooking the valley and the town. Local specialties. Good choice of wines and spirits.

La Favorita 🍴 ★
Richelmo, Strada S. Pietro 1,
Tel. 0184208186
www.hotelristorantelafavorita.com
Closed Wednesdays (in winter also Tuesday evenings), always open in August
Credit cards: American Express, Diners Club, Visa, Mastercard, Bancomat
Cozy restaurant in a small "locanda" with a few comfortable rooms for guests. Great views and an al fresco dining area for the warmer months. Very attentive service and excellent cuisine, with meat grilled on the fireplace in the dining room. Home-grown olive oil.

Museums

Museo della Storia di Apricale
Castello della Lucertola,
Via Castello, Tel. 0184208126
www.apricale.org
Tuesdays-Saturdays 15-18.30;
Sundays 10.30-12, 15-18.30

BORDIGHERA

> ℹ️ *IAT*
> Via Vittorio Emanuele II
> 172/174, Tel. 0184262322

Hotels

Aurora *** ♿
Via Pelloux 42/B, Tel. 0184261311
www.hotelaurora.net
30 Rooms
Credit cards: American Express, Diners Club, Visa, Mastercard, Bancomat
An attractive historic villa surrounded by greenery, centrally placed and near the sea. The hotel offers its guests comfortable rooms, spacious lounges, a café, restaurant and terrace solarium with a great view, private car park and an excellent cellar of fine wines.

G.H. del Mare ***** ★
Via Portico della Punta 34,
Tel. 0184262201
www.grandhoteldelmare.com
99 Rooms
Credit cards: American Express, Diners Club, Visa, Mastercard,

Bancomat

A large, modern hotel overlooking the sea with a spacious hanging garden which blooms all year long. Very comfortable rooms, sea views available, internet point, wellness and beauty center.

Villa Speranza ★★★
Via G. Galilei 3, Tel. 0184261717
www.hotelvillasperanza.it
12 Rooms
Credit cards: American Express, Diners Club, Visa, Mastercard
Villa Speranza was originally a British ambassador's residence, today it is an elegant hotel in a quiet position with a small number of comfortable rooms overlooking the sea or the tropical garden. The restaurant is exclusively for guests and serves classical Italian cuisine with local specialties. Vegetarian and coeliac menu available.

Restaurants

Carletto 🍴🍴🍴
Via Vittorio Emanuele 339,
Tel. 0184261725
Closed Wednesdays
Credit cards: American Express, Diners Club, Visa, Mastercard, Bancomat
This elegant, refined restaurant with its large windows only serves seafood. Try the lukewarm shellfish and asparagus salad or the local pasta trenette with prawns, scampi and baby octopi, good choice of wines and spirits.

Il Tempo Ritrovato 🍴
Via Vittorio Emanuele 144,
Tel. 0184261207
www.descurundu.it
Credit cards: Visa, Mastercard, Bancomat
A small, well-run restaurant. Advance booking is advisable to ensure a chance to enjoy its excellent meat and fish dishes.

La Via Romana 🍴🍴🍴🍴
Via Romana 57, Tel. 0184266681
www.laviaromana.it
Closed Wednesdays and Thursday midday
Credit cards: American Express, Diners Club, Visa, Mastercard, Bancomat
The Via Romana is a long, shady road which runs parallel to the main Aurelia road. It is lined with handsome 19th-century buildings and villas and one of these is home to the eponymous restaurant. Refined cuisine with fish and seafood dishes predominating. Vast choice of over 500 spirits.

Museums

Mostra Permanente Pompeo Mariani ★
Via Romana 39, Tel. 0184263601

www.iisl.it
Mondays-Fridays 9-12, 15-17.
Closed holidays

Museo-Biblioteca «Clarence Bicknell»
Via Romana 39/bis,
Tel. 0184263694
www.iisl.it
Mondays-Fridays 9.30-13, 13.30-16.45

BORGIO VEREZZI

> ℹ️ **Comune**
> *Via Municipio 17,*
> *Tel. 01961821*

Restaurants

Cà du Gregorio 🍴
Verezzi, Via Ortari 22,
Tel. 019611952
Closed Mondays-Wednesdays (Mondays-Fridays in winter)
Charming farmhouse restaurant nestling amidst terraced vineyards with a superb view over the bay below. Home cooking.

Da Caxetta 🍴🍴
Bòrgio, Via XX Settembre 12,
Tel. 019610166
Closed Tuesdays
Credit cards: American Express, Diners Club, Visa, Mastercard, Bancomat, JCB
This characteristic restaurant is in the historic downtown, oppiste the tiny church of S. Pietro. The dining room is in a cave chiselled out of the rock and in the summer guests can dine al fresco in the charming piazzetta. Local specialties in the Ligurian tradition with top quality ingredients.

Doc 🍴🍴🍴
Bòrgio, Via Vittorio Veneto 1,
Tel. 019611477
www.ristorantedoc.it
Closed Mondays and Tuesdays
Credit cards: American Express, Visa, Mastercard, Bancomat
An elegant, early 19th-century villa with two dining rooms and a large garden for al fresco dining. The DOC label is reserved for quality wines and quality is exactly what you can expect from this restaurant's refined cuisine.

CAMOGLI

> ℹ️ **IAT Punto Turistico Informativo**
> *Via XX Settembre 33,*
> *Tel. 0185771066*

Hotels

Cenobio dei Dogi ★★★★ ★
Via Cuneo 34, Tel. 01857241
www.cenobio.it

106 Rooms
Credit cards: American Express, Diners Club, Visa, Mastercard, Bancomat
This stylish hotel is in a prestigious historical palazzo, overlooking an inlet at the feet of Portofino's hills, with just the right mix of history and modernity. Rooms are spacious and the terrace café overlooks the sea. The "Dei Dogi" restaurant under independent management specializes in local cuisine.

La Camogliese ★★
Via Garibaldi 55, Tel. 0185771402
www.lacamogliese.it
21 Rooms
Credit cards: American Express, Diners Club, Visa, Mastercard, Bancomat
A family-run hotel in a completely renovated liberty-style palazzo on the seafront with a splendid view.

Restaurants

Da Paolo 🍴🍴
Via S. Fortunato 14,
Tel. 0185773595
Closed Mondays and Tuesday midday
Credit cards: American Express, Diners Club, Visa, Mastercard, Bancomat
The same family has been running this fish restaurant for the last 20 years. Local cuisine with homemade sweets and a selection of local and Italian wines.

Hostaria del Pesce 🍴🍴
Via P. Schiaffino 5,
Tel. 0185775068
www.hostariadelpesce.com
Closed Thursdays
Credit cards: American Express, Diners Club, Visa, Mastercard, Bancomat
A small, family-run restaurant in the center of this fishing village. The menu changes day by day according to what's freshest at the market every morning.

Rosa 🍴🍴🍴 ★
Largo Casabona 11,
Tel. 0185773411
ristoranterosa@hotmail.com
Closed Tuesdays and Wednesday midday
Credit cards: American Express, Diners Club, Visa, Mastercard, Bancomat
Restaurant in a liberty-style villa perched on a cliff top. Founded in 1949, it has a terrace for fresco dining and a conservatory with a stunning view over the Paradiso bay for the winter months. Freshly-caught local fish are the focal point of the excellent cuisine.

At night

Capitan Hook
Via Porto 4, Tel. 0185770411
Overlooking the port, open until 3am, excellent cocktails, whisky, rum and snacks.

CAMPOROSSO

ℹ️ Comune
Piazza Garibaldi 35,
Tel. 018428771

Rural Lodgings

Il Bausco ★
Brunetti, Tel. 0184206013
www.ilbausco.com
Closed November
Credit cards: Visa

This complex of farmhouses have been carefully renovated to provide accommodation in the Bordighera countryside, with its background of palm trees, cypresses and olive groves. Excursions on the Maritime Alps, to the coast and over the border to the Côte d'Azur.

Restaurants

Manuel ᪲
Corso italia 265, Tel. 0184205037
Closed working Mondays and Tuesdays
Credit cards: American Express, Diners Club, Visa, Mastercard, Bancomat

Pleasant building on the road to Dolceacqua, sunny, airy dining room and local cuisine with an emphasis on meat. Good selection of spirits.

CASTELNUOVO MAGRA

ℹ️ Comune
Via Vittorio Veneto 2,
Tel. 0187693801

Rural Lodgings

Cascina dei Peri ★
Via Montefrancio 71,
Tel. 0187674085
www.lacascinadeiperi.com
An 8-hectare farm growing grapes for Colli di Luni, Vermentino and red Querciolo DOC wines, as well as delicious olive oil. Comfortable rooms and some independent apartments with the use of the kitchen are available as well as a small fully-equipped area for camper vans.

Monteverde
Via Molin del Piano 65,
Tel. 336442926
www.agriturismomonteverde.it
A well-looked after farm with lovingly-tended vineyards and olive groves producing excellent Colli di Luni DOC wine and extra-

virgin olive oil. The same care goes into the airy, well-equipped accommodation, with gifts of fresh eggs, vegetables, fruit and jam for guests.

Restaurants

Armanda ᪲
Piazza Garibaldi 6,
Tel. 0187674410
trattoriaarmanda@libero.it
Closed Wednesdays
Credit cards: Visa, Mastercard, Bancomat

This typical "trattoria" is a local institution. Its superb position dominates the village and part of the surrounding countryside. The "trattoria" itself is a long narrow room lined with tables each side. Typical local cuisine and a well-balanced, tasty menu.

Mulino del Cibus ᪲
Via Canale, Tel. 0187676102
Closed Mondays
Credit cards: Visa, Mastercard, Bancomat

A characteristic old mill dating back to the 1930s that has been restored to its former glory complete with all its mechanisms. The menu changes completely every week.

CERVO

ℹ️ Comune
Salita Al Castello 15,
Tel. 0183449111

Restaurant

San Giorgio ᪲᪲᪲
Via A. Volta 19, Tel. 0183400175
www.ristorantesangiorgio.net
Closed July and August only Tuesday midday
Credit cards: American Express, Visa, Mastercard, Bancomat

Positioned right at the top of the village, this cozy, well-run restaurant is best reached on foot. Al fresco dining on the terrace overlooking the sea in the summer. Fish-based menu with locally-produced olive oil.

Museums

Museo Etnografico del Ponente Ligure
Piazza S. Caterina 2,
Tel. 0183408197
Summer: Mondays-Sundays 9-12.30, 16-22.30. Winter: Mondays-Sundays 9-12.30, 15.30-18.30

CHIÀVARI

ℹ️ Punto Informativo Turistico
Corso Accorti I,
Tel. 0185325198

Hotels

Monte Rosa ★★★
Via Marinetti 6,
Tel. 0185300321
www.hotelmonterosa.com
64 Rooms
Credit cards: American Express, Diners Club, Visa, Mastercard, Bancomat

An elegant palazzo houses this hotel with its lively restaurant serving local specialties and Mediterranean cuisine open to the public in the historic medieval downtown. Extra-comfort rooms and some suites are available, together with a private garage and an internet point.

Santa Maria ★★★ ♿
Viale Tito Groppo 29,
Tel. 0185363321
www.santamaria-hotel.com
36 Rooms
Credit cards: Diners Club, Visa, Mastercard

Renovated four-story hotel on the seafront with a pretty garden and well-run restaurant. Special offers and facilities for families with children.

Restaurants

Boccondivino ᪲᪲᪲
Via Entella 18,
Tel. 0185362964
www.tigulliovino.it/boccon_divino_chiavari.htm
Closed Sundays
Credit cards: Visa, Mastercard, Bancomat

This new restaurant is in the heart of the Tigullio, along a narrow street of the historic downtown. It serves menus based on freshly-caught local fish, with a wide selection of desserts to round off the meal.

Lord Nelson ᪲᪲᪲᪲
Corso Valparaiso 27,
Tel. 0185302595
Closed Wednesdays
Credit cards: Diners Club, Visa, Mastercard, Bancomat

Stunning restaurant with a long history right on the beach. Lovely veranda overlooking the sea and various indoors dining rooms in wood recreate the suggestive atmosphere of Lord Nelson's flagship. Delicious menus with homemade bread and ice cream. Excellent list and wine shop.

Luchin ᪲
Via Bighetti 51, Tel. 0185301063
www.luchin.it
Closed Sundays and holidays
This typical local "osteria" along a typical local carruggio (street) in the historic downtown has been in business since 1907. It serves traditional cuisine and has a shop that sells the osteria's products.

Museums

Galleria Civica di Palazzo Rocca
Via Costaguta 2, Tel. 0185308577
www.comune.chiavari.ge.it
Saturdays and holidays 10-12,
16-19. Visits also by request

Museo Archeologico
per la Preistoria e la
Protostoria del Tigullio
Via Costaguta 4, Tel. 0185320829
www.archeologia.beniculturali.it/
pages/atlante/S18.html
Tuesdays-Saturdays, 2nd and 4th
Sundays of the month 9-13.30

Museo Diocesano
Piazza Nostra Signora
dell'Orto 7,
Tel. 0185590530-0185370062
www.chiavari.chiesacattolica.it
Wednesdays and Sundays 10-12.
Visits also by request, only
groups

Museo Storico, Quadreria,
Museo Garaventa, Biblioteca
Via Ravaschieri 15,
Tel. 0185324713
www.societaeconomica.com
Museo Storico: summer:
Tuesdays-Thursdays 10-12;
Fridays 9.30-11.30. Museo
Garaventa: summer: Thursdays
10-12; Fridays 9.30-11.30

DOLCEÀCQUA
Rural Lodgings

La Vecchia
Via Roma 86, Tel. 0184206024
www.locandalavecchia.com
Credit cards: Visa, Mastercard
A "locanda" surrounded by
greenery just on the edge of this
medieval village with
comfortable, color-themed
rooms. Guests can go on walks
and mountain bike excursions or
spend their days relaxing at the
seaside just 5 kms away.

Rifugio Alta Via
Pozzuolo, Strada Militare
La Colla-Gouta, Tel. 0184206754
Open April-October
The Nervia valley runs north-
south and benefits from a sea
breeze that makes growing olives
possible even at an altitude of
800 meters. The Rifiugio is a
simple house built in stone
halfway up the valley slope with
a lovely view over the sea and
the mountains.

Restaurants

L'Antico Corso †
Via Patrioti Martiri 26,
Tel. 0184206403
rist.lanticocorso@libero.it
Closed Thursdays
Credit cards: American Express,
Visa, Mastercard, Bancomat
Unpretentious restaurant serving
traditional dishes based on fresh
local ingredients.

La Vecchia ††
Via Roma 86, Tel. 0184206024
www.locandalavecchia.com
Credit cards: Visa, Bancomat
Local Ligurian starters, borrage
ravioli and vineyard snails are
just some of the specialties
available on this restaurant's
fixed price menu (including
beverages) with suggested
choices of dishes. The walls are
signed by celebrities who have
eaten here in the past.

FINALE LIGURE

> 🛈 **Punto Informativo**
> **Riviera di Ponente**
> *Via San Pietro 14,*
> *Tel. 019681019*

Hotels

Internazionale *** ★
Via Concezione 3, Tel. 019692054
www.internazionalehotel.it
32 Rooms
Credit cards: American Express,
Visa, Mastercard, Bancomat, JCB
On the seafront promenade. All
rooms are air-conditioned and
the hotel has a seaview terrace.
Restaurant with traditional menu
and local specialties. Diving
center for enthusiasts.

Medusa *** ♿
Via Bricchieri 7, Tel. 019692545
www.medusahotel.it
32 Rooms
Credit cards: American Express,
Diners Club, Visa, Mastercard,
Bancomat
Right on the seafront, just a
stone's throw from the beach,
this charming 17th-century
building has been thoroughly
renovated. Excellent traditional
Riviera-style cuisine in the
restaurant, panoramic terrace
overlooking the sea.

Park Hotel Castello ***
Via Caviglia 26, Tel. 019691320
www.parkhotelcastello.com
19 Rooms
Credit cards: American Express,
Visa, Mastercard
The family-run Park Hotel is
surrounded by greenery just 200
meters from the sea, next to the
Castelfranco fortress. Well laid-
out, sunny rooms; swimming
pool with solarium, patio and
play equipment for children.

Punta Est ****
Via Aurelia 1, Tel. 019600611
www.puntaest.com
39 Rooms
Credit cards: American Express,
Visa, Mastercard, Bancomat
Lovely position for this hotel
perched on the rocks above the
sea and set in a park. The oldest
part of the complex was
originally an 18th-century villa,

which is now flanked by a
modern building. The rooms are
air conditioned and there is a
swimming pool with a solarium,
as well as an elegant restaurant
with an open fireplace and a
very cool bar in a cave.

Restaurants

Ai Torchi ††
Finalborgo,
Via dell'Annunziata 12,
Tel. 019690531
Closed Tuesdays (except August)
Credit cards: American Express,
Diners Club, Visa, Mastercard
This smart restaurant is in a
restyled 16th-century olive press
in the medieval downtown. It
serves traditional cuisine with
some modern touches: fish
tartare with local herbs, fish
ravioli in a ricotta cream and
basil sauce; delicious desserts,
such as orange parfait, and
homegrown olive oil.

Osteria della Briga †
Le Mànie, Via Mànie 1,
Tel. 019698579
Credit cards: Visa, Mastercard,
Bancomat
An "osteria" surrounded by
greenery which specializes in the
alternative to fish in Ligurian
cuisine: vegetable starters, onion
soup, pasta and bean soup,
charcoal-grilled meat.

Museums

Museo Archeologico
del Finale ★
Finalborgo, Chiostri
di S. Caterina,
Tel. 019690020
www.museoarcheofinale.it
Summer: Tuesdays-Sundays and
holidays 10-12, 14.30-17. Winter:
Tuesdays-Sundays and holidays
9-12, 14.30-17.30. Closed 25 and
26 December

GENOVA/GENOA

> 🛈 **Genova Turismo**
> **c/o Stazione Ferroviaria**
> **Principe**
> *Piazza Acquaverde*
> *Tel. 0102462633*
> **c/o Aeroporto Cristoforo**
> **Colombo**
> *Sestri Ponente*
> *Tel. 0106015247*
> **Genova Turismo c/o**
> **Stazione Marittima –**
> **Terminal Crociere**
> *(coincides with the arrival*
> *of cruise ships)*

Hotels

Agnello d'Oro ***
Via delle Monachette 6,
Tel. 0102462084
www.hotelagnellodoro.it
20 Rooms

A five story family-run hotel in a typical "carruggio" (street) in the historic downtown, unpretentious, efficient service with a panoramic terrace. Sweet breakfast buffet.

Balbi **
Via Balbi 21/3,
Tel. 0102759288
www.hotelbalbigenova.it
13 Rooms

Centrally positioned hotel in a historical palazzo with high, frescoed ceilings; the street it stands in has recently been awarded UNESCO Heritage status. Ideal for sightseeing, offers guest rooms both comfortable and characteristic.

Best Western Hotel Metropoli *** ★
Piazza Fontane Marose,
Tel. 0102468888
www.bestwestern.it/metropoli_ge
48 Rooms

Credit cards: American Express, Diners Club, Visa, Mastercard, Bancomat

In the heart of the city, just a stone's throw from the Aquarium and the Opera House, this hotel is ideal for business or pleasure. Sweet and savory breakfast buffet.

Bristol Palace ****
Via XX Settembre 35,
Tel. 010592541
www.hotelbristolpalace.com
133 Rooms

Credit cards: American Express, Diners Club, Visa, Mastercard, Bancomat, JCB

Liberty-style palazzo built in 1902 right in the center of downtown Genoa with comfortable, cozy rooms. Some suites have whirlpool tubs. Prices on request.

Golden Tulip Moderno Verdi **** ★ &
Piazza G. Verdi 5,
Tel. 0105532104
www.modernoverdi.it
87 Rooms

Credit cards: American Express, Diners Club, Visa, Mastercard, Bancomat, JCB

A 1920s palazzo that has been restyled, but still retains its Liberty atmosphere, right in the business district of Genoa opposite the Brignole railway station. Stylish rooms decorated with careful attention to detail, spacious bathrooms all with either power showers or whirlpool tubs. The "Rigoletto" restaurant is reserved for guests' exclusive use and serves local specialties and classic Italian cuisine.

Helvetia *** ★
Piazza della Nunziata 1,
Tel. 0102465468
www.hotelhelvetiagenova.it
32 Rooms

Credit cards: American Express, Diners Club, Visa, Mastercard, Bancomat

A centrally-placed 19th-century hotel close to landmarks like the Aquarium, the Porta Principe railway station and the Genoa conference center. Sweet breakfast buffet with homemade pastries and free internet point.

Jolly Hotel Plaza **** ★ &
Via M. Piaggio 11,
Tel. 01083161
www.jollyhotels.it
143 Rooms

Credit cards: American Express, Diners Club, Visa, Mastercard, Bancomat

Housed in two buildings, the Jolly Plaza maintains the excellent standards the chain is well-known for. Individually decorated, stylish rooms with a good level of comfort; "Villetta di Negro" restaurant.

Savoia Continental **** ★
Via Arsenale di Terra 1,
Tel. 010261641
www.hotelsavoiagenova.it
44 Rooms

Credit cards: American Express, Diners Club, Visa, Mastercard, Bancomat

A completely restyled, early 20th century, Liberty building in the heart of downtown Genoa. Rooms have all amenities.

Sheraton Genova Hotel **** &
Via Pionieri e Aviatori d'Italia 44,
Tel. 01065491
www.sheratongenova.com
282 Rooms

Credit cards: American Express, Diners Club, Visa, Mastercard, Bancomat

A modern hotel with comfortable rooms and luxurious suites near the airport. The well-run "Il Portico" restaurant serves Mediterranean and Ligurian cuisine.

Torre Cambiaso **** ★ &
Pegli, Via Scarpanto 49,
Tel. 010665236
www.antichedimore.com
45 Rooms

Credit cards: American Express, Diners Club, Visa, Mastercard, Bancomat

Set in a park with a small lake and caves on the hills overlooking the sea, this hotel is fully-equipped to host business meetings and events. The rooms are air conditioned and furnished with antiques. A snooker room and the "Del Castello" restaurant complete the picture.

Rural Lodgings

Pietre Turchine
Campenave, Via Superiore dell'Olba 41/L, Tel. 0106139168
www.pietreturchine.it
Open mid June-mid September, Christmas, Easter and weekends

Accommodation close to Genoa city, but set amidst the woods of the Monte Beigua Nature Reserve. Guests enjoy comfortable rooms and local cuisine using produce directly from the farm.

Restaurants

Antica Cantina i Tre Merli ¶¶ ★
Vico dietro il Coro della Maddalena 26/r, Tel. 0102474095
www.itremerli.it
Closed Saturday midday and Sundays

Credit cards: American Express, Diners Club, Visa, Mastercard, Bancomat

A soberly stylish restaurant in what was once a Medieval stable block, which has retained its original stone walls and floors. Specialties range from traditional Ligurian dishes to creative cuisine. The pasta, "focaccia" bread rolls and the desserts are all homemade; excellent wine list and guests are welcome to tour the wine cellar.

Antica Osteria del Bai ¶¶¶
Quarto dei Mille, Via Quarto 12,
Tel. 010387478
www.osteriadelbai.it
Closed Mondays

Credit cards: American Express, Diners Club, Visa, Mastercard, Bancomat

A charming historical "osteria" with a stylish air and impeccable service. Typical local cuisine with a range of tasty, but light, dishes mostly based on fish and vegetables flavored with herbs and spices.

Antica Osteria della Castagna ¶¶
Quarto dei Mille, Via R. della Castagna 20/r, Tel. 0103990265
www.osteriadellacastagna.it
Closed Mondays and Sunday evenings

Credit cards: American Express, Diners Club, Visa, Mastercard

An old posting inn with several dining rooms and an air conditioned veranda. The kitchen stays open after 10 o'clock for late diners. A mainly fish-based menu with a selection of delicious desserts. A good choice of different olive oils.

Antica Osteria di Vico Palla ¶¶
Vico Palla 15, Tel. 0102466575
acap29@libero.it
Closed Mondays

Credit cards: American Express, Diners Club, Visa, Mastercard

This "osteria" next to the old

pier in the Porto Antico district opened at the end of the 17th century and has been in business ever since. Recently enlarged, it has managed to retain its fascinating, historic ambience. Fresh fish and seafood cooked in traditional Ligurian style dominate the menu.

Bruxaboschi ⅐⅐
San Desiderio, Via F. Mignone 8,
Tel. 0103450302
www.bruxaboschi.com
Closed Sunday evenings and Mondays

Credit cards: American Express, Diners Club, Visa, Mastercard, Bancomat

A restaurant serving mushrooms and other products of the earth to balance its fish dishes, with some innovative culinary ideas. Good choice of wines and spirits. Homemade bread and desserts.

Chichibio ⅐⅐⅐
Via David Chiossone 20/r,
Tel. 0102476191
Closed Sundays

Credit cards: Visa, Mastercard, Bancomat

A restaurant in a mid 15th-century palazzo with a couple of clever chefs in the kitchen producing fish dishes and meat menus that change with the seasons. Excellent wine list.

Creuza de Ma ⅐⅐⅐
Piazza Nettuno 2,
Tel. 0103770091
www.ristorantecreuzadema.it
Closed Sundays and Monday midday

Credit cards: American Express, Diners Club, Visa, Mastercard, Bancomat

The name for this characteristic, nautical-style restaurant comes from a song by folk singer Fabrizio De Andrè. It is set in a great position on the small Boccadasse harbour and has a cozy veranda. Local cuisine with a lot of fish and seafood dishes and some meat. Finish up with the house specialty dessert of hazelnut semifreddo with hot chocolate sauce.

Enoteca Sola ⅐
Via C. Barabino 120/r,
Tel. 010594513
www.vinotecasola.it
Closed Sundays

Credit cards: American Express, Diners Club, Visa, Mastercard, Bancomat

Enoteca wine bar serving snacks and light meals. Try the fish tartare with crudités, trenette pasta al pesto, freshly-made tagliolini pasta with grouper sauce and the homemade desserts, all washed down with appropriate wines selected from among the 500 labels in the cellars. Good choice of spirits with the accent on rum.

Gran Gotto ⅐⅐⅐
Viale Brigata Bisagno 69/r,
Tel. 010564344
www.mangiareinliguria.it
Closed Saturday midday and Sundays

Credit cards: American Express, Diners Club, Visa, Mastercard

A cozy, but stylish restaurant (with an important collection of contemporary art) which upholds its long-standing tradition of fine wines and fine dining. Coeliac menu available on request. Extensive wine and spirit list.

I Tre Merli ⅐⅐ ★
Area Porto Antico,
Palazzina Millo, Tel. 0102464416
www.itremerli.it

Credit cards: American Express, Diners Club, Visa, Mastercard, Bancomat, JCB

A spacious restaurant in a restyled tobacco warehouse in the Porto Antico Marina district. Specialized in fish but with some meat dishes; the focaccia di Recco, farinata, pasta and desserts are all homemade.

Il Violino Rosso ⅐
Via Donghi 172/r, Tel. 010511412
Closed Mondays

Credit cards: American Express, Diners Club, Visa, Mastercard, Bancomat

A rather unusual restaurant run by two energetic young people who are both passionate about their chosen professions. Unpretentious décor with a small terrace for al fresco dining. Interesting, innovative menu based on fresh local ingredients.

La Buca di San Matteo ⅐⅐⅐
Via D. Chiossone 5/r,
Tel. 0108690648
www.labucadisanmatteo.it
Closed Sundays

Credit cards: American Express, Diners Club, Visa, Mastercard, Bancomat

A very smart restaurant in the Medieval Piazza di S. Matteo, with several cozy corners and a private dining room. Guests can watch their meals being prepared in the open plan kitchen and the menu changes with the seasons. Stylish food and impeccable service.

La Cantina di Colombo ⅐⅐
Via di Porta Soprana 55/r,
Tel. 0102475959
www.lacantinadicolombo.it
Closed Sundays and Saturday midday

Credit cards: American Express, Visa, Mastercard, Bancomat

In a rustic 16th-century palazzo in the historic downtown, this cozy restaurant has a partially glass floor that gives guests a glimpse of its amazing cellars with over 1000 labels. The traditional menu follows the seasons.

Le Cantine Squarciafico ⅐
Piazza Invrea 3/r,
Tel. 0102470823
www.squarciafico.it

Credit cards: American Express, Diners Club, Visa, Mastercard

In a renovated 16th-century palazzo in what were once the cisterns, now transformed into two dining rooms with vaulted ceilings and marble and slate floors. The kitchen is open until midnight for late diners and the chef recommends his assortment of vegetable pies, Ligurian-style fish and the chocolate cake.

Le Terrazze del Ducale ⅐⅐
Piazza Matteotti 8,
Tel. 010588600
www.leterrazzedelducale.it

Credit cards: American Express, Diners Club, Visa, Mastercard, Bancomat, JCB

A very stylish, centrally-located restaurant on the 5th floor of Palazzo Ducale with beamed ceilings and a terrace for al fresco dining. Perfect for working lunches or after cinema or theater suppers.

Maxela ⅐⅐
Vico inferiore del Ferro,
Tel. 0102474209

Credit cards: American Express, Diners Club, Visa, Mastercard, Bancomat

Meat reigns supreme at Maxela's. Guests choose their cut directly from the butcher's counter next to the entrance.

Rina ⅐⅐
Mura delle Grazie 3/r,
Tel. 0102466475
www.ristorantedarina.it
Closed Mondays

Credit cards: American Express, Diners Club, Visa, Mastercard, Bancomat, JCB

The oldest restaurant in town with 15th-century cap-vaulted ceilings, it has been under the same cheerful management since 1946 and specializes in freshly-caught fish and seafood dishes. A favorite haunt of the red carpet crowd.

Museums

Castello D'Albertis Museo delle Culture del Mondo ★
Corso Dogali 18,
Tel. 0102723820-0102723464
www.castellodalbertisgenova.it
April-September: Tuesdays-Fridays 10-18; Saturdays and Sundays 10-19. October-March: Tuesdays-Fridays 10-17; Saturdays and Sundays 10-18. Closed Mondays

Musei di Strada Nuova-Palazzo Bianco ★
Via Garibaldi 11,
Tel. 0102759185
www.museidistradanuova.it
Tuesdays-Fridays 9-19;
Saturdays and Sundays 10-19.
Closed Mondays

Musei di Strada Nuova-Palazzo Rosso ★
Via Garibaldi 18,
Tel. 0102759185
www.museidistradanuova.it
Tuesdays-Fridays 9-19;
Saturdays and Sundays 10-19.
Closed Mondays

Museo Civico di Storia Naturale «Giacomo Doria» ★
Via Brigata Liguria 9,
Tel. 010564567-010582171
www.museodoria.it
Tuesdays-Fridays 9-19;
Saturdays and Sundays 10-19.
Closed Mondays

Museo del Tesoro della Cattedrale di San Lorenzo ★
Cattedrale, Piazza S. Lorenzo,
Tel. 0102471831
www.museosanlorenzo.it
Mondays-Saturdays 9-12, 15-18

Museo di Palazzo Reale
Via Balbi 10,
Tel. 0102710236
www.palazzorealegenova.it
Tuesdays, Wednesdays 9-13;
Thursdays-Sundays 9-19

Museo di Sant'Agostino ★
Piazza Sarzano 35/r,
Tel. 0102511263
www.museosantagostino.it
Tuesdays-Fridays 9-19;
Saturdays and Sundays 10-19.
Closed Mondays

Palazzo Ducale-Mostre ★
Piazza Matteotti 9,
Tel. 0105574000
www.palazzoducale.genova.it

At night

Jasmine
Via D'Annunzio 19,
Tel. 010541273
www.jasminecafe.it
Well-known disco specializing in '70s, '80s and '90s disco music.

Liquid Art Café
Via Mura delle Grazie 25
Trendy décor, excellent service and lounge music, top quality drinks.
Milk Club dedicated to avante-garde music: Indian, reggae and electronic.

IMPERIA

> ℹ️ **Punto Informativo Turistico**
> Viale Matteotti 37,
> Tel. 0183660140

Hotels

Croce di Malta *** ♿
Porto Maurizio,
Via Scarincio 148,
Tel. 0183667020
www.hotelcrocedimalta.com
39 Rooms
Credit cards: American Express, Diners Club, Visa, Mastercard, Bancomat
A comfortable hotel right on the seafront overlooking the port, ideal for business or pleasure. The "I Cavalieri" and "Le Polene" restaurants serve high quality local cuisine and are both open to the public. Parking is charged separately.

Kristina ***
Spianata Borgo Peri 8,
Tel. 0183293564
www.hotelkristina.com
34 Rooms
Credit cards: American Express, Diners Club, Visa, Mastercard, Bancomat
The Kristina is an owner-run hotel right on the seafront with elegant rooms of various sizes and a classic décor. Its restaurant serves regionally-inspired Italian cuisine

Miramare **** ★ ♿
Porto Maurizio,
Viale Matteotti 24,
Tel. 0182667120
www.rhotels.it
22 Rooms
Credit cards: American Express, Visa, Mastercard, Bancomat
A small hotel in a renovated Liberty villa in the historic downtown, ideal for business or pleasure. Swimming pool with whirlpool and private beach.

Rossini al Teatro **** ★ ♿
Oneglia, Piazza Rossini 14,
Tel. 018374000
www.hotel-rossini.it
49 Rooms
Credit cards: American Express, Diners Club, Visa, Mastercard, Bancomat
An extremely exclusive hotel in what was once the Rossini theater; both the rooms and public areas are decorated in contemporary style.

Restaurants

Didù ⅋ ★
Oneglia, Viale Matteotti 76,
Tel. 0183273636
www.ristorantedidu.it
Closed Sundays
Credit cards: Visa, Mastercard, Bancomat
A small, family-run restaurant with stylish, well-thought out décor. The same style applies to the kitchen, where good home-made food using organic flours is the rule.

Hostaria ⅋
Porto Maurizio,
Piazza S. Antonio 9,
Tel. 0183667028
Closed Mondays and Tuesday midday (except in summer)
Credit cards: American Express, Diners Club, Visa, Mastercard, Bancomat
This stylish restaurant in what was once a 13th-century church has a fantastic ambience. Excellent cuisine based on traditional recipes which lean heavily on fish and vegetable dishes, although meat is included on the menu every now and again.

Museums

Museo dell'Olivo
Oneglia, Via Garessio 13,
Tel. 0183295762
www.museodellolivo.com
Mondays-Saturdays 9-12, 15-18.30. August: Mondays-Saturdays 9-12.30, 15.30-19

Museo Navale Internazionale del Ponente Ligure
Piazza Duomo 11,
Tel. 0183651541-3356399861
www.sullacrestadellonda.it/museoimperia
Summer: Wednesdays, Saturdays 21-23. Winter: Wednesdays, Saturdays 15-19

Pinacoteca Civica
Piazza Duomo 11/a,
Tel. 0183701551-0183701556
www.comune.imperia.it/
Wednesdays, Saturdays 16-19 (July-August: also 21-23). Visits also by request

LA SPÈZIA

> ℹ️ **Punto Informativo Turistico**
> Viale Mazzini 45,
> Tel. 0187770900
> c/o Stazione Centrale,
> Tel. 0187718997

Hotels

Genova *** ★
Via F.lli Rosselli 84/86,
Tel. 0187732972
www.hotelgenova.it
37 Rooms
Credit cards: American Express, Diners Club, Visa, Mastercard, Bancomat, JCB
A comfortable, traditional-style hotel in the historic downtown next to the pedestrian area. Sweet and savory breakfast buffet.

Jolly Hotel **** ★
Via XX Settembre 2,
Tel. 0187739555
www.jollyhotels.it
110 Rooms

Credit cards: American Express, Diners Club, Visa, Bancomat

A modern, efficient hotel with well-furnished, spacious rooms and suites and all comforts just a stone's throw from the port. The "Del Golfo" restaurant has a summer terrace for al fresco dining.

My Hotels La Spezia **** &
Via XX Settembre 81,
Tel. 0187738848
www.myhotels.it
68 Rooms
Credit cards: American Express, Diners Club, Visa, Mastercard, Bancomat

A modern hotel on one of the characteristic carrugio (street), with comfortable rooms and excellent conference facilities making it ideal for business or pleasure. Extensive sweet and savory breakfast buffet.

Rural Lodgings

Golfo dei Poeti - Fattorie Bedogni Von Berger
Via Proffiano 34,
Tel. 0187711053
www.agriturismogolfo
deipoeti.com

A holiday with a view over the Golfo dei Poeti in these two 17th century, stone farmhouses nestling amidst vineyards, olive groves and woods. Accommodation in characteristic apartments with open fireplaces, plus two outdoor swimming pools with whirlpool and waterfall. Well-placed for excursions.

Restaurants

Antica Trattoria Dino ⁝⁝
Via Cadorna 18,
Tel. 0187736157
trattoriadino@yahoo.it
Closed Sunday evenings and Mondays
Credit cards: American Express, Diners Club, Visa, Mastercard, Bancomat, JCB

This smart "trattoria" with its open air dining area for al fresco summer meals is just 200 meters from the wharf. Fresh fish and organic meat. Local and national wines.

Il Centro ⁝⁝
Cadimare,
Via della Marina 54,
Tel. 0187738832
www.trattoriailcentro.it
Closed Mondays
Credit cards: Diners Club, Visa, Mastercard, Bancomat

A typical "trattoria" both in looks and cuisine in a characteristic little fishing district. Fish straight from the boat. During the summer fine wine tasting sessions.

Museums

Musei Civici/Biblioteca
Currently in *Palazzo Crozza, Corso Cavour 251,*
Tel. 0187738279
Mondays-Fridays 8-13, 14,15-19;
Saturdays 8-12; 14,15-19

Museo Civico d'Arte Antica, Medievale e Moderna «Amedeo Lia» ★
Via Prione 234, Tel. 0187731100
www.castagna.it/musei/mal
Tuesdays-Sundays 10-18

Museo Civico di Etnografia e Antropologia «Giovanni Podenzana» e Museo Diocesano
Via Prione 156, Tel. 0187258570
www.laspeziacultura.it
Wednesdays, Thursdays 10-12.30;
Fridays-Sundays 10-12.30, 16-19

Museo Civico Archeologico Ubaldo Formentini ★
Castello di S. Giorgio,
Via XXVII Marzo, Tel. 0187751142
www.laspeziacultura.it
Summer: Wednesdays-Mondays 9.30-12.30, 17-20. Winter: Wednesdays-Mondays 9.30-12.30, 14-17

Museo Tecnico Navale della Marina Militare
Viale Amendola 1,
Tel. 0187783016-0187770750
www.museotecniconavale.it
Mondays-Saturdays 8-18.45;
Sundays 8-13. Closed 15 August, 1 November, 8, 24-26, 31 December

LAVAGNA

> ℹ️ **Azienda di Promozione Turistica del Tigullio**
> *Piazza Torino 35,*
> *Tel. 0185395070*

Hotels

Arco del Sole *** &
Via Aurelia 1992,
Tel. 0185390036
www.albergoarcodelsole.com
24 Rooms
Credit cards: American Express, Diners Club, Visa, Mastercard, Bancomat

A family-style hotel with cozy, simply-furnished rooms in a quiet position surrounded by greenery. Direct access to the beach, small private gym and a restaurant specializing in fish and seafood.

La Scogliera **
Cavi, Via del Cigno 4,
Tel. 0185390072
www.hotelscoglieradicavi.it
19 Rooms
Credit cards: American Express, Diners Club, Visa, Mastercard, Bancomat

A modern recently-renovated hotel in a panoramic position. Restrained, functional décor. Continental breakfast.

Villa Fieschi ***
Via Rezza 12, Tel. 0185304400
www.hotelvillafieschi.it
13 Rooms
Credit cards: American Express, Visa, Mastercard, Bancomat

A late 19th-century patrician villa with a cozy, comfortable air, set in all the quiet of its own splendid park. Excellent local cuisine in the restaurant for guests and the public.

Restaurants

All'Ulivo ⁝⁝
Barassi, Via Chiesa 9/B,
Tel. 0185390458
Closed Mondays
Credit cards: Visa, Mastercard, Bancomat

A delightful, hidden-away spot well worth taking the pain to find. Attractive dining rooms and traditional local dishes.

Cà Melia ⁝ ★
Cavi, Via Brigate Partigiane 40/42,
Tel. 0185390770
Closed Wednesdays (in low season)
Credit cards: Visa, Bancomat

Charming, informal restaurant serving traditional Italian food. Vegetable quiches a specialty.

Rajeu ⁝⁝ ★
Cavi, Via Milite Ignoto 23,
Tel. 0185390145
beboro@libero.it
Closed Mondays
Credit cards: American Express, Diners Club, Visa, Mastercard, Bancomat

A pleasant, nautical-style restaurant which first opened in 1960. The kitchen stays open until after 10:00 pm and specializes in simple, traditional dishes using local ingredients.

LÉRICI

> ℹ️ **Punto Informativo Turistico**
> *Via Biaggini 6, Tel. 0187967346*

Hotels

Del Golfo **
Via Gerini 37,
Tel. 0187967400
www.hoteldelgolfo.com
20 Rooms
Credit cards: American Express, Visa, Mastercard, Bancomat

A modern hotel in the town center, but in a quiet position. Spacious veranda for breakfast and dining, perfect for families with children.

Doria Park Hotel ★★★
Via Doria 2, Tel. 0187967124
www.doriaparkhotel.it
42 Rooms
Credit cards: American Express, Diners Club, Visa, Mastercard
A well-run hotel in a panoramic position surrounded by greenery. All rooms are air conditioned and sound-proofed. Sweet and savory breakfast buffet and shuttle bus service for local trips. The "I Doria" restaurant serves local food with a creative twist.

Shelley & delle Palme ★★★ ★
Lungomare Biaggini 5,
Tel. 0187968204
www.hotelshelley.it
49 Rooms
Credit cards: American Express, Diners Club, Visa, Mastercard, Bancomat
A centrally-located hotel with a terrace overlooking the sea and comfortable rooms with all amenities. The new "Shelley" restaurant is open to guests and the general public.

Villa Maria Grazia ★★
Tellaro, Via Fiascherino 7,
Tel. 0187967507
www.villamariagrazia.it
7 Rooms
Credit cards: Bancomat
Quiet, small hotel set in olive groves close to the sea. Comfortable rooms and a cool garden to relax in.

Rural Lodgings

Gallerani ★
Zanego 5, Tel. 0187964057
A farm set in the woods just inland from the sea with a view over the La Spezia and Lerici bays. Perfect for lazing on the beach or trekking in the mountains.

Restaurants

Due Corone ⛟
Via Vespucci 1, Tel. 0187967417
www.duecorone.com
Closed Tuesdays (in July-August Tuesday midday)
Credit cards: American Express, Diners Club
Elegant fish restaurant with a veranda overlooking the sea near the castle. Good selection of wines and spirits.

Vecchia Lerici ⛟
Piazza Mottino 10,
Tel. 0187967597
Closed Mondays (except in summer)
Credit cards: Diners Club, Visa, Mastercard, Bancomat
Pleasant fish restaurant with a large veranda. Carefully chosen selection of white and dessert wines.

Museums

Museo del Castello di Lerici ★
Piazza S. Giorgio 1,
Tel. 0187969042-0187969114
www.castellodilerici.it
Spring and fall:
Tuesdays-Sundays and holidays 10.30-13, 14.30-18.
Summer: Tuesdays-Sundays and holidays 10.30-12.30, 18.30-24. Winter: Tuesdays-Fridays 10.30-12.30; Saturdays, Sundays, holidays and 26 December-6 January 10.30-12.30, 14.30-17.30

LÈVANTO

> ℹ **Punto Informativo Turistico**
> *Piazza Cavour,*
> *Tel. 0187808125*

Hotels

Al Terra di Mare ★★★★ ♿
Gallona, Tel. 0187807672
www.alterradimare.it
31 Rooms
Credit cards: American Express, Diners Club, Visa, Mastercard, Bancomat
A cluster of buildings echoing the old villages huddled on the slopes of the surrounding mountains. A romantic piazzetta is the social hub of the complex where guests relax or dine al fresco on local specialties.

Palace ★★★
Corso Roma 25,
Tel. 0187808143
www.hotelpalacelevanto.com
43 Rooms
Credit cards: American Express, Diners Club, Visa, Mastercard, Bancomat, JCB
A stylish, historical hotel with an unspoilt Liberty atmosphere. Smart, but cozy, it is centrally placed near the sea with a spacious dining room to enjoy local cuisine.

Rural Lodgings

Il Frantoio ★
Lavaggiorosso,
Via S. Sebastiano 10,
Tel. 0187803628
www.agriturismoilfrantoio.it
Credit cards: Visa, Mastercard
Accommodation available in the rustic "Gelsomino" with kitchenette and bathroom or the historic, renovated "Fiordaliso" village house with its open fireplace, spacious kitchen and veranda in a sunny position in an inland village with great views amidst the olive groves of the Lèvanto countryside. Ideal for exploring the Cinque Terre national park.

Museums

Mostra Permanente della Cultura Materiale
Via S. Nicolò, Ospitalia del Mare,
Tel. 0187817776-0187808336
Temporarily closed

LUNI

Museums

Museo Archeologico Nazionale
Via S. Pero, Tel. 018766811
www.archeoge.arti.beniculturali.it
Tuesdays-Sundays 8.30-19.30

MANAROLA

Restaurants

Marina Piccola ⛟ ★
Via Lo Scalo 16,
Tel. 0187920923
www.hotelmarinapiccola.com
Closed Tuesdays
Credit cards: American Express, Diners Club, Visa, Mastercard, Bancomat
A pleasant fish restaurant serving the daily catch in a variety of mouth-watering dishes. The chef's special is taglierini pasta with cuttlefish, prawn, scampi and pepper sauce. Sunny veranda and terrace overlooking the sea.

MILLÈSIMO

> ℹ **Comune**
> *Piazza Italia 1,*
> *Tel. 019565937*

MONTEROSSO AL MARE

> ℹ **Associazione Pro Loco**
> *Via Fegina,*
> *Tel. 0187817506*

Hotels

La Colonnina ★★★
Via Zuecca 6,
Tel. 0187817439
www.lacolonninacinqueterre.it
19 Rooms
Well-run, centrally-positioned hotel with a great view. Simply-furnished, comfortable rooms. Sweet and savory breakfast buffet with some organic products.

Porto Roca ★★★★
Via Corone 1, Tel. 0187817502
www.portoroca.it
44 Rooms
Credit cards: American Express, Diners Club, Visa
Elegant, comfortable hotel surrounded in greenery set in a marvellous clifftop position. Spacious dining room, well-equipped beach and solarium.

Restaurants

Miky ⌘⌘
Via Fegina 104, Tel. 0187817608
www.ristorantemiky.it
Closed Tuesdays (except August)
Credit cards: American Express,
Diners Club, Visa, Mastercard,
Bancomat
Characteristic restaurant with a
garden for al fresco dining and a
veranda overlooking the sea. The
kitchen is open until midnight
and serves fresh pasta
specialties and traditional fish
dishes, accompanied by fine
wines from the carefully selected
wine list.

NOLI

> ℹ️ **Ufficio Turistico Noli**
> Corso Italia 8,
> Tel. 0197499003

Hotels

El Sito *** ♿
Via La Malfa 2, Tel. 019748107
www.elsito.it
14 Rooms
Credit cards: Visa, Mastercard
A small hotel on a green
mountain plateau complete with
all comforts for a pleasant,
relaxing stay.

Miramare ***
Corso Italia 2, Tel. 019748926
www.hotelmiramarenoli.it
28 Rooms
Credit cards: American Express,
Diners Club, Visa, Mastercard,
Bancomat
14th-century hotel just a stone's
throw from the sea and historic
downtown. Traditional hospitality
for a relaxing stay. The
independently-managed
"U Portellu" restaurant serves
local and Italian cuisine.

Restaurants

La Scaletta ⌘⌘
Via Verdi 16, Tel. 019748754
Closed Wednesdays
Credit cards: American Express,
Diners Club, Visa, Mastercard,
Bancomat, JCB
Extremely cozy restaurant where
guests can dine on fish and
seafood to the accompaniment
of soft jazz.

Lilliput ⌘⌘
Voze, Via Zuglieno 49,
Tel. 019748009
Closed Mondays
Credit cards: American Express,
Visa, Mastercard
Smart, country-style restaurant
with a spacious terrace set in the
midst of a Mediterranean pine
wood. Regional specialties
prepared with the freshest local
ingredients.

PIGNA

> ℹ️ **Comune**
> Piazza Umberto I 1,
> Tel. 0184240013

Hotels

G.H. Antiche Terme **** ♿
Regione Lago Pigo,
Tel. 0184240010
www.termedipigna.it
97 Rooms
Credit cards: American Express,
Diners Club, Visa, Mastercard
Elegant architecture and wood
finishings characterize this spa
and wellness hotel with its
comfortable rooms and suites.
Its two restaurants, the "San
Michele" and the "il Bistrot del
Lago" (open during the summer),
serve traditional local and Italian
cuisine with special menus for
guests on a diet.

PORTOFINO

> ℹ️ **Azienda di Promozione**
> **Turistica del Tigullio**
> Via Roma 35,
> Tel. 0185269024

Hotels

Eden ***
Vico Dritto 18, Tel. 0185269091
www.hoteledenportofino.com
8 Rooms
A hotel with a great atmosphere
just a step away from the
famous "piazzetta". Classically
furnished rooms and an
independently-run restaurant,
although guests can bill their
meals to their rooms.

San Giorgio-Portofino
House **** ♿
Via del Fondaco 11,
Tel. 018526991
www.portofinohsg.it
18 Rooms
Credit cards: American Express,
Diners Club, Bancomat, JCB
Very smart, stylish hotel with
attentive service and spacious
rooms well-equipped with
cutting edge technology.
Guests can order from the room
service menu and breakfast at
the buffet.

Splendido ***** ♿
Viale Baratta 16,
Tel. 0185267801
www.hotelsplendido.com
64 Rooms
Credit cards: American Express,
Diners Club, Visa, Mastercard,
Bancomat, JCB
This 19th-century villa is now a
hotel surrounded by greenery
with a great view. It combines
elegant décor with attentive
service. Air conditioned rooms,

excellent facilities and a beauty
center. Courtesy shuttle bus to
and from downtown Portofino.

Splendido Mare ****
Via Roma 2, Tel. 0185267802
www.hotelsplendido.com
16 Rooms
Credit cards: American Express,
Diners Club, Visa, Mastercard,
Bancomat, JCB
A typical local-style hotel right
on the famous "piazzetta",
combining a great atmosphere
with modern comfort. Stylish
rooms with a sea view.

Restaurants

Chuflay ⌘⌘⌘
Via Roma 2, Tel. 0185267802
www.hotelsplendido.com
Credit cards: American Express,
Diners Club, Visa, Mastercard,
Bancomat, JCB
A refined, elegant restaurant
with an open air dining area
right on the stunning harbour.
Freshly-caught fish and feather-
light cuisine combine with
attentive service and a good
selection of wines and spirits.

La Terrazza ⌘⌘⌘⌘⌘
Viale Baratta 16, Tel. 0185267801
www.hotelsplendido.com
Credit cards: American Express,
Diners Club, Visa, Mastercard,
Bancomat, JCB
Attractive, prestigious restaurant
in a splendid position with a
panoramic terrace. The refined
menu includes dishes such as
lobster and prawn salad drizzled
with rosemary-scented olive oil,
asparagus tip ravioli served in
truffle sauce and mouth-watering
desserts.

PORTOVÈNERE

> ℹ️ **Associazione**
> **Turistica Pro Loco**
> Piazza Bastreri 7,
> Tel. 0187790691

Hotels

Belvedere ***
Via Garibaldi 26, Tel. 0187790608
www.belvedereportovenere.it
18 Rooms
Credit cards: American Express,
Diners Club, Visa, Mastercard,
Bancomat, JCB
Cute, Liberty-style palazzo
overlooking the sea in the
historic downtown, comfortable
rooms and sweet and savory
breakfast buffet.

Della Baia ***
Le Grazie, Via Lungomare 111,
Tel. 0187790797
www.baiahotel.com
34 Rooms
Credit cards: American Express,
Visa, Mastercard, Bancomat, JCB

⌘⌘⌘ ⌘⌘ ⌘⌘ *** ** * Hotels   ⌘⌘⌘⌘⌘ ⌘⌘⌘⌘ ⌘⌘⌘ ⌘⌘ ⌘ Restaurants   ♿ Disabled   ★ Special TCI Rates

Modern hotel overlooking the sea enhanced by exhibitions of contemporary art. Some rooms have spacious panoramic terraces. The "La Nave Rossa" restaurant serves Mediterranean cuisine.

G.H. Portovenere ★★★★
Via Garibaldi 5,
Tel. 0187792610
www.portoverehotel.it
54 Rooms
Comfortable hotel in a renovated 17th-century convent with a beauty center running wellness programmes. The "Il Convento" restaurant is independently managed.

Restaurants

Antica Osteria del Carugio ⸗ ★
Via Cappellini 66,
Tel. 0187790617
www.anticaosteriadelcarugio.com
Closed Thursdays
In a building with over a hundred years of history, this unpretentious restaurant serves traditional specialties.

Dei Poeti ⸗
Via dell'Ulivo 345,
Tel. 0187790326
www.royalsporting.com
Credit cards: American Express, Diners Club, Visa, Mastercard, Bancomat, JCB
Elegant restaurant with a relaxed atmosphere serving local specialties and international cuisine.

Museums

Museo Archeologico dell'Isola del Tino
Insel Tino, Tel. 0187794890-0187790691-0187794885
Open only 13 September (Fest of St Venerius) and the following Sunday

Museo della Chiesa di San Lorenzo
Piazza S. Lorenzo,
Tel. 0187790684
Visits by request

RAPALLO

> ### ⓘ Punto Informativo del Tigullio
> *Lungomare V. Veneto 7,*
> *Tel. 0185230346*

Hotels

Astoria ★★★★
Via Gramsci 4, Tel. 0185273533
www.astoriarapallo.it
22 Rooms
Credit cards: American Express, Diners Club, Visa, Mastercard
Elegant Liberty villa overlooking the sea, sweet and savory breakfast buffet. The hotel has a special arrangement with the

nearby "Osteria Vecchia Rapallo" restaurant for its guests.

Canali ★★★
Via Pietrafraccia 15,
Tel. 018550369
www.hotelcanali.com
24 Rooms
Comfortable hotel in a historic villa with an excellent restaurant serving local specialties and Italian cuisine. New relax area with solarium and whirlpool aromatherapy tub in the garden.

Europa ★★★★ ★ ♿
Via Milite Ignoto 2,
Tel. 0185669521
www.thi.it
60 Rooms
Credit cards: American Express, Diners Club, Visa
18th-century palazzo in the historic downtown transformed into comfortable hotel with a fitness center. The "Il Trattato" restaurant serves local specialties.

Italia e Lido ★★★
Via Montebello 2, Tel. 018550492
www.italiaelido.com
50 Rooms
Credit cards: American Express, Diners Club, Visa, Mastercard, Bancomat
Historical hotel in an enchanting position overlooking the sea, sunny rooms with all mod cons and a complete range of services for a pleasant, relaxing stay. The panoramic "Grande Italia" restaurant serves typical local dishes.

Stella ★★★
Via Aurelia Ponente 6,
Tel. 018550367
www.hotelstella-riviera.com
29 Rooms
Credit cards: American Express, Diners Club, Visa, Mastercard, JCB
Typical Ligurian house under family management near the sea with pleasant, restrained décor.

Rural Lodgings

La Bicocca
Madonna Nera,
Salita S. Agostino 57,
Tel. 0185272380
www.labicocca.eu
Closed February and November
Admire the panorama at sunset while dining al fresco on the terrace after a day spent walking, doing sport or just relaxing.

Restaurants

Luca ⸗⸗
Via Langano 32, Tel. 018560323
ristoranteluca@yahoo.it
Closed Tuesdays
Credit cards: Visa, Mastercard, Bancomat

Elegant fish restaurant with a nautical flavor serving local specialties. Good choice of wines and spirits.

U Giancu ⸗
San Massimo, Tel. 0185260505
www.ugiancu.it
Closed Wednesdays
Credit cards: Diners Club, Visa, Mastercard, Bancomat
Half-restaurant half-museum with original drawings by cartoonists from all over the world, where the food matches the cordial atmosphere. Home-grown vegetables and home-made breads and ice cream.

RECCO

> ### ⓘ Punto Informativo Turistico
> *Via Ippolito d'Este 2A,*
> *Tel. 0185722440*

Hotels

Da O' Vittorio ★★★ ♿
Via Roma 160, Tel. 018574029
www.daovittorio.it
35 Rooms
Credit cards: American Express, Diners Club, Visa, Mastercard
Modern, family-run hotel 500 meters from the sea with comfortable rooms and balconies.

La Villa ★★★★ ★ ♿
Via Roma 274, Tel. 0185720779
www.manuelina.it
23 Rooms
Credit cards: American Express, Diners Club, Visa, Mastercard, Bancomat
Lovely, typical two-story house linked to the more modern part of the hotel by a glass-encased lift. Pleasing décor and good facilities, air-conditioned rooms, fully-equipped for sports and leisure activities.

Restaurants

Manuelina ⸗⸗⸗ ★
Via Roma 278, Tel. 018574128
www.manuelina.it
Closed Wednesdays
Credit cards: American Express, Diners Club, Visa, Mastercard, Bancomat
Since 1885 four generations of Emanuela (Manuelina) Capurro's descendants have carried on her tradition of first class local cuisine, backed up by an interesting wine list.

Vitturin 1860 ⸗ ★
Via dei Giustiniani 48,
Tel. 0185720225, www.vitturin.it
Closed working Mondays
Credit cards: American Express, Visa, Mastercard, Bancomat
The Vitturin has been run by the

same family since 1860 and has maintained its high standard of fish and mushroom dishes, along with Recco's specialty, its cheese focaccia. Quality assortment of local salamis and cheeses.

RIOMAGGIORE

Hotels

Cà dei Duxi
Via Colombo 36, Tel. 0187920036
www.duxi.it
6 Rooms
Credit cards: American Express, Diners Club, Visa, Mastercard, Bancomat, JCB
A "locanda" in a 17th-century palazzo where modern comforts have been added to the charm of the historic architecture. Some rooms have wooden-beamed ceilings, while others have little terraces. Breakfast buffet served in what was once the cellar, where the extremely rare Sciacchetrà wine used to be produced.

Luna di Marzo *** &
Volastra, Via Montello 387/C,
Tel. 0187920530
www.albergolunadimarzo.com
10 Rooms
Credit cards: Diners Club, Visa, Mastercard, Bancomat
In the cool of the hills close to the sea, a sunny hotel with big picture windows and comfortable rooms. The garden nestles amidst the olive groves and the hotel terrace boasts a truly stunning view.

Villa Argentina **
Via De Gasperi 170,
Tel. 0187920213
www.hotelvillargentina.com
15 Rooms
Credit cards: American Express, Visa, Mastercard, Bancomat
A traditional, comfortable hotel in a dominant position. Guests can order breakfast in their rooms or go down to the buffet; the hotel restaurant serving local cuisine is for guests only.

Rural Lodgings

Riomaggiore
Via de' Battè 61, Tel. 3404174905
www.cinqueterreedintorni.it
Two rooms and an apartment to rent in the village of Riomaggiore, very conveniently placed for exploring the paths that criss-cross the Cinque Terre and the nearby coast.

Restaurants

Cappun Magru ▯▯
Groppo, Via Volastra 19,
Tel. 0187920563
www.cappunmagru.it
Closed Mondays and Tuesdays
Credit cards: American Express, Visa, Mastercard, Bancomat

Booking is recommended to ensure a table in one of the three tiny dining rooms in this brightly colored Marin house. Modern, colorful cuisine based on fresh local seasonal produce centered around fish and vegetable combinations.

La Lanterna-da Massimo ▮ ★
Via S. Giacomo 10,
Tel. 0187920589
www.lalanterna.org
Closed Tuesdays (in winter)
Credit cards: American Express, Diners Club, Visa, Mastercard, Bancomat, JCB
A rustic restaurant just a stone's throw from the sea. Fish reigns supreme here and diners might like to wind up their meals with basil-flavored panna cotta dessert.

SANREMO

> ℹ **Punto Informativo Turistico**
> *Largo Nuvoloni,*
> *Tel. 018450059*

Hotels

Bel Soggiorno ***
Corso Matuzia 41, Tel. 0184667631
www.belsoggiorno.net
36 Rooms
Credit cards: Visa, Mastercard, Bancomat
An unpretentious, comfortable hotel centrally located just a stone's throw from the sea. The restaurant serves traditional local cuisine.

Europa **** ★
Corso Imperatrice 27,
Tel. 0184578170
www.hoteleuropa-sanremo.com
65 Rooms
Credit cards: American Express, Diners Club, Visa, Bancomat
A well-designed, comfortable 19th-century hotel whose restaurant serves local specialties and international cuisine. For the last word in comfort and service eight suites are also available.

Morandi ***
Corso Matuzia 51, Tel. 0184667641
www.hotelmorandi.com
32 Rooms
Credit cards: American Express, Visa, Mastercard, Bancomat
A four-story Liberty hotel which has been renovated to provide modern comfort and amenities located on the western promenade. The hotel restaurant serves local and Italian cuisine.

Paradiso *** &
Via Roccasterone 12,
Tel. 0184571211
www.paradisohotel.it
41 Rooms

Credit cards: American Express, Diners Club, Visa, Mastercard, Bancomat
A sunny, comfortable hotel with an open-air swimming pool in a quiet, green area not far from the sea and the historic downtown. The "Magnolia" restaurant serves traditional local and Mediterranean cuisine.

Royal Hotel *****L
Corso Imperatrice 80,
Tel. 01845391
www.royalhotelsanremo.com
127 Rooms
Credit cards: American Express, Diners Club, Visa, Mastercard, Bancomat, JCB
This charming, extremely luxurious hotel is tucked away in its own large subtropical park and gardens, which flowers all year round. There are three restaurants, the "Fiori di Murano", the "Corallina" at the swimming pool and the "Giardino", which is open during the summer months. New Royal Wellness center.

Sole Mare **
Via Carli 23, Tel. 0184577105
www.solemarehotel.com
21 Rooms
Credit cards: Visa, Mastercard, Bancomat
A modern hotel on the seafront a stone's throw from the casino, with a restaurant serving local and traditional Italian cuisine.

Restaurants

Da Nicò ▯▯▯
Piazza Bresca 9, Tel. 0184501988
Closed Wednesdays
Credit cards: American Express, Diners Club, Visa, Mastercard, Bancomat
This restaurant is on one of the prettiest piazzette in the historic downtown, it serves quality local and Calabrian regional cuisine.

Paolo e Barbara ▯▯▯▯
Via Roma 47, Tel. 0184531653
www.paolobarbara.it
Closed Wednesdays and Thursdays (except holidays)
Credit cards: American Express, Diners Club, Visa, Mastercard
Hidden along the "City of Flowers'" main street is a small door with a bell. Open the door to discover a restaurant which is a gourmet heaven.
Mediterranean-style fish tartare and pasta in meat and eggplant sauce are just two of its must-try dishes.

Museums

Museo Civico
Corso Matteotti 143,
Tel. 0184531942
Tuesdays-Saturdays 9-12, 15-18

SANTA MARGHERITA LIGURE

Punto Informativo del Tigullio
Via XXV Aprile 2B,
Tel. 0185287485

Hotels

Continental ****
Via Pagana 8, Tel. 0185286512
www.hotel-continental.it
70 Rooms
Credit cards: American Express, Diners Club, Visa, Mastercard, Bancomat, JCB
A lovely turn-of-the-century hotel right on the sea, in a park dotted with Mediterranean oaks and palm trees. Spacious, sunny rooms for a quiet, comfortable stay and a restaurant on a terrace overlooking the sea.

G.H. Miramare ****
Lungomare Milite Ignoto 30,
Tel. 0185287013
www.grandhotelmiramare.it
84 Rooms
Credit cards: American Express, Diners Club, Visa, Mastercard, Bancomat, JCB
One of the Ligurian Riviera's best-known hotels. A Liberty building right in front of the sea set in a tropical park with an open-air seawater swimming pool. The suites and rooms are extremely comfortable and guests can use the new Espace wellness and beauty center.

Imperiale Palace Hotel ** ★ ♿***
Via Pagana 19, Tel. 0185288991
www.hotelimperiale.com
89 Rooms
Credit cards: American Express, Diners Club, Visa, Mastercard, Bancomat, JCB
This luxurious, stylish hotel occupies a late 19th-century villa set in a stunning, mature park that runs down to the sea. Guests can enjoy candlelit dining on the terrace and in the charming dining room of the panoramic "Novecento" restaurant.

Rural Lodgings

Gnocchi
San Lorenzo della Costa
Via Romana 53, Tel. 0185283431
roberto.gnocchi@tin.it
Open mid April-October
Credit cards: American Express, Diners Club, Visa, Mastercard
A small farm specialized in olives, fruit and market gardening in the Tigullio hills, set in the woods with a view down to the sea. Guests are welcome to help out on the farm or they can fish, play golf and tennis, or go horse riding.

Restaurants

***Cambusa* 🍴🍴 ★**
Via Bottaro 1, Tel. 0185287410
www.liguriaplanet.com
Closed Thursdays (in winter)
Credit cards: American Express, Diners Club, Visa, Mastercard, Bancomat
A characteristic restaurant on the seafront with a lovely veranda overlooking the harbour. Tasty, simple cuisine carefully prepared using fresh fish and meat.

***Il Faro* 🍴**
Via Maragliano 24/A,
Tel. 0185286867
Closed Tuesdays
Credit cards: American Express, Visa, Mastercard, Bancomat
A restaurant with a nautical flavor on the road to Portofino, serving traditional local cuisine.

***Lo Spinnaker* 🍴🍴🍴**
Via Pescino 16,
Tel. 0185286739
www.lospinnaker.com
Closed Tuesdays
Credit cards: American Express, Diners Club, Visa, Mastercard, Bancomat
Quality and style are the keynotes in the cuisine and elegant décor that combine to make this one of the best-known restaurants along the Liguria riviera. Unusual food combinations and creative recipes characterize the menu.

SANTO STÉFANO D'ÀVETO

Comune/Ufficio Turismo
Piazza Del Popolo 1,
Tel. 018588046

Hotels

Leon d'Oro **
Via Razzetti 52,
Tel. 018588073
www.albergoleondoro.net
35 Rooms
Credit cards: American Express, Diners Club, Visa, Mastercard, Bancomat, JCB
Comfortable hotel with a great view over the Apennines and a restaurant serving local and Emilian regional specialties.

Restaurants

***Hosteria della Luna Piena* 🍴**
Via Ponte dei Bravi 7,
Tel. 018588382
Credit cards: American Express, Diners Club, Visa, Mastercard, Bancomat
An unpretentious, cozy restaurant serving traditional cuisine. In the evening guests can order delicious pizzas.

SARZANA

Rural Lodgings

La Bianca Fattoria
Ponticello, Via Turi 120,
Tel. 0187607301
www.labiancafattoria.com
Open by reservation
Credit cards: Bancomat
A renovated traditional farmhouse with a portico set on the hillside in an oasis of peace and quiet. Cozy rooms, dining room with an open fireplace and home cooking complete the picture.

Restaurants

***Girarrosto-da Paolo* 🍴**
Via dei Molini 388,
Tel. 0187621088, dcargio@tin.it
Closed Wednesdays
Credit cards: American Express, Diners Club, Visa, Mastercard, Bancomat
A typical, country "trattoria" set in the green of the hills under family management since 1953. Typical local cuisine.

***La Cantina del Vescovo* 🍴🍴**
Via Mazzini 82, Tel. 0187621943
www.cantinadelvescovo.it
Closed Mondays
Credit cards: American Express, Diners Club, Visa, Mastercard, Bancomat
A 13th-century restaurant with its original well in the characteristic historic downtown. Fish and meat dishes are the house specialty.

SASSELLO

Provincia/ Ufficio Turistico
Via Giambattista Badano 45, Tel. 019724020

Restaurants

***Pian del Sole* 🍴🍴**
Pianferioso 23,
Tel. 019724255
www.hotel-piandelsole.com
Closed Mondays from October to March
Credit cards: Visa, Bancomat
Sunny restaurant surrounded by greenery. Home-cured hams and salamis for starters and home-made bread. Fixed menu at an attractive price. Prestigious wine list.

Museums

***Museo Perrando* ★**
Via del Perrando 33,
Tel. 019724100
www.sasselloweb.it
Thursdays, Fridays and Sundays 16-18. Closed November-March. Visits also by request

SAVONA

Hotels

Ariston ★★★
Via Giordano 11, Tel. 019805633
www.hotelaristonsavona.it
16 Rooms
Credit cards: American Express, Diners Club, Visa, Mastercard, Bancomat
A modern, family-run hotel in a quiet position on the seafront.

Mare Hotel ★★★★
Via Nizza 89/r, Tel. 019264065
www.marehotel.it
66 Rooms
Credit cards: American Express, Diners Club, Visa, Mastercard, Bancomat
A hotel right on the beach with comfortable rooms complete with whirlpool tubs and balconies overlooking the sea. Private beach with canoe school.

Riviera Suisse ★★★ ★
Via Paleocapa 24,
Tel. 019850853
www.rivierasuissehotel.it
80 Rooms
Credit cards: American Express, Diners Club, Visa, Mastercard, Bancomat
A historic palazzo strategically located midway between the harbour and the railway station. Nicely-furnished rooms with all amenities.

Restaurants

A Spurcacciun-a ▒▒▒
Via Nizza 89/r, Tel. 019264065
www.marehotel.it
Closed Wednesdays
Credit cards: American Express, Diners Club, Visa, Mastercard, Bancomat
A lively restaurant with a lovely garden. The wholly fish-based menu is creative and the vegetables are all home-grown.

La Playa ▒▒
Via Nizza 103, Tel. 019883533
laplaya@iol.it
Closed Mondays
Credit cards: American Express, Diners Club, Visa, Mastercard
A fish restaurant with a pleasant open-air dining area overlooking the sea. Good wine list.

Museums

Civico Museo Storico-Archeologico del Priamar
Corso Mazzini 1, Tel. 019822708
www.museoarcheosavona.it
June-September: Tuesdays-Saturdays 10-12, 17-19; holidays 17-19. October-May: Tuesdays-Fridays 9.30-12.30, 15-17; Saturdays 10-12, 15-17; holidays 15-17

Collezione d'Arte «Sandro Pertini»
Corso Mazzini 1, Tel. 019811520
www.comune.savona.it
Saturdays and Sundays 10-12

Collezione Renata Cuneo
Corso Mazzini 1,
Tel. 0198387391-0198310256
www.comune.savona.it
Temporarily closed

Museo del Tesoro della Cattedrale di Nostra Signora Assunta
Via Manzoni 11, Tel. 019813003
Temporarily closed

Museo del Tesoro del Santuario di Nostra Signora della Misericordia
Santuario, Piazza del Santuario 6, Tel. 019879025
www.santuariosavona.it
Visits by request

Pinacoteca Civica ★
Palazzo Gavotta
Piazza Chabrol 1-2,
Tel. 019811520-0198387391
www.comune.savona.it
Mondays, Wednesdays, Fridays 8.30-13; Tuesdays, Thursdays 14-19; Saturdays 8.30-13, 15.30-18.30 (Summer: 8.30-13, 20.30-23.30); Sundays 10-13

SESTRI LEVANTE

Hotels

Due Mari ★★★
Vico Coro 18, Tel. 018542695
www.duemarihotel.it
55 Rooms
Credit cards: American Express, Diners Club, Visa, Mastercard, Bancomat
A renovated 17th-century patrician villa right on the tip of the peninsula that divides the Baia delle Favole from the Baia del Silenzio.

G.H. dei Castelli ★★★★ ♿
Via Penisola 26, Tel. 0185487220
www.hoteldeicastelli.com
48 Rooms
Credit cards: American Express, Diners Club, Visa, Mastercard
A Medieval castle set in a huge park with all the amenities and attentive service necessary for a comfortable stay. The independently managed "Ai Castelli" restaurant serves traditional local and Italian cuisine.

Mira ★★★
Viale Rimembranza 15,
Tel. 0185459404
www.hotelmira.it
18 Rooms
Credit cards: American Express, Diners Club, Visa, Mastercard, Bancomat
The Mira has been impeccably managed by the same family since 1890; it offers its guests both comfort and a lovely view over the Baia delle Favole and Portofino mountain. Its popular restaurant serves traditional local cuisine.

Restaurants

Asseü ▒▒
Riva Trigoso, Via G.B. da Ponzerone 2, Tel. 018542342
www.asseu.it
Closed Wednesdays
Credit cards: American Express, Diners Club, Visa, Mastercard, Bancomat
In what was once a 1920s railroad house, this sunny restaurant with its lovely terrace serves haute cuisine based entirely on fish and seafood. It has been family-run since 1960.

Olimpo ▒▒
Via della Chiusa 28,
Tel. 018542661
www.hotelvisavis.com
Credit cards: American Express, Diners Club, Visa, Mastercard, Bancomat, JCB
This elegant, stylish restaurant is on the top floor of the hotel with the same name. Specialized in fish and seafood, it serves traditional local cuisine. Delicious desserts.

Polpo Mario ▒▒
Via XXV Aprile 163,
Tel. 0185487240
www.polpomario.it
Closed Mondays
Credit cards: American Express, Diners Club, Visa, Bancomat
In what used to be the summer residence of popes and princes, this restaurant serves freshly-caught fish straight from its own fishing boat.

Terrazza ▒
Piazza Bo 23/25,
Tel. 0185481796
Credit cards: American Express, Diners Club, Visa, Mastercard, Bancomat
Elegant, Liberty-style restaurant with a terrace overlooking the beach. Local recipes dominate the menu with some traditional Italian favorites.

Museums

Galleria Rizzi
Via Cappuccini 8, Tel. 018541300
18 April-30 April, 1-24 October:

Sundays 10-13. 1 May-19 June, 11-30 September: Wednesdays 16-19. 20 June-10 September: Fridays, Saturdays 21.30-23.30

TOIRANO

> ### ℹ *Comune*
> *Via Braida 35,*
> *Tel. 018292101*

Restaurants

Al Ravanello Incoronato ⊗
Via Parodi 27/A, Tel. 0182921991
www.alravanelloincoronato.it
Closed Tuesdays and midday (except June-September)
Credit cards: American Express, Diners Club, Visa, Mastercard, Bancomat
A restaurant in a historic palazzo in the Medieval downtown serving traditional local fare. Excellent value for money.

Museums

Museo Etnografico della Val Varatella
Scuderie del Palazzo del Marchese, Via Polla 10, Tel. 0182989968
www.toiranogrotte.it/museo/museo_intro.html
Mondays-Sundays 10-13, 15-18

TRIORA

Hotels

Colomba d'Oro ** ★
Corso Italia 66, Tel. 018494051
www.colombadoro.it
37 Rooms
Credit cards: Visa, Mastercard, Bancomat
A renovated 16th-century Franciscan monastery with comfortable rooms overlooking either the Valle Argentina or the village. This hotel has a friendly atmosphere and specializes in home cooking. Spacious terrace for al fresco dining during the summer.

Museums

Museo Regionale Etnografico e della Stregoneria ★
Corso Italia 1, Tel. 018494477
www.comune.triora.im.it/italia/museo/museo.htm
Summer: Mondays-Fridays 15-18.30; Saturdays and holidays 10.30-12, 15-18.30. Winter: Mondays-Fridays 14.30-18; Saturdays and holidays 10.30-12, 14.30-18

VENTIMÌGLIA

> ### ℹ *Punto Informativo Turistico*
> *Via Cavour 61,*
> *Tel. 0184351183*

Hotels

Calypso **
Via Matteotti 8, Tel. 0184352742
www.calypsohotel.it
31 Rooms
Credit cards: American Express, Visa, Mastercard
A restrained style characterizes this recently renovated hotel conveniently located close to the sea and the local park. Breakfast buffet.

La Riserva di Castel d'Appio ***
Castel d'Appio, Via Peidaigo 71, Tel. 0184229533
www.lariserva.it
19 Rooms
Credit cards: American Express, Diners Club, Visa, Mastercard, Bancomat, JCB
A lovely historic residence perched on the cliffs above the sea that has been transformed into a comfortable hotel with excellent amenities and a superb view. Sunny, comfortable rooms and a restaurant with a swimming pool and terrace for al fresco dining.

Restaurants

Baia Beniamin ⊗⊗
Grimaldi Inferiore, Corso Europa 63, Tel. 018438002
www.baiabeniamin.it
Closed Sunday evenings (in low season) and Mondays
Credit cards: American Express, Diners Club, Visa, Mastercard
An enchanted spot just on the Italian side of the French border. Turn off the main road and head downhill until reaching a lush green bay. The restaurant has a splendid terrace and the refined cuisine is mainly fish-based.

Balzi Rossi ⊗⊗
Ponte San Ludovico, Via Balzi Rossi 2, Tel. 018438132
ristorantebalzirossi@libero.it
Closed Mondays, Tuesday midday (in August also Sunday midday)
Credit cards: Visa, Bancomat
An elegant and pleasant restaurant with a dining room overlooking the sea, just a stone's throw from the French

border. Top quality ingredients and traditional local cuisine.

Museums

Museo Archeologico «Girolamo Rossi» ★
Via Verdi 41, Tel. 0184351181
www.fortedellannunziata.it
Tuesdays-Saturdays 9-12.30, 15-17; Sundays 10-12.30

Museo Preistorico dei Balzi Rossi
Ponte San Ludovico, Via Balzi Rossi 9, Tel. 018438113
www.archeoge.arti.beniculturali.it
Tuesdays-Sundays 8.30-19.30

VERNAZZA

Hotels

Gianni Franzi **
Piazza Marconi 1,
Tel. 0187821003
www.giannifranzi.it
25 Rooms
Credit cards: American Express, Diners Club, Visa, Mastercard
In the main village piazza. Some of the rooms are in the historic main building and others are in the next-door annex, most have views out over the bay. Romantic clifftop garden. Local cuisine specializing in fish in the hotel's "trattoria".

Rural Lodgings

La Rocca
Belvedere di Corniglia,
Via Fieschi 222, Tel. 0187812178
larocca.corniglia@libero.it
As is often the case in the Cinque Terre, this farm is actually in the village. Guests usually spend the first few days exploring the fascinating network of steep lanes and then are spoilt for choice with all the art and nature the coastal region abounds in.

Restaurants

Gambero Rosso ⊗
Piazza Marconi 7,
Tel. 0187812265
www.ristorantegamberorosso.it
Closed Mondays (except August)
Credit cards: American Express, Diners Club, Visa, Mastercard, Bancomat
Freshly-caught fish reign supreme in this pleasant historic restaurant. Excellent wine list.

METRIC CONVERTIONS

DISTANCE

Kilometres/Miles

km to mi	mi to km
1 = 0.62	1 = 1.6
2 = 1.2	2 = 3.2
3 = 1.9	3 = 4.8
4 = 2.5	4 = 6.4
5 = 3.1	5 = 8.1
6 = 3.7	6 = 9.7
7 = 4.3	7 = 11.3
8 = 5.0	8 = 12.9

Meters/Feet

m to ft	ft to m
1 = 3.3	1 = 0.30
2 = 6.6	2 = 0.61
3 = 9.8	3 = 0.91
4 = 13.1	4 = 1.2
5 = 16.4	5 = 1.5
6 = 19.7	6 = 1.8
7 = 23.0	7 = 2.1
8 = 26.2	8 = 2.4

WEIGHT

Kilograms/Pounds

kg to lb	lb to kg
1 = 2.2	1 = 0.45
2 = 4.4	2 = 0.91
3 = 6.6	3 = 1.4
4 = 8.8	4 = 1.8
5 = 11.0	5 = 2.3
6 = 13.2	6 = 2.7
7 = 15.4	7 = 3.2
8 = 17.6	8 = 3.6

Grams/Ounces

g to oz	oz to g
1 = 0.04	1 = 28
2 = 0.07	2 = 57
3 = 0.11	3 = 85
4 = 0.14	4 = 114
5 = 0.18	5 = 142
6 = 0.21	6 = 170
7 = 0.25	7 = 199
8 = 0.28	8 = 227

TEMPERATURE

Fahrenheit/Celsius

F	C
0	-17.8
5	-15.0
10	-12.2
15	-9.4
20	-6.7
25	-3.9
30	-1.1
32	0
35	1.7
40	4.4
45	7.2
50	10.0
55	12.8
60	15.5
65	18.3
70	21.1
75	23.9
80	26.7
85	29.4
90	32.2
95	35.0
100	37.8

LIQUID VOLUME

Liters/U.S. Gallons

l to gal	gal to l
1 = 0.26	1 = 3.8
2 = 0.53	2 = 7.6
3 = 0.79	3 = 11.4
4 = 1.1	4 = 15.1

Liters/U.S. Gallons

l to gal	gal to l
5 = 1.3	5 = 18.9
6 = 1.6	6 = 22.7
7 = 1.8	7 = 26.5
8 = 2.1	8 = 30.3

INDEX OF NAMES

GENERAL INDEX

GLOSSARY

Ambo
Stone pulpit with steps dating from the Romanesque period

Amphitheater
An oval or round building with tiers or seats around a central arena, used in Ancient Roman times for gladiatorial contests and spectacles

Apse
A semi-circular or polygonal projection of a building, especially at east end of a church

Architrave
The lowermost division of a classical entablature, resting directly on the column capitals and supporting the frieze

Atrium
The forecourt of an early Christian church, flanked or surrounded by porticoes. Also an open-air central court around which a house is built

Basilica
Rectangular-shaped building: in Roman times, used for the administration of justice; in early Christian times, used for worship, and generally with a central nave and side aisles, possibly with apse/s

Borgo
Medieval town

Cantoria
Gallery for the choir in a church, often containing the organ

Capital
Part which links a column to the structure above. In classical architecture, capitals were Doric, Ionian, or Corinthian

Carolingian
Referring to a Frankish dynasty from about 613 AD, which ruled between 774 and 961 in Italy chemin-de-ronde: internal raised pathway in medieval fortifications

Ciborium
Casket or tabernacle containing the host; also a canopy above the altar

Colombarium
A building, usually underground, with niches for urns containing the ashes of the dead

Confessio
Crypt below the high altar, usually containing the relics of a saint

Dosseret
Supplementary capital set above a column capital to receive the thrust of the arch

Embrasure
With a splayed (angled) opening, usually the doorway of a church

Ghibelline
Term used in the Middle Ages to refer to supporters of the Holy Roman Emperor

Grotesque
Decorative art characterized by fanciful, incongruous or fantastic human or animal forms

Guelph (or Guelf)
Term used in the Middle Ages to refer to supporters of the Papacy

Incunabula
Book printed before 1501

Loggia
A colonnaded or arcaded space within the body of a building but open on one side

Lunette
An area in the plane of a wall framed by an arch or vault containing a painting or sculpture

Lunigiana
Name for the area around the once flourishing town of Luni, now ruined

Majolica
A type of early Italian earthenware covered with an opaque tin glaze

Matroneum
Overhead gallery in an early church reserved for the worship of women

Merlon
One of the solid parts between the crenellations of a battlement on a fortified medieval building

Pax Romana
The status of peace under the Roman Empire

Peristyle
A colonnade surrounding a building or courtyard.

Piano Nobile
Upper floor occupied by the nobility

Pilaster
A shallow, rectangular feature projecting from a wall, with a capital and a base and architecturally treated as a column

Polyptych
Altar-piece consisting of a number of panels. A diptych has two panels; a triptych has three

Presbytery
The part of a church reserved for the officiating clergy

Pronaos
A vestibule before
the main part of the
church

Risorgimento
The period of turmoil in
the 19th century leading up
to the Unification of Italy
(1861)

Riviera del Levante
The coast of eastern
Liguria

Riviera del Ponente
The coast of western
Liguria

Sacristy
Part of church where
furnishings and vestments
are kept, and where clergy
prepare for services

Tessera (pl. tesserae)
Small square of stone
or marble used in to make
mosaics

Tiburium
Architectural structure
enclosing and supporting
a dome, used in early and
Romanesque Lombard
churches

Tympanum
The triangular space at the
top of the facade of a
temple, often recessed and
decorated with sculpture

Transept
The major transverse part
of a cruciform church

Triptych
A painting or panel with a
main central part and two
lateral parts

Volute
A spiral, scroll-like
ornament

PICTURE CREDITS

Notes

Notes

Notes

Isola Gallinara - Albenga (Savona)

LIGURIA: THE SEASIDE FIT FOR FAMILIES.

n Liguria, nothing is missing for a perfect
amily holiday.
he sea: undisputed protagonist of the
igurian territory, with its crystal clear waters
urrounded by a breathtaking landscape.
Small hidden bays and long sandy beaches,
afe and provided with all kinds of reliable
ervices, along with the sincere hospitality
f the sea folk.
So this year, let Liguria excite you, and get
eady for a great family holiday!

n Liguria
GENZIA REGIONALE

LIGURIA
ITALIA

terradamare

www.turismoinliguria.it

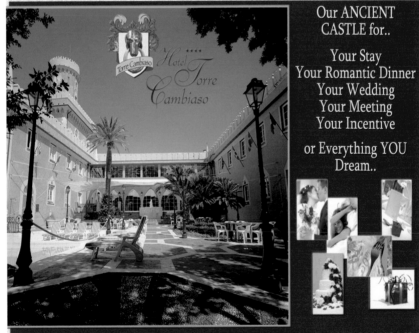